Safety in Catering

A Guide for Supervisors and Managers

Roy Hayter

Brewers and Licensed Retailers Association

TRAINING
COMPANY

M
MACMILLAN

Acknowledgements

Industry liaison, research and supervision of photography

Pam Frediani

Reviewing the text

Ronald Bolton, principal environmental health officer, environment department, London Borough of Camden

Photographer

Tom Stockill

Graphics

Tom Lines

Photographic locations

The Bellhouse, Beaconsfield, De Vere Hotels
The Whittington, Pinner, Whitbread Chiltern Inns
Colour-coded chopping board and knife loaned by Staines Catering Equipment Limited

Articles reproduced from industry magazines

Caterer & Hotelkeeper
Health & Safety at Work
Health & Safety in the Office
Hotel & Restaurant Magazine
Hotels
IEHO Food Forum
Inside Hotels
Publican
The Safety Practitioner
Voice

Loan of photographs

Health at Work Picture Library
National Medical Slide Bank
Nisbets
St John's Institute of Dermatology, London
Topham

Reproduction of material

Diversey Limited
Formecon Services Limited, Crewe
S C Johnson Professional
Lever Industrial Limited
Procter & Gamble Food Services Division
Signs & Labels Limited, Stockport
Stocksigns Limited, Redhill, Surrey

Every effort has been made to trace all the copyright holders. If any have been inadvertently overlooked, the publishers will be pleased to make the necessary arrangements at the first opportunity.

The publishers gratefully acknowledge the contribution of:

Commenting on the text

Department of Health: John Barnes, principal environmental health officer
Fire Protection Association: Helen Bonar, senior information officer
Health & Safety Executive, Local Authority Unit: James Barrett, principal inspector
Institution of Environmental Health Officers: Ann Goodwin, assistant secretary
Local Authorities Coordinating Body on Food and Trading Standards: Mark Du Val, senior principal executive
National Health Service: Anne Tofts, director development programmes

Academic reviewers

Bournemouth University: Professor Peter A Jones, head of department of service industries
The Colchester Institute: Barrie Mills, head of school of hotel and catering studies
The Manchester Metropolitan University: Bill Nevett, head of department of hotel, catering and tourism management
Napier University, Edinburgh: Sandra Watson, assistant head of department of hospitality and tourism management, and Alex Watson, lecturer
South Devon College: Sheila Morrison Smith, head of department of hotel and catering

Environmental Health Officers contributors

Manchester, Alec Grocott
Newbury, John Parfitt, John Guild, Grant Courteney
Plymouth, Michael Studden
Rushmoor Borough Council: David Quirk, David Belford, Mrs Barbara Hancox
Borough of Southend-on-Sea, Richard Evans
South Oxfordshire, Ken Calcutt
Surrey Heath Borough Council, Derek Gould

Advice with the text and contributing material

Allied-Lyons Retailing Limited: Michael Hall, Caroline Smethurst
Bass Taverns Limited: Allan Powers, David Plant
The Boddington Group plc: Frank Blanchard, Chris Gillespie
Department of Health: Alison Crook
Health & Safety Executive: Keith Broughton, Jean Flanagan, Ian Greenwood, Harry Lester, Mary McAleese, Stuart North, Barry Watkinson
International Safety Media, Braintree: Andrew Ings
Metropole Hotels: Eddy Williams, group security manager
Ministry of Agriculture, Fisheries and Food: Sharon Taylor
Morland & Co plc: Marcus Harborne
Scottish & Newcastle plc: Jim Stark
The Whitbread Beer Company: John Reade
The Wolverhampton & Dudley Breweries plc: John Beerjeraz

Contributing industry procedures and other material

Ansells Limited: Jeff Dixon
CCG Services Limited: Barbara Cummin
County of Avon: Maggie Tiltman, senior client officer school meals
Crieff Hydro Hotel: June McIntosh
De Vere Hotels Limited: Alan Makinson, Nicki Fincham
Employers Association of Catering Equipment Engineers Limited (ACE): Be Goulden
Everards Brewery Limited: Marshall Hodgkinson
Forte (UK) Limited: John Forte
Gleneagles Hotel: Mrs Anne Holley
Hotel Catering & Institutional Management Association: Rosemary Morrison, Kalpana Amin
Hudson's Coffee Houses Limited: Timothy Penrose
Ind Coope Retail Limited: Lee Hubbucks
Institute of Hotel Security Managers: Brian Waight
Jarvis Hotels Limited: Pauline Brown
McDonald's Restaurants Limited: Jill Barnes, Mark Hathaway, Kathleen Henry
Merrychef Limited: Helen Stephens
Metropolitan Police Hotel Security Squad David Williams
North Middlesex Hospital NHS Trust: Elizabeth Stalley, Charlotte Hatton
Rank Leisure Limited: Mark Lindsell
Roadchef Motorways Limited: Kathie Thomas
St John's College, Cambridge: Nigel Bruc
Scotland Yard Crime Prevention Unit: Mike Gillette
Scottish & Newcastle Breweries plc: Chris Ripper
Stakis plc: Douglas Cameron
The University of Edinburgh: Caroline Strathie
University of St Andrews; Hamish Johnsto
The University of Sheffield: David McKown
J D Wetherspoon plc: Jane Biss, Geoff Taylor, Pat Terry
Whitbread Inns: Chris Jefferies, Mike Cowan

Also helped with information and material

Alan Nuttall Limited; ARA Services plc: Jackie Glass; Autobar Limited: Roger Davies; Automobile Association Developments Limited; Breadwinner Foods: Peter Bartlett; Compass Services (UK) Limited: Nicki Rees; Courage Limited: Keith Johnson; Electricity Contractors Association: Terry Cann, Graham Wool; Food National Interest Group: Richard North; Institute of Baths & Recreational Management: Ralph Riley Local Authority Pollution Control Department: Helen Snellings; Whitbread Technical Centre: Dr David Rosie, Geoff Foster

CONTENTS

1   Towards a safer workplace **1**

*Your attitude 1 • Human capabilities and human failings 2 •
Building a safety-first attitude 4*

2   Getting the framework right **5**

*How the law is enforced 5 • Managing health and safety 7 •
Assessing health and safety risks 10 • Communicating
safety 11 • What you need to report officially 14*

3   Workplace safety and welfare **19**

*Workplace regulations 19 • Noise 23 • First-aid arrangements 24 •
Manual handling 26 • Hazardous substances 29 • Protective
clothing 32 • Waste disposal 33 • Violence in the workplace 34*

4   Safety with equipment **35**

*Work equipment 35 • Dangerous machinery 36 • Electrical
equipment 37 • Gas equipment 39 • Play areas and equipment 40*

5   Fire prevention and safety **41**

*Getting a fire certificate 43 • Reducing the risk of fire breaking
out 44 • Preparing for an emergency 46*

6   Security of property and people **51**

*Basic rules of security 51 • Cooperating with the police 54 •
Bomb threats and terrorism 55*

7   Managing food safety **57**

*Food safety legislation 57 • Food safety management 66 •
Food hygiene inspections 74*

8   Workplace safety by area of operation **77**

*In the bar 77 • In the cellar 80 • In the kitchen 82 •
In the restaurant 86 • In housekeeping 88 • In reception,
portering and administration 89 • In leisure 90*

9   Other issues of security and safety **93**

*Fraud and other security issues 93 • Safety with display screen
equipment 96 • Precautions against Aids 98 • Precautions
against legionnaires' disease 99 • Building services 99*

0   Reviewing your safety performance **101**

*Re-looking at safety and security procedures 102 •
Monitoring and maintaining standards 111 • Towards
a healthier and safer environment 114 • NVQ/SVQ level 3
checklist 115 • Comments on case studies/activities 116*

index and index to legislation **123**

First published 1994 by

THE MACMILLAN PRESS LTD
Houndmills, Basingstoke, Hampshire RG21 2XS
and London
Companies and representatives throughout the
world

in association with

HOTEL & CATERING TRAINING COMPANY
International House, High Street, Ealing,
London W5 5DB

BREWING PUBLICATIONS LTD
42 Portman Square, London W1H 0BB

ISBN 0–333–61639–1

A catalogue record for this book is available
from the British Library

Designed and typeset by the author

Printed in Great Britain by
Scotprint Ltd, Musselburgh

About this book

This book guides you through your legal responsibilities towards health and safety, and gives ideas and practical guidance on how you can establish safe working practices.

Much of this guidance is from industry employers. There are examples from hospitals, as well as from night clubs, university catering, restaurants, hotels and pubs. Some will seem very different from your operation (or the sector of the industry you intend to join). Nevertheless, you will find ideas and principles that can be readily adapted to your own situation.

The structure

The book is divided into ten sections. The role of people in safety forms the substance of *Section 1* and you will find this theme returned to throughout the book.

From the overall management of health and safety in *Section 2*, the text then proceeds through the workplace in *Section 3*, equipment in *Section 4*, fire in *Section 5*, security in *Section 6* and hygiene in *Section 7*. The focus switches in *Section 8* to each of the main areas of operation: bar, cellar, kitchen, restaurant, housekeeping, reception, portering, administration and leisure. *Section 9* returns to deal with issues that affect some of the industry or some styles of establishment more than others, such as display screen equipment and Aids. Finally, in *Section 10*, you are invited to review the whole context of safety.

Case studies, activities and checklists

The case studies are included to provoke thought, to make a point and to encourage discussion. Each one describes a situation that really happened. The other activities serve a similar purpose, but are more practical so that the work you put into them will directly help you in your job. Some provide the framework for the assessment of risks required by law. Comments on the case studies and activities are included in *Section 10*, with discussion points and follow-on activities.

Help towards NVQ/SVQ level 3

Working through *Sections 1* to *6*, and *Sections 8* to *10*, will help you achieve the core unit which is required for all level 3 NVQ/SVQ qualifications in Catering and Hospitality Supervisory Management: *3D1 Monitor and maintain the health, safety and security of workers, customers and other members of the public*. The NVQ/SVQ checklist on page 115 will help you identify the points you need to pay special attention to as you work through the book, the activities and case studies analysis. The text of *Section 10* is cross-referenced to the performance criteria and to earlier sections in the book.

Checklists in the book

Assessing risks 10

Bomb threats by telephone 56

Cash security 53

Cellar delivery check 80

Closing time (managing in pub) 78

Display screens/computers:
overcoming problems 96

Display screens/computers:
workstation requirements 97

Door safety 20

Drug abuse 79

Electrical equipment: in-house
inspection 38

Equipment: instructions for using 39

Fire certificate, what it specifies 43

Fire notices 47

Fire responsibilities 46

Fire training 48

First aid: selecting people
to be trained 25

First-aid boxes 24

Floors and personal traffic routes 20

Food premises, equipment,
hygiene, etc. 58, 59, 61

Inspection by EHO 75

Legal requirements 103

Lighting 20

Manual handling, carrying 27

Manual handling, reducing risk 26

NVQ/SVQ 115

Portering staff training 89

Safety signs 13

Security coordinator's role 55

Staff toilets and washing facilities 22

Traffic routes 21

Training: safe use of equipment 114

Waste disposal 33, 59

Are safety and security procedures in your workplace examined only after something has gone wrong, or when new legislation has been introduced, or an enforcement officer is due for a visit? Or is the whole area of health and safety an on-going priority for everyone, from top management down to the most junior member of staff, and including part-timers?

Prioritising health and safety is something you cannot do on your own. And the process will be difficult to manage, given all the other priorities in business. However, there are two areas where you can begin to exert influence immediately:

- demonstrating by your attitude and what you do, that you consider the health, safety and welfare of everyone in your workplace as fundamentally important

- taking proper account of human capabilities and human failings when you supervise and manage your staff.

Towards a safer workplace

Contents guide

Your attitude .... this page

Human capabilities and
human failings 2

Building a safety-first attitude 4

Your attitude

If you give the impression that safety is only of passing concern to you, your staff are likely to place even less importance on this aspect of their own work. If you don't follow correct procedures yourself, why should others do so? It won't be enough simply to say: 'I am the manager, so do as I say.'

The proper way often takes longer, or requires more effort. If you haven't explained the reasons for the particular approach, your staff can't be blamed for thinking: 'Oh, what's the point. My supervisor doesn't seem sufficiently bothered to tell me why I need to take all these safety precautions, so why should I?'

When customers need serving, or there are other pressures, shortcuts that get the job done more quickly seem attractive to everyone, even if they involve risks to safety. By allowing or positively encouraging this to happen, you are as good as saying to your staff: 'For those at the sharp end, all these safety rules and procedures are unrealistic. We're sensible enough to find our own way, which is both safe and quick.'

When a minor accident occurs, e.g. someone slips but does not get hurt, it may be tempting to dismiss the incident to other staff as 'bad luck', over-hastiness or personal stupidity. But what if the real reason (which your staff know) was that the floor often gets slippery yet you have never done anything about it?

Behind most accidents is human error. Often there may be understandable excuses by the person or people most directly involved – a rush of customers, over-tiredness, need to save time, or by the managers and supervisors – too much to do, or lack of information from head office. The safest workplaces are those where the risks of human failings are recognised from the outset, and planned for when systems and procedures are established.

Human capabilities and human failings

As a good manager, you will not ask a member of staff to do something unless you are satisfied that he or she has the ability. Part of this process of checking capability – which may well be automatic when you know your staff well – is an assessment of any 'human failings' which might interfere with their work.

Health and safety issues need to be uppermost in your mind when you decide who does what, when you supervise the carrying out of these tasks, and when you become involved in setting up work systems and procedures.

Mistaken priorities

Get the food to the customers while it is hot, or mop up the gravy you have just spilled on the floor? The following thoughts might run through your mind:

- the chef will get cross with me if I don't take the food straight to the customers
- it'll take too long to put the food down somewhere, go and find the mop and bucket, clean the floor, then return everything and finally deliver the food
- if I see John the kitchen porter I'll ask him to mop it up
- it's only a small spill and no one's likely to slip on it
- this could be very dangerous, 'Chef, I'm sorry I've dropped some gravy – could you please ask John to mop it up while I deliver this food. I'll be back to help in a moment.'

You will recognise various priorities here including customer service, vanity or pride, personal convenience and safety. If the spill was not immediately attended to, and no accident occurred, there would probably never be any questioning of which was the right priority.

False assumptions

Just as priorities may not be recognised as mistaken until something goes wrong, so the sort of assumptions that people make every day can go unquestioned:

- she's a regular customer, I won't bother with that cheque guarantee card routine
- the engineer came to fix the waste disposal unit only yesterday. He said the unusual vibration and noise were nothing serious – I'll ask the chef later to report them, but there is no reason to hold us up now
- when the kitchen gets hot the temperature monitor on the freezer often gives a warning – but it always sorts itself out
- it's usually about this time of the week that there is a fire alarm, it won't be anything serious.

Lifting and carrying

Cellar flaps and deliveries

Faulty cellar flaps can be dangerous to you, your employees, delivery crew and the public.

As licensee you are responsible for the design and maintenance of the premises and equipment where goods are delivered, including cellar flaps.

You also have a responsibility to cooperate with the employers of delivery crews in reducing the risk of injury.

- Care must be taken when cellar flaps and hatchways are open. A suitable barrier should be erected to keep passers-by away from the cellar opening.
- Cellar flaps must have adequate holding bolts or fasteners.
- Hinges should be oiled regularly.

Beware of broken glass!

- Never plunge your hand into a bottle crate.
- Look first! There may be a bottle broken.
- Look for broken glass when washing up.
- Do not pile dirty glasses in sinks.
- Look out for cracked and chipped glasses when drying.
- If you break the rim of a bottle when removing the crown cork, dispose of bottle contents and temporarily put in crate, neck first.
- Dispose of all broken glass by wrapping up in plenty of paper and place in metal receptacle, unless you have special arrangements.

Humour is often very effective at reinforcing safety messages. But even the most appealing material loses its impact after a time. To win the battle, you need to use all your skills of communication, leadership and motivation.

Inadequate information

Poor communications can turn an emergency into a disaster, or a potential hazard into the cause of an accident. The telephone operator in the Woolworth store fire (see box) thought she was being told about a fight, not a fire. If the vacuum cleaner develops a fault while you are using it, don't put it back in the usual cupboard thinking to yourself 'I'll have to get that repaired before I can use it again.' What happens if someone else needs to use the cleaner? How will that person know the cleaner is unsafe to use, unless you put it away where it cannot be used, and clearly marked out-of-order?

Playing out roles

How people react to a situation can depend on how they see their role:

- a customer may not mention the suspicious behaviour of some youths in the car park: 'It's the security officer's business to catch them'

- the dishwasher operator ignores a chipped glass: 'The bar staff should check glasses before they use them'

- an assistant notices the power cable to the cash till is damaged: 'No worry, Janet the supervisor does the safety checks – it'll make a change for her to find something.'

Underestimating risk

The attitude 'It never happens here, our management is much too careful' might be rather flattering, but if people have too much confidence in systems and equipment they can:

- fall into bad habits – not check temperatures of chilled food from the regular supplier: 'It's a good company and they have always been correct'

- fail to pass on information because it seems unimportant at the time – a customer asking many questions about the business (in preparation for a robbery)

- miss danger signals – frosting on the outside of carbon dioxide cylinders.

Equally dangerous are the viewpoints of:

- the unofficially recognised/self-appointed do-gooder – 'Management never complains, and it does help everyone if we keep our costs down by reducing wastage.' A typical example of this is the unsafe and illegal practice of pouring the over-spills or slops from the draught beer back into the cask

- the fatalist – 'If a major disaster like a fire is going to happen, it will, and nothing we do can prevent it'

- the expert – 'These use-by dates on food always allow for a margin of safety. I have never had a problem with items two or three days out of date.'

Key word misheard

In the Woolworth store fire (Manchester, 1979), the telephone operator failed to call the brigade when given insufficient information: 'He came in and the door didn't shut behind him and he shouted something and then went back out again. I thought he said "There's a fight on the 2nd floor." I just continued working on the phone. I wasn't aware of anything untoward.'

David Canter, *Studies of Human Behaviour in Fire*, Fire Research Station/University of Surrey

---

Ladder safety

A hotel handyman had been told to erect a new sign by the hotel owner, who had then gone on holiday.

The ladder was approximately 5 metres long, made of wood and belonged to the hotel. The man was using an electric drill to make a hole in the hotel wall when the rung on which he was standing gave way, and he fell to his death on the pavement below.

The investigation

The electric drill and the extension lead showed no signs of malfunction. However the ladder had been strengthened with telephone cable and the rungs were badly worn. The rung which had broken (3rd from the top) showed signs of a break at both ends. It seems likely that it gave way when the deceased applied extra pressure on the drill to penetrate the wall.

Accidents in Service Industries 1988/89, Health and Safety Executive

ANALYSIS

1 What precautions should have been taken?

2 What human failings might have led to the accident?

Building a safety-first attitude

Human failings cannot be easily put into categories, and many accidents result from a complex mix of failures. There are limits to the range of abnormal circumstances which can be planned for, and not much can be done to anticipate equipment breakdowns caused by a design or manufacturing fault.

What this discussion of human failings should do is help you focus on how you might encourage your staff to:

1 Ensure safety is always a key priority.

2 Not make assumptions when safety is at risk.

3 Respond to the information they are given (and you have a key role to play in ensuring the information is adequate and accurate).

4 Ask for more information, instruction and training when they need it.

5 Not close their eyes to safety matters which are the usual responsibility of other staff or management.

6 Not use safety matters as a way of testing management, or causing difficulty for unpopular individuals.

7 Recognise that most customers and new members of staff will not know what to do if there is a safety crisis, and will usually expect others to take control.

8 Avoid becoming complacent about safety risks.

Safety at work for managers and supervisors

Jarvis HOTELS

• When planning each operation, take into account the safety aspect.

• Make sure your staff are properly instructed in the potential hazards of their job and how to avoid them.

• Where appropriate, seek assistance and guidance from a senior manager.

• Essential safety equipment and devices must be provided and used on each job performed under your supervision.

• Take prompt corrective action when conditions and/or activities become unsafe, or problems are reported to you by staff.

• All injuries must be promptly treated and reported. You should help investigate the cause of every accident, even minor ones.

• Periodically check the safety status of all operations under your control, ideally by doing a safety checklist. Inform senior management about any hazard which you cannot correct.

• Maintain comprehensive records of all health and safety training undertaken by employees reporting to you.

⚡ ACTION

The scenes in these photographs are not particularly unusual. All of them might be within your experience at some time in your career. Take the subjects they illustrate, consider what human factors might have contributed to the problem, and what you as a manager or supervisor could do to counteract them.

Forced to evacuate their hotel after a bomb scare, these American tourists had flown into London just the day before.

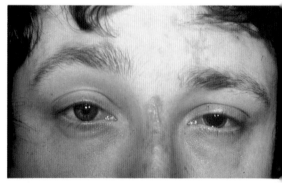

Ammonia burns after a cleaning substance had splashed.

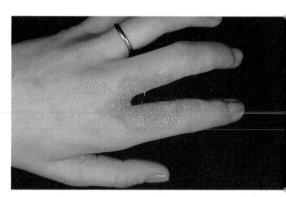

Contact dermatitis, a condition often set off by constant hand washing and contact with detergents and harsh cleaners.

Everyone at work – employers, self-employed, employees, contractors and trainees – has a statutory duty to look after the health and safety of colleagues and anyone else affected by their work – guests, clients, customers, visitors and members of the public. The overall responsibilities of employers and employees are set out in the Health and Safety at Work etc. Act 1974 (summarised overleaf). The Act provides the framework for various regulations relating to more specific health and safety issues, e.g. reporting accidents, electricity at work, hazardous substances, workplace equipment and manual handling.

How the law is enforced

In pubs, hotels, restaurants and most other catering establishments, the environmental health officer (EHO) of your local authority or council will deal with any problems relating to the Health and Safety at Work etc. Act, and the various regulations made under it.

For catering facilities in schools, hospitals, prisons, factories, sports and leisure clubs and arenas, theatres and cinemas, health and safety law is enforced either by an EHO or by an inspector from the Health and Safety Executive. (Food safety law is the responsibility of the EHO in all premises.)

An enforcing officer may carry out an inspection of your premises at any reasonable time (reasonable in a general sense for your sort of business – it is not necessary that the time should be convenient for you). The officer has wide powers (explained in the summary of the law overleaf). If you have a good record of complying with the law and doing suggested works, the inspector may notify defects to you informally, by letter.

Where advice is likely to be ignored, and/or the problem is considered serious, the officer may issue an *improvement notice*. This gives you a time limit for making changes, and details what changes are required (see example overleaf).

If there is risk of serious personal injury, a *prohibition notice* may be issued. This stops specified activities (e.g. you might be prevented from using the kitchen) unless remedial action is taken. The notice can take immediate effect.

Alternatively, or as well, the officer may decide to prosecute you for breaking the law. The fines can be very substantial – there is no limit in the upper courts, and prison is a possibility – a sentence of up to two years.

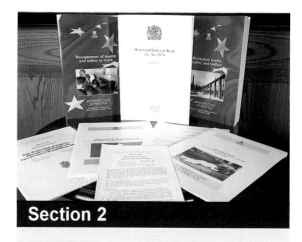

Section 2

Getting the framework right

Contents guide

How the law is enforced .... this page

Managing health and safety 7

Assessing health and safety risks 10

Communicating safety 11

What you need to report officially 14

The safest workplaces are those where health and safety is given top priority at all times by all management and staff.

The most effective safety measures are those which you and your staff are well motivated towards. Rules handed down from 'on high' get ignored.

HEALTH AND SAFETY AT WORK ETC ACT 1974
Sections 21, 23 and 24
LONDON BOROUGH OF CAMDEN
IMPROVEMENT NOTICE

Reference number

To:

I Ronald Bolton one of the
of the London Borough of Camden En
Health and Safety Team Town Hall,
London WC1H 8EQ Tel: 071 278 44

HEREBY GIVE YOU NO

you as an employer are contravening

Sections 2(2)a and 2(2)
and Safety at Work etc

The reasons for my said opinion are

SCHEDULE

The reasons for my opinion

There is a hatchway in the floor of the ground
floor food preparation area, which provides
access to the basement which is used as a store.

The hatch is approximately 1 metre square. It
has a wire handle at one end by which the hatch
is lifted. During inspection, the hatch was at an
angle of 60 degrees to the floor, supported by a
metal rod in one corner.

The method of getting down through the hatchway is to put both hands on the floor to support
the body, then move the feet approx. 1 metre
down to touch the top rung of a vertical metal
ladder; finally, while standing on the top rung, to
move the feet and body round to face the
opposite direction and climb down. The person
would often be carrying stock at the same time.

The hatchway is dangerous for 3 reasons:

1 There is a risk of a person falling while trying
to get from one floor to the other, and
particularly while carrying goods.

2 There is a risk that a person will accidentally
fall into this hole. This is particularly likely
for staff who stand at the food preparation
table with the back less than 0.3 metre from
the floor opening.

3 There is a risk that the hatch will collapse on
someone's foot or on a person climbing
through the hatchway.

**You must remedy the said contraventions a
follows:**

Provide a safe system of work so that:

1 staff can get from the ground floor to the
basement and back; and

2 goods can be moved from the ground floor to
the basement and back;

all in such a way that working in the premises
does not cause a significant risk to the health of
any person.

A traditional staircase would be acceptable for
the above purpose, if suitably located and
guarded.

Send drawings and details of all proposed works
to me for approval before carrying out any
works.

Your proposals must be received by me within 6
weeks of today's date. Work must be completed
within 16 weeks of today's date.

nald Bolton
incipal Environmental Health Officer
ndon Borough of Camden

If you are served an
improvement or prohibition
notice, the detailed notes
accompanying it explain the
procedure for an appeal.

Health and Safety at Work etc. Act 1974

Employer's responsibilities

Employers must ensure, so far as
reasonably practicable, the health, safety
and welfare of all their employees and
other people (non-employees) affected
by the work of their business or
operation. As part of these responsibilities, employers must:

• provide safe equipment and safe ways
of carrying out jobs

• ensure that the use, handling, storage
and transport of articles and substances are safe and without health
risks

• provide information, instruction, training and supervision to ensure health
and safety

• maintain the workplace in a safe
condition, and provide and maintain
safe ways of getting into and out of the
workplace

• provide a working environment which
is safe, without risks to health and has
adequate facilities and arrangement
for the welfare of employees

• prepare and, as often as necessary,
revise a written statement of general
health and safety policy, which should
also describe the organisation and
arrangements for carrying out that
policy, and bring the statement and any
revisions to the notice of all
employees.

Employee's responsibilities

Every employee while at work has a duty
to:

• take reasonable care for the health and
safety of himself/herself and of others
who may be affected by what he or she
does, or does not do, at work

• perform health and safety-related
duties and comply with health and
safety requirements imposed by the
employer or any other person with
health and safety responsibilities.

Everyone in the workplace

Everyone has a duty not to interfere with
or misuse anything provided in the
interests of health, safety or welfare.

Powers of enforcing officers

• take with them a police constable
there are reasonable grounds fo
fearing obstruction, and any othe
person duly authorised by the
enforcing authority

• make such examination as they
consider necessary

• direct that the premises or part of them
are left undisturbed

• take measurements and photographs

• take samples of articles and sub
stances

• require articles or substances to be
dismantled or subjected to tests, and
detain these as long as is necessary

• question anyone who might provide
information

• take copies of documents which migh
relate to the incident

• seize and render harmless articles o
substances which might pose
imminent danger.

Managing health and safety

With much at stake and many requirements to meet, health and safety arrangements can only work smoothly when they are given the same attention as any other management activity. This involves planning:

- identifying priorities

- setting objectives, e.g. accident reduction targets, number of people to be trained

- eliminating risks, e.g. through careful selection and design of equipment, facilities and work procedures.

It involves control – ensuring that what has been planned has been implemented. It involves monitoring and review:

- checking performance against plans and targets

- assessing the effectiveness of health and safety policies

- adjusting policies and procedures as required.

And it involves organisation: appointing a health and safety manager or adviser (see box), and deciding who does what.

A typical arrangement is to develop the health and safety policy statement to cover all these issues. Unless you have fewer than five employees, both the policy and your health and safety arrangements must be recorded in writing.

 Writing your own health and safety policy statement: Guide to preparing a safety policy statement for a small business, published by the Health and Safety Executive (see page 12), provides the structure and blank spaces so that you can keep the completed booklet as your statement: ISBN 0 11 885510 7.

Features of the policy statement

- signed and dated by the director or chief executive of the organisation

- communicate values, beliefs and commitment to health and safety

- explain the benefits, e.g. reduced injuries and ill health, better conditions of work

- put health and safety objectives on the same level of importance for everyone as other business objectives

- identify responsibilities of directors, managers, supervisors, staff, etc.

- set out the procedure for consultation/ participation in health and safety matters

Health and Safety Company Policy and Procedure

Appointment of health and safety manager/adviser

The Management of Health and Safety at Work Regulations require employers to have access to competent help in applying the provisions of health and safety law, and in devising and applying protective measures. A self-employed employer or one of the partners in a partnership can undertake the measures without assistance, providing he or she has sufficient training and experience or knowledge and other qualities.

HOUSE MANAGERS

are responsible to their immediate manager for ensuring that so far as is reasonably practicable, the activities carried on in their house comply with statutory requirements for health, safety, hygiene and fire. In particular they will:

1 Ensure all house staff are adequately trained in:

- health and safety to enable them to work without risk to themselves or others

- hygiene, especially personal hygiene, so that food prepared and sold for public consumption is without risk to health

- fire precautions, including the action to be taken in the event of a fire

and that records of all such training are kept available, including a signature of each member of staff acknowledging that they have received such training.

2 Ensure that all accidents occurring in the house are recorded and where necessary reported in the appropriate manner.

3 Report to the Area Manager any defects in the building, plant or equipment which might constitute an existing or potential hazard, whether to employees or members of the public.

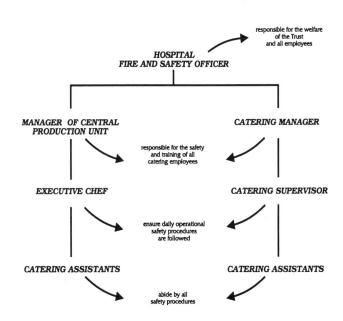

Whatever the size of organisation, it's important that everyone is clear about their responsibilities for health and safety.

Organisation chart with thanks to Catering Services, North Middlesex Hospital NHS Trust

Cooperating with suppliers, contractors and equipment engineers

Anyone visiting your workplace to carry out work has a duty under the Management of Health and Safety at Work Regulations to cooperate closely with you regarding safety (see box). This includes draymen and the delivery staff who are responsible for moving stock to your cellar or storage room, as well as builders and painters doing repairs, re-building or re-decoration work.

When the contract is negotiated, or before work starts, you should discuss and agree with the other party a safety plan to cover such matters as:

1   Safe work practices – particularly important if contractors are working on the premises when members of the public and staff are present.

2   Security – proof of identity on arrival, wearing of identity badges/uniform, entrances which should be used.

3   First aid – who will provide.

4   Fire – any particular hazards which will be caused by the work, and if so whether special fire extinguishers will be needed to deal with these.

5   Emergency evacuation – who will take the roll-call for the contractor's employees.

6   Hazardous substances – safety precautions for any which will be brought on site.

7   Waste disposal – who will arrange and accept responsibility.

8   Communications – arrangements for reporting problems, or stopping work where there is serious risk of personal injury.

9   Respect for your work procedures – checking when it is convenient to enter a public or work area, wearing suitable over-clothing in food preparation areas.

Design and maintenance of the premises and equipment where goods are delivered

The person in control of the premises is responsible for this. However, if you are considering improved handling methods (e.g. installing powered lifting equipment for kegs and casks, or new access to the cellar) then you have a duty to cooperate with the employers of the delivery crew who would have to use the new equipment (the brewery in this example).

If contractors or other non-employees work in your workplace

You have a duty under the Management of Health and Safety at Work Regulations to provide health and safety information to anyone visiting your workplace to carry out work (e.g. contractors carrying out repair or maintenance of equipment), and their employer. This should include any risks, the health and safety measures in place to address those risks, and who should be contacted in the event of an emergency.

If there are health and safety risks arising from the work being undertaken by persons visiting your workplace (e.g. from equipment or hazardous substances), you (or your employer) should be informed by their employer of those risks.

Temporary workers

Temporary workers – including those employed by you on fixed term contracts, and those employed by another employer (e.g. engineer doing maintenance work on your central heating system) – need to be informed of:

- any special occupational qualifications or skills required to carry out the work safely
- specific features of the job which might affect health and safety (e.g. work at heights).

Where you do not employ the temporary worker, you have a duty to inform that worker's employer, and to check that the information is received by the employee.

More on employees' duties

Employees' duties under the Health and Safety at Work etc. Act are made more specific in the Management of Health and Safety at Work Regulations. Your staff have a duty to:

- use correctly all work items provided by their employer, in accordance with their training and the instructions they receive to enable them to use the items safely
- inform, without delay, their employer (or the person with responsibility for health and safety matters) of any work situation which might present a serious and immediate danger to health and safety (whether this is to the employee concerned, or, if it results from the employee's work, to others)
- notify their employer (or appropriate person) of any shortcomings in the employer's protection arrangements for health and safety.

The duties placed on employees do not reduce the responsibility of the employer to comply with the regulations. Furthermore, employers need to ensure that employees receive adequate instruction and training to enable them to comply with their duties.

Shared workplaces

Many contract caterers are based in the premises of their client. Eating and drinking outlets in a shopping centre share the premises.

The Management of Health and Safety at Work Regulations place a specific duty on those in this situation, to cooperate with each other to ensure their respective obligations under the health and safety legislation are met.

Where a particular employer controls the worksite (e.g. the client of a contract caterer), other employers should assist the controlling employer in assessing shared risks and coordinating measures.

If there is no controlling employer, joint arrangements should be agreed between all employers. It may be appropriate to appoint a health and safety coordinator. This person can then set about bringing together the efforts of individual employers across the workplace to the benefit of everyone. He or she can also take a lead role in establishing and communicating specific health and safety arrangements, for example when contractors are re-decorating the common areas, or drawing up the evacuation procedure in the event of a bomb alert.

Emergency procedures

Clear guidance on when to stop work in an emergency, and how to move to a place of safety, must be available to all employees and others at work under the Management of Health and Safety at Work Regulations.

The procedures should set out the role and responsibilities of the person who will take charge if the emergency occurs, and those who have other, specific responsibilities (e.g. to evacuate guests from a certain area).

A forensic expert searches the interior of The Sussex, a pub in Covent Garden, following a bomb blast inside the building at lunchtime.

Disaster plans

To be put into operation after a serious fire, bomb, bomb threat, serious flooding, building collapse, etc.

Factors to consider

- how long the premises might have to remain empty
- how many people are/will be involved
- climatic conditions prevailing/expected.

Arrangements

Short duration: hot drinks etc. upon return.

Longer duration: arrange accommodation.

Pick-up point for transport, and contact details for contractor who provides emergency cover.

Guidelines for evacuation

In the event of a fire in one area of the hotel, evacuation to an unaffected area can be considered. This must be agreed by the senior fire officer at the scene.

Full evacuation

All personnel will rendezvous at X. Senior managers will report to the Fire Panel.

With the exception of the hotel minibuses, no vehicle to be moved from the car park, except on the direction of the emergency services.

Hotel minibuses will assist in transporting elderly or infirm guests. Thereafter they will be used to provide a shuttle service for other guests as required.

A member of staff will accompany each bus and be responsible for the bus party. On arrival at the temporary accommodation, a registration card will be completed for each guest.

Details of all guests evacuated will be collated by the senior manager present at the accommodation and communicated to the chief security officer.

Dependent on the number of staff available, efforts will be made to divide guests into parties of about 25 persons, each group being accompanied by a member of staff.

With thanks to Metropole Hotels

Assessing health and safety risks

First, the key terms. Take electrical equipment. Contact with electricity is dangerous, so such equipment is a *hazard* – it has the potential to cause harm. Hazards cannot be avoided. What can be controlled or managed is the *risk* – the likelihood that a particular hazard will cause harm.

You will be aware of the general hazards posed by equipment you use, and activities you undertake. And when you ask a member of staff to do a task, you will take account of the risks which might be involved – to the person concerned, as well as to fellow-workers, customers, contractors and anyone else in the workplace. This process is in effect a risk assessment.

The Management of Health and Safety at Work Regulations 1992 require all employers and the self-employed to assess the health and safety risks to which anyone in their workplace is exposed: employees, contractors, customers, members of the public, etc. The assessment should establish:

- what has the potential to cause harm (see checklist)

- the control measures in place and the extent to which they control the risks

- who might be affected.

Here are some ways to approach the assessment:

- *by level of risk* – in a simple case there might be just two categories: risks so great that substantial alterations are essential, e.g. new staircase to basement storage area; and risks which require use of day-to-day controls, e.g. training, work procedures, guards on equipment.

- *by type of risk* – this could concentrate on the areas known to present the highest level of risk in catering: slips, trips and falls; being struck by moving objects; lifting and manual handling; contact with harmful substances; contact with hot surfaces.

- *by operation or activity* – linen handling, food deliveries, setting up banquet rooms, etc.

- *by workplace area* – dispense bar, restaurant, etc.

The assessment should establish what measures need to be taken to comply with health and safety legislation. It must be updated as necessary, for example if:

- the nature of the work has changed, or new equipment been introduced

- an accident investigation identifies hazards which had previously been overlooked.

You may have to establish to your EHO that your assessment meets the legal requirement 'suitable and sufficient'. Make a record of the assessment process and the outcome, so that you can do this. If you have five or more employees, this should be written.

CHECKLIST

Who should be involved in assessing risks?

- supervisors and staff – as sources of information
- advisers and consultants – if/as necessary for their knowledge of specialist subjects

What has potential to cause harm?

- equipment, e.g. microwave oven
- substances used, e.g. dishwasher rinse-aid
- workplace design, e.g. low ceilings in cellar
- fittings and fixtures, e.g. goods lift
- methods of work, e.g. cleaning grease filters
- work organisation, e.g. lack of supervision of staff

Have you covered everything?

- non-routine events, e.g. equipment breakdowns
- instances where practices differ from procedures
- accident records to analyse what went wrong
- emergency procedures
- existing preventive or precautionary measures – e.g. are they working properly?
- groups of workers who might be particularly at risk, e.g. trainees, disabled persons
- night staff, maintenance department, office staff

RISK TYPE	ITEM	DEGREE OF RISK AND DETAILS
Burns	Hot plates on kitchen equipment	Serious: burns to hands
	Air blast from hot ovens	Serious: burns to face, hands and arms
Scalds	Fat/oil fryers	Serious: scalds from oil/fat at high temperatures
	Collision of food handlers collecting/delivering	Minor: scalds/cuts/bruises from collision
	Kettle/glass/dishwasher	Minor/serious: scald from escaping steam/boiling water
Cuts	Clearing breakages	Minor/serious: cuts from broken glass or crockery
	Using knives	Minor/serious: cuts
Gases	Carbon dioxide cylinders in drink dispense system	Risk to life: leakage of gas could cause drowsiness/unconsciousness

This risk assessment is organised by type of risk. It is also an example of a basic 'model' risk assessment. The original form has a further column on the right, in which preventive action, precautions and special training are listed.

Such an approach is particularly useful to companies or organisations which have a number of similar workplaces. It is then the responsibility of the manager of each pub, restaurant, hotel, etc. to add or amend the model to take account of hazards particular to that workplace, e.g. a children's play area, or spa pool, and to add any extra preventive action, precautions or training which is required.

Taking measures to reduce risks

The most effective step is to avoid the risk altogether, for example by changing to smaller containers of cooking oil which can be lifted more easily.

In some areas, the law will determine your action. Fire safety (covered in Section 5) is an example of this. The fire certificate which many establishments are required to have, will detail a wide range of requirements from notices on fire doors to staff instruction. Other steps include:

- combating the risks at source – e.g. moving a computer to avoid annoying glare from the window

- adapting work to the individual – e.g. introducing task rotation, so that concentration levels improve

- taking advantage of new products and techniques – e.g. switching to a less hazardous cleaning agent which can achieve the same level of hygiene.

Give priority to measures which:

- protect a lot of people or the whole workplace, e.g. better lighting outside the staff entrance

- control significant risks

- protect special risk groups.

Communicating safety

There are three aspects to communications where the law makes certain minimum requirements:

- providing information for your employees

- establishing a consultation framework, so that employees and others concerned with safety in your workplace can contribute effectively. In workplaces where there is no trade union recognition, it is up to the employer to decide how this is done

- using signs and markings to indicate danger, the need for caution, give information, or to prohibit something.

Information to employees

One basic requirement is to display a copy of the Health and Safety Executive poster *Health and safety law: what you should know* (available from HSE) in a position where employees will see it easily. In the space provided on the poster you should give the address of your local enforcing authority (e.g. the Environmental Health Department) and the Employment Medical Advisory Service.

Alternatively, you can give each employee a copy of the HSE leaflet HSC5, and a separate note of the two addresses. There is probably every advantage in displaying a poster (which

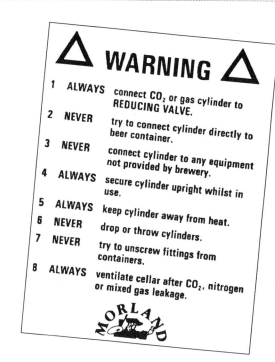

The safety poster reproduced above (originally published by the Brewers and Licensed Retailers Association) has been adopted throughout the industry.

 **ACTION**

The poster is one of the ways in which staff can be reminded of the dangers of carbon dioxide cylinders. Either for this substance, or for another serious hazard in your workplace (e.g. dangerous machinery, burns from hot kitchen equipment):

1. review what communications methods you currently use to encourage safe practice

2. check individual staff awareness

3. investigate what other methods would be useful in reinforcing the messages

4. introduce these as soon as possible.

Capabilities and training

In entrusting tasks to employees, you must take into account their capabilities as regards health and safety (Management of Health and Safety at Work Regulations). Employees must also be provided with health and safety training (during working hours) when they:

- join your employment, e.g. as part of the induction training, when arrangements for first aid, fire and evacuation would also be explained

- are being exposed to new or increased risks, e.g. because of a change of responsibilities, or introduction of new equipment.

The training should be repeated and updated as appropriate to ensure continued competence. Refresher training will be particularly useful for employees who occasionally deputise for others.

establishes quite clearly that you have met the requirements of the Health and Safety Information for Employees Regulations 1989), and issuing a leaflet. Another precaution would be to get yourself on the HSE mailing list, so that you can get revised issues of the poster or leaflet without delay (six months is the outside time limit for displaying/issuing revised information).

Under the Management of Health and Safety at Work Regulations, all employees, including trainees and those on fixed-duration contracts, must be provided with such information as they need to ensure their health and safety. The information should be in a form that will be effective and comprehensible, so consider the level of training, knowledge and experience of the individuals concerned.

Try and target training material carefully, bearing in mind the interest and attention span of the person it is intended for. A coordinated campaign, tackling one-by-one specific issues which cause a problem in your workplace, can be very effective. Posters, leaflets, videos and training sessions on the same theme will provide strong back-up. Quality (meaning appropriateness, not necessarily glossiness) is better than quantity (posters everywhere, leaflets by the dozen).

Consulting on safety

Safety considerations often make a task more difficult or more time-consuming to complete. Backed by a good explanation, this is acceptable. Introduced with the full involvement and support of those it affects, it becomes common-sense. Depending on the number of staff involved, approaches you could consider are:

- small discussion groups of staff

- regular safety seminars

- putting safety on the agenda of your team meetings

- at such seminars or meetings, choosing a safety topic to be tackled in the coming period, agreeing a target, and at the subsequent meeting reviewing progress

- regular safety tours of the workplace – to show your commitment and interest, and in conversations with staff, encouraging them to make suggestions on safety matters

- following up accidents with a discussion of what went wrong, identification of how the problem could have been avoided, and then being seen to take action

- including safety awareness in incentive schemes (e.g. a star system, employee of the month award)

- health and safety suggestion scheme

- setting up a health and safety committee. In workplaces where a recognised trade union has negotiating rights, the Safety Representatives and Safety Committee Regulations 1977 apply. Further requirements are set out in the 1992 management of health and safety regulations.

HSE Enquiry Point
For information and advice about health and safety at work. The staff will handle general enquiries (Monday to Friday, 9 a.m. to 5 p.m.), provide special information and help you find your way around HSE.

Health and Safety Executive, Information Centre, Broad Lane, Sheffield S3 7HQ

Tel: 0742 892345   Fax: 0742 892333
HSE Free Leaflet Line   Tel: 0742 892346

Here the carbon dioxide safety poster (page 11) is in place on the cellar wall of a Whitbread pub.

Some ways to increase safety awareness

- competitions: posters, slogans

- health and safety quiz between departments, or with teams from other establishments in the company or the locality

- hazard spotting by representatives of one department in another department – being less familiar with that area of the workplace, can be a help in spotting problems, but watch that the exercise does not lead to bad feeling

- features about health and safety in your in-house news bulletin

- participation in national award schemes which have a high public and industry profile, such as Investors in People, National Training Awards and quality management schemes (e.g. BS 5750)

Safety signs and markings

Certain hazards cannot be avoided. Some are temporary, e.g. a slippery floor while it is being mopped. Some exist because of the age or structure of the building, e.g. a low doorway in an historically interesting building. Some are there because of the nature of the work or the business, e.g. pressurised gas cylinders for drink dispensers.

Safety signs and markings (e.g. a black and yellow striped band to mark the edge of a step) must be provided in these circumstances – the proposed Safety Signs at Work Regulations 1994 require the use of a safety sign for any risk you cannot adequately control by other means.

You must also provide a sign where some element of risk remains after following standard precautionary procedures, e.g. warning of the corrosive nature of a cleaning fluid, and perhaps to remind staff to wear gloves when handling it.

In this example, the sign acts as a reminder, and supports workplace training. It would not be accepted as an alternative to proper procedures, nor would it be accepted if there was a way of avoiding the hazard altogether, e.g. switching to a different cleaning fluid which gave the same results.

If you are buying new safety signs of any type, including illuminated ones and fire alarms (defined as signs in the regulations), you should check with your supplier that they comply with the new regulations. There is no need to replace existing signs, assuming you obtained them from a reputable supplier and they conformed with British Standard 5378 (as specified in the Safety Signs Regulations 1980), or, in the case of fire safety signs, BS 5499.

If you think that some of your existing signs are pre-1980, check their design against an up-to-date catalogue from one of the safety sign suppliers.

If self-employed, you do not have to erect safety signs for risks which you are already aware of. But you should remember your duty under the Health and Safety at Work etc. Act to protect the safety of customers, visitors, staff, etc. Signs can play an important role.

The triangular shape and yellow and black colour scheme is a warning sign – i.e. there is a risk of danger.

The crossed-through red circle is a prohibition sign – i.e. stop/you must not do something.

The solid blue round shape with white pictogram is a mandatory sign – i.e. obey/carry out the action.

The sign for an emergency escape or first aid is a rectangular or square, white on a green background. Fire-fighting signs are rectangular or square, white on a red background.

 CHECKLIST

Using safety signs

- appropriate for the purpose – amusing and effective perhaps to put a radioactive material warning sign on your office door, but not appropriate!
- readily visible – an illuminated or reflective sign might be necessary in a dark area
- properly maintained – not covered with graffiti, clean, light bulb working
- of a permanent nature – made of durable material, securely attached
- in the case of movable signs for temporary hazards (e.g. slippery floor) – durable and functional. Don't add to the hazard by propping the sign against the mop bucket!
- located appropriately – where the first-aid equipment is actually kept, removed when the situation to which it refers no longer exists
- located effectively – too many signs together will confuse the message
- used correctly – staff responsible for positioning temporary or permanent signs should receive instruction and training on their correct use
- understood by those they affect – particularly important where a sign supports safe workplace procedures, e.g. on manual handling
- conforming to the standards set out in the regulations and/or the British Standard – reputable suppliers of safety signs will see that their products do this

With thanks to:
Stocksigns Limited, Ormside Way, Redhill, Surrey RH1 2LG

What you need to report officially

If you work for a company or organisation, you are likely to have detailed guidance on the reporting procedure for accidents and other incidents (e.g. an explosion). There are four basic rules which apply to every type and size of operation and a further explanation of these follows:

- a record must be made of all accidents, even minor ones, which involve a member of staff or a trainee. You can devise your own form for this, or use the accident record book available from HMSO, BI 510 (shown below)

- establish promptly whether the matter is one of those that must, by law, be reported to your Environmental Health Department, give immediate notification if required, and submit the official form, F2508 (shown on opposite page)

- provide any information requested by the Department of Social Security in relation to claims by an employee

- get expert advice (via head office if appropriate) if you receive an insurance claim or solicitor's letter about the incident.

There are no shortcuts. The list of accidents, incidents and diseases which have to be reported is long and complex. Much of the information may have to be repeated on two or three different forms – but if you get things right from the start, you will certainly cut down on the difficulties that can occur as the various parties and authorities make their investigations.

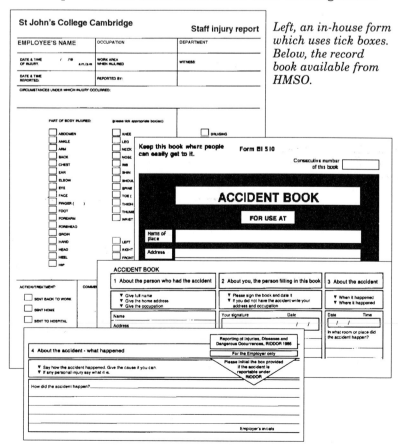

Left, an in-house form which uses tick boxes. Below, the record book available from HMSO.

Accident with borrowed bandsaw not reported for two months

A restaurateur in Oxfordshire was fined £5500 plus £870 costs in September 1993 after an accident involving a bandsaw.

A chef at the restaurant severed the knuckle of his left hand in January while cutting a veal bone with a bandsaw. The restaurant had run out of pre-cut bones and was using a saw borrowed from a local supplier.

The defending solicitor told the court the accident might still have happened if a guard had been in place, because the chef's finger had slipped on to the blade's cutting edge.

The wound eventually became infected and had to be operated on, though at the time it seemed the knuckle had been merely cut, not severed, and when the company tried to report the accident to the council it was told there was no need to do so.

An official report was made to the council in March, and it was then that environmental health officers visited the restaurant and later issued summonses.

The restaurateur was fined £5000 for failing to provide a guard on the saw and £500 for not reporting the accident within seven days.

Caterer & Hotelkeeper, 30 September 1993

ANALYSIS

Consider the events at the restaurant. What went wrong? What questions does this report leave unanswered? Here are some to start you thinking:

1 Why do you think the impression was given/received that the accident did not have to be reported?

2 What led the accident to be reported in March, at least two months after the event?

3 What circumstances may have led to the guard being removed?

4 As the machine was borrowed, who should have checked that it had a guard?

5 What could have been the reason for borrowing a bandsaw, as opposed to obtaining an alternative supplier of cut veal bones?

6 What weaknesses does the incident suggest in the management of health and safety at the restaurant?

7 Why do you think the fine was so high?

Accident books

You should record in the accident book or on a suitable form at least the following details:

- date and time of incident
- full name, address and occupation of persons involved
- nature of the injury or illness or dangerous occurrence
- place where the incident happened and a brief description of the circumstances
- names (and if necessary addresses) of any witnesses
- details of the person making the report, and time and date the report was made.

The accident book should be kept in a place where employees can easily have access to it. While employees are required by law to tell you as soon as they have had an accident, they can do this by writing about their accident in the accident book. Anyone else can do this on their behalf.

Accident records must be kept for three years.

For matters which have to be reported

You are required to report to your environmental health department (or health and safety inspector, as appropriate) any of the matters covered by the Reporting of Injuries, Diseases and Dangerous Occurrences Regulations 1985 (RIDDOR). Here is a summary of the rules:

1 In the event of death, major injury or acute illness (see box) notification must be made by the quickest practicable means (i.e. by telephone – note the name of the person you spoke to, and the time of the call, or fax – which has the advantage that you have a record). You must also follow this procedure for a dangerous occurrence, e.g. a serious explosion, irrespective of whether it causes any injury. The reporting form (see step 3) has a full list.

2 Notifiable accidents and incidents are those arising out of or in connection with work. Thus the emphasis is on where the problem occurred, and less on whom it affected. You should certainly follow the procedure for employees, trainees and contractors, and it is strongly recommended that you do so when a customer, visitor or other member of the public is involved.

3 This must be followed up within seven days by a written report using form F2508.

4 The employer should submit the report – alternatively, the person who is in control of the premises, or for trainees who are not employees, the person whose undertaking makes the immediate provision of the training. A self-employed person who suffers a major injury at his or her workplace is exempted from the need to make immediate notification, but should see that the form is sent in within seven days, if necessary completed by some other person.

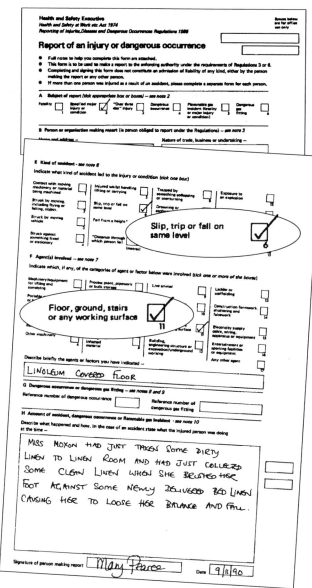

Reportable injuries and illnesses

- any injury which results in the person being admitted immediately into hospital for more than 24 hours
- fracture of the skull, spine or pelvis
- fracture of any bone in the arm, wrist, leg or ankle (but not a bone in the hand or foot)
- amputation of a hand, foot, finger, thumb or toe or any part of these if the bone or joint is completely severed
- loss of eyesight, a penetrating injury to an eye or a chemical or hot metal eye burn
- burn or other injury resulting from an electric shock which requires immediate medical treatment or results in a loss of consciousness
- loss of consciousness which results from lack of oxygen, or absorption of any substance by inhalation, ingestion or through the skin
- acute illness requiring medical treatment where there is reason to believe it has resulted from exposure to a pathogen (any agent that can carry disease) or infected material, or absorption of any substance by inhalation, ingestion or through the skin

'Three-day injuries' or 'Lost-time accidents'

A report on form F2508 must also be made within seven days for all injuries which incapacitate a person for more than three consecutive days after the day of the accident (i.e. prevents the person from doing work of a kind he or she would normally be expected to do). The day of the accident is not counted. Intervening days off do count. So, if an accident occurs on a Friday and the person returns to work on Tuesday, you would have to report it, even if that person normally had the weekend off: Saturday *day 1*, Sunday *day 2*, Monday *day 3*.

Subsequent death

If death occurs later and within one year of the accident, notification must be given in writing as soon as you learn of the death. You must do this whether or not the accident was reported at the time.

Reportable diseases

Where a person at work has a reportable disease and his or her work involves an activity where that disease is likely to be a particular problem, a report must be sent to the environmental health department (or your nearest Health and Safety Executive office) on form F2508A (shown below). The examples of reportable diseases given in the box are the only two you are ever likely to come across in catering, but there is a full list in the guidance notes which accompany the reporting form.

The report should be completed once the employee's doctor has confirmed diagnosis of the disease to you. If you are self-employed, you should submit the form (or get someone to submit it on your behalf) as soon as the doctor has told you that you are suffering from a reportable disease. You do not have to wait for written confirmation.

Reportable diseases linked to work activities in catering establishments

cataract – in work involving exposure to electromagnetic radiation, including radiant heat

occupational asthma – in work where dusts arise from processing, handling, transporting or storing barley, oats, rye, wheat or maize and meal or flour made from them

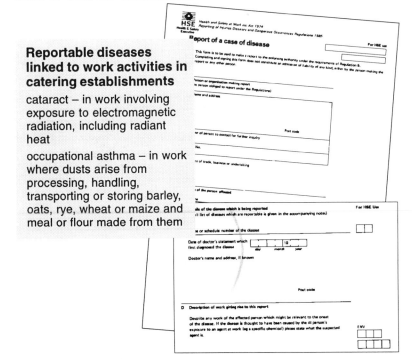

Customer dies after falling down steps in pub

An item in the *Camden New Journal* caught the attention of officers at the London Borough of Camden's Environmental Health Division, as it reported the death of a customer at the Wolsey Tavern (since renamed) in Kentish Town. The customer had fallen down the staircase leading to the men's toilets in the basement shortly before closing time on 3 December 1992.

Ronald Bolton, principal EHO with Camden, visited the pub on 8 February 1993. His inspection of the staircase revealed that it was dangerous. Made of solid concrete, it was steep, with steps of different heights. The metal covers over the front of each step were not fixed into the concrete but just stuck on. The metal cover to the top step was missing, another was loose, and many of the rubber strips in the metal covers were loose or missing.

When interviewed, the manageress said she had not been given any guidance, instructions or documents on health and safety matters by the company (Taverns of London Ltd. – a British subsidiary of an Australian company).

Camden brought charges against the company and against two of its senior officers, one of whom had been sent from Australia to run the company.

The hearing before Wells Street Magistrates Court lasted three days. The court heard that new metal covers to the stairs had been fixed days after Mr Bolton's first visit. Subsequently the whole staircase had been replaced. This work had been paid for by the Australian parent company, even though the British operation was in a 'parlous financial position' with losses of £2 million.

The company was fined £10,000 plus £2200 costs. Its two senior officers were fined £1000 each plus £2200 costs each.

Ronald Bolton, London Borough of Camden, Environment Department

ANALYSIS

1 Identify what went wrong at the Wolsey Tavern. Why might this have happened?

2 Camden brought four charges against the company and its senior officers. What do you think these might have been?

3 What are the main costs (financial and other) of this accident?

Notifiable diseases

Under the public health control of diseases legislation, there is a separate requirement not knowingly to expose other persons to the risk of infection. As an employer this means that you should take reasonable precautions to check that your staff are not suffering from a notifiable disease. There are three practical ways of doing this:

- questionnaires which staff complete when they first start work

  information in your staff handbook and on the staff noticeboard

- questionnaires which staff complete after returning from holidays abroad.

Through these steps you will encourage staff with symptoms to see their doctor. In the meantime, they should be taken off any duties or work which might spread the disease. The doctor is required to report the disease to your environmental health department.

Food poisoning is also a notifiable disease. That means if the doctor of one of your customers or staff becomes aware or suspects that his or her patient is suffering from food poisoning, and the diagnosis is confirmed, the doctor will inform the local authority and you can expect a visit from the environmental health officer.

Under the Food Safety (General Food Hygiene) Regulations 1994, a food handler (and that would include barstaff) suffering from food poisoning symptoms must tell the proprietor of the food business. You should immediately contact your environmental health department, to report the matter. (This requirement overlaps with the public health control provisions, but emphasises the need for extreme care in such situations.)

Notifiable disease in an establishment with accommodation for guests and/or staff

If you become aware that one of your guest or staff bedrooms has been occupied by a person with an infectious disease, you must have the room and everything in it properly disinfected before the room is occupied by anyone else. 'Properly disinfected' means disinfected to the satisfaction of the environmental health department, medical officer of health or other registered medical practitioner, and confirmed in a certificate issued by that person.

Suitable precautions should also be taken to ensure that you or your staff or external contractors are not infected, e.g. laundering the bedlinen or disposing of the rubbish. The person suffering from the disease has a duty not to put other people at risk.

Routine screening of food handlers who are returning from sick leave or from abroad

Name ....
Address ....
Workplace ....
Name and address of GP ....

Tick as appropriate, please

	YES	NO
Have you been suffering from sickness, diarrhoea or bowel disorder?	☐	☐
If so, did you see your doctor?	☐	☐
If so, did your doctor do any stool culture tests?	☐	☐
Have you had hepatitis?	☐	☐
If so, did you see your doctor for clearance?	☐	☐
Have you been suffering from infections of skin, nose, eyes, throat or ears?	☐	☐
If so, did you see your doctor?	☐	☐
If so, did your doctor do any tests?	☐	☐
Did your doctor give treatment for any condition?	☐	☐
Are you still on treatment?	☐	☐
Have you been outside the UK?	☐	☐
If so state which countries you visited:		
Were you in contact with anyone who had typhoid, paratyphoid, salmonella or cholera?	☐	☐
Were you ill during your stay?	☐	☐
Whilst away, did you have any flu-like symptoms?	☐	☐
Have you any symptoms now?	☐	☐
If not, how long have you been free of symptoms?		

Employee's signature ....
Manager's signature ....
Date ....

A questionnaire which staff complete when they first start working for you, and another after returning from a holiday or visit abroad can provide valuable early-warning.

With thanks to County of Avon, Senior Client Officer for School Meals

---

Notifiable diseases

The requirements are set out in the Public Health (Control of Disease) Act 1984 and the Public Health (Infectious Diseases) Regulations 1988. There are similar provisions in Scotland.

Diseases you might encounter include:

typhoid, paratyphoid and other salmonella infections, amoebic and bacillary dysentery, and staphylococcal infections likely to cause food poisoning

viral hepatitis, tuberculosis, poliomyelitis

the mainly childhood illnesses:

chickenpox, measles, mumps.

Diseases people who have lived or travelled abroad are more likely to have contacted include: malaria, rabies, tetanus, cholera, plague, yellow fever.

Accident-related claims for Social Security benefit

Your accident reporting procedure should ensure that appropriate details are available if one of your staff submits a claim to the Department of Social Security for benefits in respect of personal injury, or work-related illness. Take care that you complete the Department's form BI 76 very carefully. It could be used in evidence if the employee decides to make a separate claim against you for the accident.

If you have any doubts at all regarding whether the accident happened as claimed by the employee, mention this on the form.

The answers to the questions you will be asked on the form should be available from your accident book or personnel records. But check that you record sufficient information to answer these particular questions (as weeks or months may have passed since the incident occurred):

- On the day of the incident, what hours was the claimant expected to work?

- What hours did the claimant actually work?

- At the time of the incident, what was the claimant doing?

- At the time of the incident was the claimant authorised for the purposes of work to be where he/she was? You are asked to explain if the answer is no.

- Was the claimant authorised to do what he/she was actually doing? Explain if not.

- Did anyone see the claimant's injuries at, or shortly after, the time of the incident? If yes, describe the injuries clearly, stating left or right where appropriate.

- Did the claimant report any injuries which were not seen? If yes, what were these?

Keeping details of DSS enquiries

Any enquiries from the Department of Social Security regarding claims made by your employees in respect of a disease for which they are claiming State benefit must also be recorded. Details should include: name, sex, age, occupation, nature of the disease for which the claim was made, date of first absence from work, and date of diagnosis of the disease.

Records should be kept at the relevant workplace, or, if this is not reasonably practicable, at the employer's usual place of business. They must be kept for at least three years, and the enforcing authorities/Department of Social Security officials given extracts/allowed access as and when required.

Fall in corridor brings damage claim

On 9 November 1990 a room attendant, Marina Moxon, fell in the corridor of the hotel. She was returning from the linen room with clean linen, when she 'brushed her feet against some newly delivered linen' causing her to lose her balance and fall.

On 10 April 1991 the Department of Social Security sent form BI 76, in connection with industrial injuries benefits.

On 28 March 1992, the hotel received a letter from solicitors, under instructions from Miss Moxon to claim damages for her personal injuries and consequential losses.

In the next year came visits from insurance inspectors and much correspondence. The hotel was asked to give details of Miss Moxon's pre-accident earnings over a period of 13 weeks.

On 30 March 1992, a County Court Summons arrived, claiming damages in excess of £5000 plus costs. The hotel was accused of negligence under the Offices, Shops and Railway Premises Act 1963, for failing to ensure that all floors, passages and gangways were kept free of obstruction. The particulars of this charge included:

- instituted or devised a system whereby room attendants left the linen unstacked and/or unfolded in the passageway

- failed as aforesaid despite complaints to one Larry Chetto about the state of the passageway.

The summons, supported by a 4-page letter from the orthopaedic registrar of the hospital where Miss Moxon had treatment, claimed that Miss Moxon 'is and has been unable to work. She is at a grave disadvantage on the open labour market.'

In July 1992, the hotel was asked to provide the earnings details of a 'comparable earner'. Mrs Wayne did similar work to Marina Moxon, and had given her permission for the details to be disclosed. The details requested had to cover the two years since the accident occurred, and the six months up to the accident.

The matter concluded, the hotel's solicitors presented their final bill on 1 March 1993.

With thanks to Pauline Brown, Jarvis Hotels. Names and details have been changed or omitted for confidentiality.

ANALYSIS

1 What records would be needed to provide the information asked for at various stages?

2 How easy would it have been for you to provide all the information required?

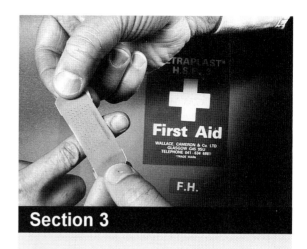

Issues which relate to workplace safety and welfare inevitably overlap with more specific requirements – notably on first aid, noise and waste disposal (considered in this section) and equipment safety, fire and security (dealt with in Sections 4, 5 and 6).

Workplace safety and welfare

Workplace regulations

The Workplace (Health, Safety and Welfare) Regulations 1992 impose wide-ranging requirements on all new workplaces, and on those which have been modified, extended or converted (the checklists on pages 20–22 are based on some of these). Otherwise, existing workplaces have until 1 January 1996 to comply.

The regulations expand on employers' duties under the Health and Safety at Work etc. Act 1974 to protect everyone in the workplace. They also ensure that adequate welfare facilities are provided for people at work.

The term workplace includes all areas of the premises, indoors as well as out-of-doors (e.g. the delivery bay or car park) to which your employees have access while at work. It also includes areas your employees use to get to their work area – e.g. corridors and staircases, private paths and entrance ways. The regulations do not apply to work areas used solely by self-employed persons.

While wide-ranging, the requirements set out in the regulations are less prescriptive – and certainly more up-to-date – than those of the Offices, Shops and Railway Premises Act 1963, which they replace. To a large extent therefore, the onus is on employers to establish, provide and maintain in good condition the facilities and conditions which ensure a safe and healthy workplace for everyone.

Managers and supervisors have a similar duty in respect of matters under their control (including any modification, extension, etc. for which they are responsible).

If you rent or lease your premises, or your workplace is on the premises of the client (as in a contract catering situation), the owners are responsible for ensuring that facilities and services within their control comply with the regulations.

Contents guide

Workplace regulations.............. this page

Noise 23

First-aid arrangements 24

Manual handling 26

Hazardous substances...................... 29

Protective clothing............................ 32

Waste disposal 33

Violence in the workplace 34

During the six-year period 1986–92, the hotel and catering industry reported 10,604 injuries to employees – probably less than one-third of those that occurred. Of these, 8700 led to absences from work of over three days. Seven were fatal.

Slips, trips and falls accounted for 35% of reported injuries, 16% resulted from handling, lifting or carrying, and 11% were caused from chemical burns.

Health and Safety in Service Industries, 1991–2, Health and Safety Executive/Local Authority Enforcement Liaison Committee

Maintenance work

Regular maintenance makes for a safer workplace. It also makes good business sense. Equipment which becomes faulty is not only dangerous to use, but it can cause unnecessary expense and disrupt the level of service you give customers. Badly worn carpets are a tripping hazard, and they give customers a poor impression.

To meet both needs, you should have:

- a planned maintenance programme for equipment, fixtures and fittings and the premises themselves, so that they are inspected, tested, adjusted, lubricated, cleaned, etc. as appropriate and at suitable and regular intervals

- records of what maintenance work is carried out and when, including non-routine maintenance (e.g. because equipment has become faulty)

- a review procedure for checking that the maintenance system is properly implemented and to help identify where improvements can be made

- a reporting system which all staff follow, to ensure that potentially dangerous defects are remedied immediately they are discovered

- emergency procedures, with responsibility clearly understood, in order that no one is put at risk in the interval between discovery of a dangerous defect and its repair – e.g. closing off part of the workplace until the fault is repaired.

Cleanliness

Hygiene considerations and the need to give a good impression to your customers demand high standards of cleanliness at all times. But pressures of business mean that back-of-house areas can fall below standard. Rapid deterioration will follow if you allow staff to get away with untidiness, or if they feel insufficient attention is paid to the cleanliness of work areas.

The regulations (see previous page) require:

- the workplace – including furniture and fittings – to be kept sufficiently clean

- waste materials should not be allowed to accumulate, except in suitable containers

- apart from regular cleaning, action should be taken when necessary to clear up spillages, or to remove unexpected soiling of surfaces.

Door safety
- ☐ if door swings in both directions, a vision panel (made of appropriate thickness and type of glass) provides a clear view of the space close to both sides
- ☐ on main traffic routes, conventionally hinged doors fitted with vision panel
- ☐ vision panel position makes it possible to see a person in a wheelchair on the other side
- ☐ sliding doors have means of preventing door coming off the end of the track, or falling out if the suspension system fails
- ☐ upward opening door has device to prevent it falling back unexpectedly
- ☐ safety features on power operated doors and gates prevent anyone being struck or trapped, and allow operation in the event of a power failure

---

Floors and personal traffic routes
- ☐ slopes (e.g. for people with disabilities) provided with secure handrail
- ☐ open sides of staircases securely railed or fenced
- ☐ changes of level (e.g. step between floors) which are not obvious, marked to make them conspicuous
- ☐ slip-resistant surfaces for floors and traffic routes likely to get wet
- ☐ effective drainage provided for floors likely to get wet
- ☐ likelihood of spillages minimised through efficient design of workplace, work surfaces and work systems
- ☐ floors not overloaded (e.g. by converting a room on the first floor of an old building to a store)

Safe lighting
- ☐ stairs well lit, shadows not cast over the main part of the treads
- ☐ car parks adequately lit, shadows not creating danger areas
- ☐ outdoor routes used by pedestrians adequately lit after dark
- ☐ local lighting provided where necessary at individual workstations
- ☐ dazzling light and annoying glare (from lights or windows) avoided
- ☐ lights and light fittings maintained to avoid causing hazards
- ☐ light switches where they can be found and used easily
- ☐ lights and windows not obscured, e.g. by stacked goods
- ☐ lights replaced, repaired or cleaned before level of lighting becomes insufficient
- ☐ fittings or lights replaced immediately if they become dangerous, electrically or otherwise
- ☐ windows and skylights cleaned regularly
- ☐ emergency lighting where sudden loss of light would present a serious risk

Preventing slips, trips and falls

Slips, trips and falls account for more than half of the accidents which occur in the catering industry. Regularly inspect floors, corridors, staircases, pathways, car parks, drives, etc. for defects or obstructions which might cause:

- a person to slip, trip, fall, or to drop or lose control of anything being lifted or carried

- instability or loss of control of vehicles and/or their loads, e.g. when deliveries are made.

Get repairs done promptly, where necessary closing off the area in the meantime.

Poor storage practices also lead to many serious accidents. Check that materials and objects are stored and stacked in such a way that they are not likely to fall and cause injury.

Ventilation, temperature and lighting

Enclosed workplaces require sufficient ventilation, a reasonable temperature during working hours, and adequate lighting to enable people to work, use facilities and move from place to place safely and without experiencing eye-strain. The lighting should be by natural light, so far as is reasonably practicable.

Generally, 16°C is considered to provide reasonable comfort without the need for special clothing (although air movement and relative humidity may require a slightly higher or lower temperature). Thermometers should be available so that anyone at work can check the temperature for themselves.

In unusually hot or cold weather, you may need to provide fans or extra heaters for staff, especially if their job involves a lot of sitting, or if they have to work in a normally unoccupied storeroom, for example. Check that the equipment is in good working order, and that staff are aware of the dangers, e.g. from overloading electric sockets, or creating a tripping hazard with the cable. Portable room heaters are a notorious fire hazard.

Opening windows and doors provides an effective way of cooling an area, but watch that this does not create a different hazard:

- hygiene – from flies and insects entering the kitchen

- fire – propping open a fire door

- security – allowing unauthorised entry to the building.

In areas where the temperature has to be kept lower than 16°C, or where it is not practicable to warm or cool the work area (e.g. outdoor delivery bay), you should provide suitable protective clothing, rest facilities and where practical, a system of task rotation, e.g. for staff stocktaking in a cold room or very cool cellar.

CHECKLIST

Safe traffic routes
- kept free from obstructions
- where temporary obstructions are unavoidable, warning signs are used
- immediate steps taken to prevent spillages or leaks creating a slipping hazard
- snow and ice cleared off entrance steps, external fire escapes, etc.
- paths and roadways cleared of snow or gritted or route closed off
- areas made unsafe by damage, or wear and tear, cordoned off

Smoking rules in work areas

In catering establishments smoking will be forbidden in the kitchen, cellar, behind the bar and other work areas for reasons of hygiene and safety. Other work areas such as the bar lounge or restaurant are also customer areas, and although staff will not usually be allowed to smoke in those areas, any rules on whether customers can smoke will largely depend on marketing considerations.

In exclusive staff areas, such as rest rooms (see next page), offices and similar parts of the workplace where hygiene, safety and marketing considerations do not apply, you should consider the advice of the Health and Safety Executive:

- all employers, after consultation with employees, should develop and implement a policy on smoking in work areas

- as part of such a policy, non-smoking should be regarded as the norm in enclosed workplaces and special provision should be made for smoking, rather than vice-versa.

Health at Work Picture Library

Welfare facilities for people at work

Your staff obviously need to have the use of suitable sanitary conveniences and personal washing facilities. Where the same facilities are used by customers, the number must be increased to ensure that staff can use them without undue delay.

For between one and five people at work, there should be at least one WC and one wash station; for 6 to 25 people, two WCs and two wash stations. If separate accommodation is provided, e.g. men and women, a separate calculation must be made for each group. In this case, one WC and one urinal is sufficient for up to 15 men, and two WCs and one urinal for 16 to 30 men.

Washing facilities must be provided in the immediate vicinity of every sanitary convenience, and in the vicinity of changing rooms, with clean hot and cold water (or warm water) supply, soap and towels (or other suitable means of cleaning and drying). No room containing a sanitary convenience should communicate directly with a room where food is processed, prepared or eaten.

Changing rooms and lockers

Staff who have to change out of their personal clothes into a uniform should be able to do so in reasonable comfort and privacy, and be able to store their own clothes safely (e.g. in their own lockable locker). Otherwise, the minimum requirement is a separate hook or peg for each person.

The storage facilities provided for personal clothing should enable it to hang in a clean, warm, dry, well-ventilated place where it can dry out during the course of a working day if necessary. Where work clothing which is not taken home becomes dirty, damp or contaminated due to the work, provision should be made for it to be stored separately from personal clothing. Where work clothing becomes wet, the facilities should enable it to be dried by the beginning of the following work period unless other dry clothing is provided.

Rest and eating facilities

One or more designated rest rooms should be provided at readily accessible places. The facilities should be suitable for:

- staff to eat meals where it is not desirable or appropriate for food to be eaten in the workplace

- non-smokers to avoid discomfort caused by tobacco smoke (e.g. by providing separate facilities, or making rest facilities non-smoking zones all or some of the time)

- pregnant women and nursing mothers to rest (including, where necessary, the facility to lie down)

- staff who have to stand to carry out their work, to sit from time to time (if their work gives them the opportunity).

Staff toilets
- ☐ well ventilated so that offensive odours do not linger
- ☐ offensive odours prevented from entering other rooms (e.g. by ventilated lobby area, mechanical ventilation)

Water closets (WCs)
- ☐ connected to a suitable drainage system, with an effective means for flushing with water
- ☐ toilet paper in a dispenser or holder
- ☐ coat hook
- ☐ means for disposing of sanitary dressings (in facilities used by women)

Washing facilities
- ☐ hot and cold, or warm water
- ☐ large enough to enable effective washing of face, hands and forearms
- ☐ showers or baths provided where the work is particularly strenuous, dirty, or results in contamination of the skin by harmful or offensive materials
- ☐ showers fitted with a device to prevent users being scalded by very hot water

Privacy
- ☐ each WC is a separate room or cubicle with a door which can be secured from the inside
- ☐ not possible to see urinals, or into communal shower or bathing area from outside the facilities when any entrance or exit door opens
- ☐ separate rooms containing conveniences for men and women (unless each convenience is in a separate room)
- ☐ windows obscured (e.g. frosted glass, blind or curtain) unless it is not possible to see into them from outside
- ☐ doors at entrances and exits (or other measure to ensure equivalent degree of privacy)

Noise

f you provide noisy entertainment (including discotheques), r regularly have a bar full of people enjoying themselves, vith juke boxes etc. in the background, you will need to take teps to protect your staff from suffering damage to their tearing. There is likely to be a problem if your staff:

have to shout to each other when they are two metres or less apart

complain their ears are still ringing after leaving the workplace.

)amage to hearing depends on the level of noise – measured n decibels units as dB(A) – and how long you are exposed to he noise on any day, and over a longer timescale (since the ffect can be cumulative).

:mployers have a duty to reduce the risk of damage to the earing of employees to the lowest level practicable. Steps vhich might be appropriate for staff at a noisy disco (where ound levels could be 100 dB(A) and over) include:

regular breaks during shifts and/or shorter shifts

arranging rotas so that the same staff are not on duty at the disco every session, but work in less noisy environments on alternate days, for example

locate the bar further away from the music, or in an adjacent room or, if this is not possible, incorporate sound bafflers or barriers to reduce the noise penetration into the bar servery.

'he Noise at Work Regulations 1989 require employers to arry out a noise assessment where any employee is exposed o a noise above 85 dB(A) (equivalent to a noisy bar) on verage, for eight hours continuously. For shorter periods han this, the allowable noise level is higher (see box). The egulations also make requirements for the provision of ear rotectors, information, instruction and training to mployees likely to be exposed to risk.

Noise as a statutory nuisance

'he Environmental Protection Act 1990 strengthened those rovisions of the Public Health Act 1936 under which steam utlets from boilers, smells and noise from extractor fans, etc. ould be regarded as a statutory nuisance. The fine increases ach day a nuisance persists.

or licensed premises, perhaps a more important onsideration is the view that will be taken when the licence s due to be renewed, or when special licences are applied for.)bjections on the grounds of noise nuisance (from the police, r from other businesses or residents in the locality) are sually taken very seriously.

Allowable noise levels	
Level dB(A)	*Hours of exposure*
90	8
93	4
96	2
99	1
102	½

Bass Taverns

Control of noise

Among the special problems of noise associated with the business which can cause nuisance to the local community are: early morning deliveries, customers leaving the premises (on foot and by car), children's play areas, extraction ventilation and refrigeration equipment, and entertainment.

New installations

1 Manufacturers will be required to indicate noise levels of equipment prior to installation.
2 Designers and installers will take into consideration noise levels related to siting and the neighbourhood, with particular reference to night time.

On completion of the installation it should be monitored to ensure noise emissions do not exceed those set in British Standard 4142.

Existing equipment and installations

The licensed house manager is responsible for the operation of the outlet without nuisance to customers and the general public and must take action to resolve any known nuisance within his/ her control:

• reduce/control amplified music (live entertainment/juke box/disco)
• encourage customers to leave the premises quietly
• use mechanical means for ventilation, rather than opening doors and windows
• liaise with suppliers regarding delivery noise.

Complaints from the general public must be acknowledged as soon as possible, and the complainant informed the matter will be responded to by the retail operations manager.

First-aid arrangements

You have a duty under the Health and Safety (First-Aid) Regulations 1986 to make adequate first-aid provision for employees and trainees who are injured or fall ill while at work. If you are self-employed, you should have a first-aid box in a place where it might be needed.

Your legal responsibilities to provide first aid do not extend to non-employees (guests, customers, visitors, contractors, etc.) – but not to offer first aid in such circumstances would probably be thought unreasonable. Where first aid is provided for non-employees, this should not cause the standard of provision for employees to fall below the required minimum.

Where a number of employers share the same workplace (as might happen if you were running the bar at a regatta or similar outdoor event), one of these (e.g. the largest) can accept responsibility for the first-aid provision (including first-aiders) for all the employers, thus avoiding unnecessary duplication and costs. A written agreement should set out the arrangements, with a copy for each employer. All employees should be told about the arrangements.

First-aid equipment and facilities

All establishments need at least one first-aid box kept in a readily accessible place. Larger workplaces may need a number of first-aid boxes at different locations.

The first-aid box should contain appropriate supplies (see box) and nothing else. Tablets for headaches etc. must never be kept in the first-aid box. Anyone suffering from such a complaint should seek their own treatment, otherwise you could be held responsible if a pain killer, for example, led to a side effect.

Soap, water and disposable drying materials should be available for first-aid purposes. If this is not possible (e.g. in the travelling kit for the sales manager), individually wrapped moist cleaning wipes (of the type not impregnated with alcohol) must be provided.

First-aid boxes in kitchens should include blue plasters for protecting cuts. This means you can tell quickly if someone has suffered an injury, and where necessary rearrange responsibilities.

There is a second practical purpose: if the plaster does fall off, then being brightly coloured it is more likely to be spotted before it finds its way into a dish of food.

As a protection against Aids, or any other infection which might be carried in the blood of the patient, the person administering first aid must ensure that any cuts or open wounds on his or her hands are covered with a plaster, or wear sterile gloves.

CHECKLIST

First-aid boxes

- box will protect the contents from damp and dus▪
- box clearly identified as a first-aid container: whit▪ cross on a green background
- contains suitable first-aid materials and nothin▪ else (if the dressings are of the recommende▪ type, there should be no need to keep scissors i▪ the box)
- contents replenished promptly after use
- no items past their expiry date (as marked o▪ packaging)
- contains only those items which the first-aider ha▪ been trained to use

Contents

Should contain sufficient quantities of each item. I▪ most cases these will be:

- 1 card giving general first-aid guidance
- 20 individually wrapped sterile adhesive dressings (assorted sizes, blue for use by food preparation staff, so they are detectable)
- 2 sterile eye pads, with attachment
- 6 individually wrapped triangular bandages
- 6 safety pins
- 6 medium-sized individually wrapped unmedicated sterile wound dressings (approx. 10 cm x 8 cm)
- 2 large individually wrapped unmedicated sterile wound dressings (approx. 13 cm x 9 cm)
- 3 extra large wound dressings (as above, approx▪ 28 cm x 17.5 cm)

if mains tap water is not readily available:

3 x 300 ml disposable containers of sterile water or sterile normal saline (0.9%) (seal mus▪ be unbroken)

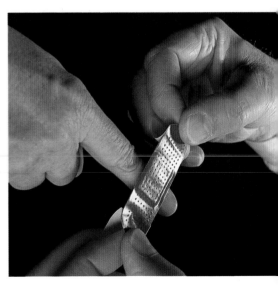

Number of first-aiders required

This will depend on the nature of the work being carried out (large catering kitchens would generally be regarded as high risk), ease of access to outside medical services, the number of employees, their distribution within the establishment, whether shift work is involved, etc. You cannot consider just the number of employees:

- when access to medical treatment outside the workplace is difficult (e.g. long distance to nearest accident and emergency facilities), one or more first-aiders will generally be required, irrespective of the nature of the work or the number of employees

- in high risk situations where working hours extend over a long period, two first-aiders will usually be required, their duties being arranged so there is cover at all times when employees are at work

- in hazardous situations there should be not less than one first-aider for every 50 employees.

Recording first-aid treatment

A record should be made of all first-aid treatment given in the workplace. A clear cross-reference to the accident book may avoid duplication of some of the information required, i.e. full name, address and occupation of the person treated, date, time, place and circumstances of the accident, details of injury, signature of person making the entry and address if different.

Appointed person to take charge in the absence of a first-aider

In a workplace with few employees, readily accessible to emergency services, where there are no specific hazards, and a qualified first-aider is not available, it may be sufficient to appoint a person to take charge (e.g. to call an ambulance) if a serious injury or illness occurs, and to be responsible for first-aid equipment. Ideally, an appointed person should be trained to give first aid for the minor injuries most likely to occur in your workplace, e.g. burns and cuts.

In other workplaces, the occasions when it is necessary to appoint a person to take charge should be limited to exceptional and temporary circumstances which result in the absence of a first-aider.

Informing employees of first-aid arrangements

Employees should be told of the location of first-aid equipment and facilities, and how to contact the first-aider, as part of their induction programme, and if they move to a different work location. At least one notice, conspicuously placed, should remind staff of this information. Different language versions of the notice may be needed.

The actual location of the equipment should be clearly marked.

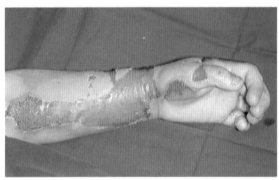

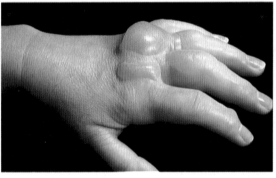

The Wellcome Trust/National Medical Slide Bank

Burns and scalds accounted for 6% of all reported injuries in the hotel and catering industry over the six-year period 1986–92. Unless prompt action – and the correct action – is taken to relieve the burn, the damage can be much worse. Would you know what to do?

CHECKLIST

Selecting people to be trained as first-aiders

- reliable
- likely to remain calm in an emergency
- able to cope with physically demanding duties
- able to leave work duties immediately to go to the scene of an emergency
- able to cope with an intense course of study (the initial course is usually four days) and able to use the knowledge and skills learnt during the course

Manual handling

A common misconception is that the weight of the load is the main, or only, factor you should consider before judging whether it is safe to lift, hold, move or carry an object. But there are many other factors that make manual handling a potential risk. These include the size and shape of the load, what sort of movement is involved in handling it, your own strength, and the working environment. What is safe one day might lead to serious back injury the next, because you are over-tired, or the lighting is poor, or you had to make an awkward movement to negotiate a small space.

Responsibilities

The Manual Handling Operations Regulations 1992 require employers to:

- eliminate manual handling operations which involve the risk of injury

- assess the risk for those operations which cannot be avoided – this means analysing every activity involving manual handling, looking at sickness and injury reports, and usually involves a formal, written report

- take steps to minimise the risk – the risk assessment will provide a basis for action.

The self-employed should take similar steps to safeguard themselves.

If none of the operations in your workplace involves a significant risk of injury, you do not need to make a formal assessment. This might be the situation in a small restaurant, where you mostly buy from a cash and carry (packages small and easily lifted), and anything awkward or heavy to handle is put in position by the delivery person.

Carrying out an assessment

1 List every task or activity which involves manual handling. A useful way of tackling this is by work area, e.g. kitchen/catering, cellar/stores, bar, housekeeping.

2 For each, consider not just the task and the load, but the working environment and individual capabilities – the activity on page 28, which is based on the Health and Safety Executive example assessment checklist, provides a framework to help you.

3 Discuss and consult with your staff the activities they are involved in. This can give a valuable insight into problems and possible solutions. Do not overlook the tasks you perform yourself.

4 The assessment need go no further if you establish that only low risks are involved. This might be the case in modern premises, where loads are light, and the staff concerned have had training in manual handling techniques.

Moving a keg

1 Wear sturdy shoes and gloves to protect against metal splinters.

2 Stand in front of the upright keg, feet apart to give you balance. Place hands at 'ten to two' position on top rim of keg.

3 Use your body weight to tilt the keg slightly towards you so that it is balanced on the rim. Move smoothly, do not jerk!

4 Use your hands to turn the keg so that it moves on its rim to the required position. Move your feet as you go to avoid twisting your body. Allow to return to the upright position.

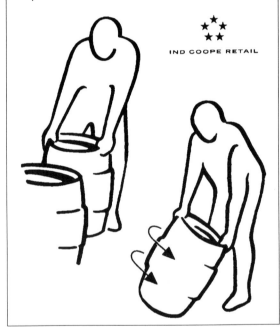

These instructions can easily be adapted to apply to a drum of oil or dishwashing fluid, for example.

 **CHECKLIST**

Reducing the risk of injury

- store loads at waist height (the optimum height)
- use good handling techniques
- improve work routines and introduce job rotation so that lifting tasks are spread among more people/over a longer time interval
- make the load smaller and easier to handle
- provide adequate room for manoeuvre
- provide information
- provide training

For medium and high risks, you should consider what methods there are of avoiding the hazard, e.g.:

- ordering small packages from suppliers
- rearranging the stores, so that heavier items are at waist level
- training the staff involved in manual handling techniques
- using team handling
- providing trolleys
- arranging for suppliers of heavy items to deliver them to the place they are used, e.g. by the dishwasher or in the cellar, ready for connection.

You will, in these cases, need to make follow-up checks to confirm that the result is satisfactory.

For activities which are medium or high risk and cannot be avoided, or which require changes to the building, you will need to seek the advice of your senior management.

Other practical steps you can take

The assessment will provide a framework for action, but there is much that can be done on a day-to-day basis as part of your supervisory/management role, e.g.:

- discourage staff from feeling they need to prove their strength (to you or to colleagues)
- make allowance for reduced strength as a result of tiredness or poor health, or particular circumstances, e.g. pregnancy – and encourage the person concerned to do so
- see that assistance is given to staff carrying loads which are bulky, difficult to hold (e.g. smooth sides, person wearing gloves, greasy hands), sharp, hot or otherwise potentially dangerous

  encourage staff to try the load first, not to make assumptions (an old oil container may not be empty, the rubbish bin could be much heavier than usual), to make more journeys with smaller loads where necessary, and to check in advance that their way is clear and suitably lit

- be alert to the dangers introduced by unusual circumstances, e.g. in outdoor areas in frosty conditions
- for team lifting, put one person in charge to ensure movements are coordinated, and use people of similar height and physical capability

  check that uniforms and protective clothing are not restricting movement, or introducing hazards (e.g. pockets or fasteners which might get tangled up with the load).

Examples of manual handling risks

☒ carrying further than 10 metres without rest and/or repeatedly

☒ a man carrying a load heavier than 25 kg (e.g. two cases of 12 bottled beers weigh 28 kg)

☒ a woman carrying a load heavier than 17 kg (a box of 12 x 75 cl bottles of wine weighs just under this limit, 15 kg)

☒ a man lifting a 10 kg load from the floor to waist height (7 kg for a woman)

☒ stacking cases of drinks or boxes of food above 5 cases high

☒ pushing, pulling, or lifting large pack goods: e.g. because kegs have been stacked on top of each other (depending on its capacity, a full keg weighs between 40 and 118 kg)

These figures are for illustrative purposes only. The regulations do not set limits.

 CHECKLIST

When carrying an object

- do some warm-up exercises, such as side bends, hula hoop, lunging to either side (these help avoid muscle strain or jarring a joint)
- examine the object
- plan the task and route
- get close to the load, feet slightly apart to give a stable base
- adopt a good posture: hands as nearly level with the waist as possible, don't bend your knees fully as this will leave little power to lift, keep your back straight (tucking in the chin helps), keep shoulders level and facing in the same direction as the hips
- keep a firm grip
- move smoothly, keeping control of the load
- keep close to the load
- use your feet if you need to turn, don't twist your body
- place the load down, then if necessary adjust its position
- check the load won't fall over, roll, etc.

⚡ ACTION

Below are some typical factors which indicate a risk in manual handling – because of the nature of the task, because of the load, because of the working environment, because of individual capabilities.

1 For those that apply to your workplace, tick **yes**, then assess the level of risk: low, medium or high.

2 Discuss with your colleagues and/or staff, what other activities occur in your workplace which involve risk, and for each of those you have rated medium or high, what action can be taken to reduce the risk.

TASK	Example	Yes	Low risk	Medium risk	High risk
Load has to be held away from the body	Large saucepan of boiling vegetables being carried to the sink to drain	☐	☐	☐	☐
Involves twisting the body	Moving crates of beer up to the bar to restock	☐	☐	☐	☐
Involves stooping	Bending under a low door while carrying a load	☐	☐	☐	☐
Involves reaching upwards	Lifting a pile of clean sheets off a high shelf	☐	☐	☐	☐
Involves a long vertical movement	Lifting boxes of tinned food after a delivery, from the floor to a high shelf	☐	☐	☐	☐
Involves carrying long distances	Carrying a room service meal order to a distant bedroom	☐	☐	☐	☐
Involves strenuous pushing or pulling	Moving a cask or keg of bitter into position	☐	☐	☐	☐
Involves risk of unpredictable movement	Carrying heavy trays through a busy bar	☐	☐	☐	☐
Involves frequent or prolonged physical effort	Rearranging the seating in a function room	☐	☐	☐	☐
Involves insufficient rest or recovery periods	Rearranging a function room between events	☐	☐	☐	☐
Involves team handling	Carrying up steps or slopes (most of the weight has to be taken by the lower person)	☐	☐	☐	☐
Involves handling while seated	Reservations assistant moving heavy files or boxes of stationery from under or over the desk	☐	☐	☐	☐

LOAD	Example				
Heavy	Carton of cleaning agents	☐	☐	☐	☐
Bulky or unwieldy	Furniture	☐	☐	☐	☐
Difficult to grasp	Shrink-wrapped object	☐	☐	☐	☐
Unstable/contents likely to shift	Heavily stacked tray of dirties from the restaurant	☐	☐	☐	☐
Sharp, hot or otherwise potentially damaging	Saucepan of boiling liquid/tray of glasses	☐	☐	☐	☐

WORKING ENVIRONMENT	Example				
Space constraints prevent good posture	Low-ceilinged storeroom	☐	☐	☐	☐
Uneven, slippery or unstable floors	Delivery area after rain	☐	☐	☐	☐
Variations in levels of floors or work surfaces	Cellar in old building	☐	☐	☐	☐
Extreme temperature, humidity or air movement	Walk-in freezers	☐	☐	☐	☐
Poor lighting conditions	Outdoor delivery area on dark winter morning	☐	☐	☐	☐

INDIVIDUAL CAPABILITIES	Example				
Does task require unusual strength, height, etc.?	House porter	☐	☐	☐	☐
Does job put at risk those who are pregnant or have health problems?	Linen room attendant	☐	☐	☐	☐
Does task require special knowledge or training?	Cellar person	☐	☐	☐	☐

Hazardous substances

Dangerous chemicals, toxic fumes and harmful dusts are not usually connected with catering. But closer examination of the cleaning cupboard, maintenance store and cellar will reveal a variety of substances that carry health warnings.

Steps to prevent and control risks from such substances are set out in COSHH (said as 'cosh'), the Control of Substances Hazardous to Health Regulations 1988.

Responsibilities

These are the steps you must take:

- carry out an assessment of the health risks which arise from the use of hazardous substances in your workplace

- prevent, or, if this is not reasonably practical, control the exposure to such substances

- provide your staff with information, instruction and training on the risks and the precautions they should take.

Employees must make full and proper use of control measures and personal protective equipment you provide, and report any defects without delay.

Manufacturers and suppliers of hazardous substances must provide safety information.

Carrying out an assessment

1 What substances are present and in what form? Itemise each of the cleaning agents used in the kitchen, cellar and housekeeping departments, and any harmful gases (e.g. carbon dioxide in a drinks dispense system).

2 What harmful effects are possible? Product information sheets and labels will generally provide this information.

3 Where and how are the substances used or handled? This should include storage and disposal after use. The aim is to identify at what stages, and in what circumstances, the substances might cause harm to those using them. This could be by breathing them in (e.g. changing carbon dioxide cylinder in cellar dispense system), absorbing them through the skin or swallowing them (directly or as a result of contact with lips, fingers, etc.), including the risks of spills, damage to containers resulting in leakages, and similar accidents.

⚠ STAFF CHECKLIST

- always follow carefully the instructions for use of cleaning agents
- never mix substances
- don't transfer a cleaning agent to another container which might result in it being mistaken for a non-hazardous product
- NEVER use food containers to store cleaning agents
- always store cleaning agents in the correct place

In a cellar

If you feel any of the following when entering the cellar, leave immediately. It is likely that a leak of carbon dioxide has occurred.

- shortness of breath
- increased heart beat
- tingling of eyes
- desire to cough
- increased breathing rate

Two of the most hazardous substances used in beer and drink dispense systems are carbon dioxide and pipe cleaners.

IND COOPE RETAIL

POTENTIALLY HAZARDOUS SUBSTANCES				
	HAZARD	PROTECTIVE CLOTHING	SPILLAGES	ADDITIONAL NOTES
Cleaning of beer lines, tanks and dispense equipment	Corrosive	Rubber gloves, eye protection	Wash away with plenty of water	Contact with acids creates toxic gas. Contact with aluminium may create a highly flammable gas
Dishwasher detergent	Corrosive	Rubber gloves	Wash away with plenty of water or dilute and lift with a mop	Keep away from aluminium, galvanised or brass containers
Descaler for dishwashing machines	Corrosive	Rubber gloves, eye protection	Neutralise spills with baking powder. Absorb on sand. Wash floor well	Keep away from other cleaners or alkaline substances
Rinsing agent in glass washing machines	Irritant	Rubber gloves	Absorb, rinse thoroughly	Acidic

There is no way of avoiding some of the hazardous products in use in catering establishments, so the assessment often takes the form of a sheet or document which details the precautions and control measures. Information can be added or updated, if procedures are changed, or different substances used (e.g. because you have changed suppliers).

Preventing exposure to hazardous substances

Is the use of the substance really necessary? Can the same result be achieved in another way? In most circumstances, for example, sanitary fittings can be kept clean and hygienic with the regular use of neutral and alkali detergents. Strong acid cleaners may only be required rarely, or not at all.

Focus on the end result required, rather than on how the task is done now. A combination of less hazardous products and different work methods might achieve the same result. Would it be safer and more effective to contract the job out to a specialist (e.g. deep cleaning of the kitchen)?

Keep up-to-date with product information. Substances considered safe when your requirements and procedures were last reviewed may since have been found to expose the user to danger.

Product Handling Information Sheet

Product Name	Diverforce L4 (QED Plus)
Manufacturer	Diversey Limited Emergency tel.: 0604 405311
Physical form	Yellow liquid
Purpose	Machine dishwashing fluid
Method of use	By automatic dispensing equipment
Hazardous contents	Sodium hydroxide
Risks	Corrosive, causes severe burns
Safety precautions	Avoid contact with skin and eyes Wear suitable gloves and eye/face protection Keep out of reach of children
Storage	Store upright in original containers, closed, cool place
Flammability	Non-flammable – compatible with water
Harmful effects	Eyes: corrosive. May cause severe permanent damage Inhalation: capable of causing irritation Skin: corrosive Ingestion: corrosive

Spillage
Wear suitable gloves and eye/face protection. Hose away with plenty of water and run to waste unless this would contaminate a water course or vegetation, in which case absorb spillage with sand or earth

First aid
Take off immediately all contaminated clothing. Eyes: rinse immediately with copious amounts of water and obtain immediate medical attention
Inhalation: remove from source of vapour or spray mist
Skin: wash thoroughly and obtain medical attention
Ingestion: remove product from mouth, give water or milk to drink if subject is conscious. Get medical advice without delay

Disposal
For small quantities, wear suitable gloves and eye/face protection. Dilute with water and run to waste, diluting greatly with running water. Disposal of larger quantities should be in line with the Control of Pollution (Special Waste) Regulations 1980

Use of hazardous substances

Ward/department	Catering
Substance name	Universal degreasing powder
What is it used for?	To remove grease from deep fat fryers
How many people use it?	2
What are their job titles?	Chef
How often is it used?	Once a week
Amount used weekly?	2½ kg per week
How is it supplied?	10 kg containers
How is it stored?	In original packaging
Where is it stored?	In locked cleaning chemical storeroom
Is it mixed with anything?	Yes, water
In what proportions?	Dependent on amount of grease and conditions – guidelines on container
What is the expiry date?	N/A
Supplier	G W Poulmans Group
What are the hazards?	Product has irritant properties
Do staff follow a safe system of work?	Yes
Is personal protective equipment (PPE) worn?	Yes, goggles and rubber gloves
Are staff trained in safe use?	All staff receive COSHH training
Is there a procedure for major spillages?	Yes
Are there first-aid arrangements?	Yes, accident book First-aid boxes Eye wash/wash hand basins Qualified first-aider on duty
How are empty/partially empty containers disposed of?	Flush to drain with copious quantities of water
Any fire hazards	Product is non-combustible

Above: product handling information from supplier (extracts from original printout).

Left: a simple COSHH assessment / information sheet.

At North Middlesex Hospital, sheets like this are kept for each hazardous product in the catering department's COSHH folder.

recautions and control measures

eview the use of personal protective equipment (PPE), e.g.
oves and face masks. Could protection be achieved in some
her way? Is the protection given by PPE adequate (e.g. do
oves protect the whole arm from splashes and drips when
eaning the inside of the oven)? Does the PPE carry the CE
ark (a requirement of more recent legislation, see page 32).

estrict access to hazardous substances to those trained in
eir use (e.g. by colour-coding and/or storing separately from
neral-purpose substances).

se dispensers which ensure correct dilution. Staff should
t have to make complicated calculations.

eview work procedures to stress safety aspects. Do they give
idance on how much to make up of a solution, is the amount
lequate for the job, is the concentration level adequate, how
e the substances carried from storage to where the task is
ne, would the risk of spillage be reduced if dilution was
ne on-site?

n't expect your staff to be chemists. For example, why
ould they know that some cleaning agents for washrooms
d toilets, none especially hazardous on its own, will
oduce a chemical reaction if they are mixed, producing a
isonous gas?

e vigilant and insist on high standards. Otherwise
miliarity with products – and never having experienced a
oblem – might lead to shortcuts, e.g. not putting on gloves.

neck shelf-life of products. Beyond the best-before date, they
n rapidly lose their effectiveness. This may lead staff to
crease concentrations, or use another product, putting
emselves unnecessarily at risk.

et help from your suppliers

any suppliers produce a range of staff communication aids:
lour-coding systems, wall charts, job cards, cleaning
hedules, etc.

e prepared

onitor extent of exposure. A substance that is only slightly
izardous in normal use (e.g. washing-up detergent) can
use serious skin complaints (dermatitis in this example, see
otograph on page 4) if exposure is increased (e.g. through
ing too much detergent, or because the amount of washing
has increased).

eep information and data sheets on harmful products in a
fe place, where they can be referred to in case of an
nergency. Ensure that you (or the designated first-aid
ficer) are familiar with the treatment required for all
irmful substances kept on the premises.

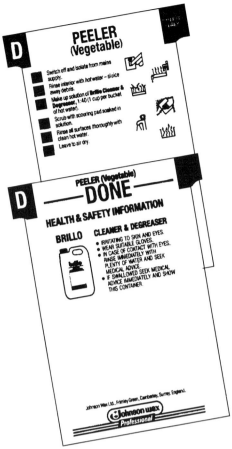

*One example of the useful communications aids
available from suppliers. The cards fit into a wall
file, which has sections and colour codes for*
Cleaning after use *(red),* **Daily cleaning**
(green) and **Weekly cleaning** *(blue – slots are
allocated to each day of the week).*

*One side has instructions for cleaning the item,
and using the recommended product, the other
side has safety information. When the task has
been completed the card is returned to its slot,
with the DONE side facing outwards.*

*A training record sheet of the sort shown here is a
useful way of reminding staff of their obligations,
once trained, to adopt the established schemes of
work, and wear appropriate protective clothing.*

Protective clothing

Although caterers will be familiar with the need to wear uniforms, gloves, goggles, safe footwear, etc., the term *personal protective equipment* or *PPE* may be less familiar.

PPE includes all equipment intended to be worn or held at work which protects against one or more risks to the health and safety of the user, and any addition or accessory designed to meet that objective. The PPE must be:

- appropriate for the risks involved and workplace conditions

- compatible with any other PPE which has to be worn (e.g. so that goggles do not reduce the effectiveness of a breathing mask)

- effective in preventing or adequately controlling the risks, without increasing overall risk (e.g. PPE used in a kitchen will need to be cleaned easily, loose fitting PPE would not be appropriate if it could be caught in equipment)

- take account of ergonomic requirements (e.g. methods of work, ability to see, talk and hear)

- fit the wearer correctly, with the minimum discomfort, and not cause any health problems (e.g. wearing a mask worsening a difficulty with breathing).

From this, it follows that the PPE should be readily available to employees, and that employees should be trained and encouraged to use it effectively.

Where PPE should be provided

PPE should only be provided where there is a risk to health and safety that cannot be adequately controlled by other means. PPE is seen as a measure of last resort because it:

- protects only the person wearing it, whereas measures controlling the risk at source benefit everyone in the workplace

- may limit the wearer's vision or mobility

- will only be effective if correctly fitted and maintained and properly used.

The regulations do not apply to ordinary working clothes and uniforms which do not specifically protect the health and safety of the wearer. Nor do they apply to protective clothing provided primarily for food hygiene purposes, e.g. chef's uniform, although this may also provide protection against splashes from hot liquids and foods.

The CE mark

This indicates that the PPE has met minimum levels of performance set out in the regulations. Any personal protective equipment which is worn under the requirements of safety legislation (e.g. COSHH) must carry the CE mark (after a transition period, ending 30 June 1995).

You also need to satisfy yourself that the equipment will work effectively in the workplace, giving genuine protection for the user and comfort.

Employer's responsibilities for PPE

The Personal Protective Equipment at Work Regulations 1992 require employers to:

- provide suitable personal protective equipment to employees who may be exposed to a risk to their health or safety while at work

- make an assessment (usually in writing) to establish that the PPE is correct for the particular risks involved and the circumstances of its use

- maintain the PPE in efficient working order (e.g. clean, periodically tested, regularly maintained, and replaced when necessary)

- provide appropriate storage for the PPE when it is not in use (e.g. safe from contamination, loss or damage)

- provide adequate information, instruction and training so that employees use the PPE correctly

- ensure that the PPE is properly used and that any problems relating to its use are reported as soon as possible.

The self-employed have similar obligations to use PPE to protect themselves while at work.

Waste disposal

As the creator of the waste, you have a duty under the Environmental Protection Act 1990 to look after it, and to see that it is disposed of safely. For any waste you hand on to someone else, you must:

- secure it – most waste should be in a suitable container; loose material loaded in a vehicle or skip should be covered

- check that the person taking your waste away is legally authorised to do so

- hand over a written description of the waste, fill in and sign a transfer note for it (explained below).

Your responsibilities do not end once you have handed over the waste. If, for example, you had used a private contractor and all the details checked correctly, but later you found some of your waste had been dumped illegally (e.g. on a local common), you should stop using that contractor and inform the waste regulation authority. To do this, telephone your local environmental health department, state that it is a general public health enquiry and you wish to be connected to the pollution department of the waste regulation authority.

The paperwork

When you arrange for your waste to be collected or disposed of, even if it is to a charitable or voluntary organisation, you must provide a *written description*. This should give as much information as someone else might need to handle the waste safely. A *transfer note* is also required. This is usually part of the same document. Once completed this must be signed by both parties. Details required are:

- what the waste is and how much there is

- what sort of containers it is in

- the time, date and place the waste was transferred; for multiple consignments give dates between, e.g. 1 April 199X to 31 March 199Y

- your name and address and that of the waste carrier/waste disposal company

- registration/licence details of the waste carrier/waste disposal company, and name of the council that issued it

- reasons for any exemption from the requirement to register or have a licence (for charities/voluntary organisation collections).

Repeated transfers of the same kind of waste between the same parties can be covered by one transfer note/description for up to a year. This sort of arrangement would cover the regular removal of your waste.

You must keep your copy of the description and transfer note for two years.

 CHECKLIST

Safe storage of waste

- container not worn or damaged and (for hygiene reasons) cleaned regularly
- liquids not liable to leak out
- not liable to be knocked or blown over
- lid will not blow open in a strong wind
- secure against animals, vandals, thieves, children, etc.
- contents will not chemically react with each other
- no fire risk
- building and demolition materials safe from scavengers

Waste left for collection

- strong containers/bags to resist wind and rain
- containers/bags secure against disturbance by animals, vandals, arsonists, etc.
- old packaging/cardboard cartons collapsed and securely bundled
- not likely to be blown away by wind
- not likely to be knocked over by passing vehicles or pedestrians
- drums (e.g. of old cooking oil) and similar containers labelled clearly and firmly closed
- items left outside for collection no longer than necessary
- skips covered

Rules of waste disposal

IND COOPE RETAIL

1 Ensure waste is contained and is stored safely, securely and protected from pests.

2 Ensure waste is collected by a recognised contractor, authorised by your area manager. This may require you to sign a long term waste transfer note. Keep the transfer note on file.

3 Where specialist waste (e.g. oil etc.) is collected by an authorised waste collector, it will require a controlled waste transfer note. A copy of this should be kept.

4 Train staff on the procedure for safe storage of waste, including hazardous items such as broken glass etc.

5 Great care must be taken when handling any hypodermics customers have left behind: not only is the needle very sharp, but it may be carrying the Aids virus or other dangers. Hypodermics should be disposed of in a specially provided *Sharps* box (available from suppliers of medical products).

Violence in the workplace .

There are three groups of people who could cause your staff physical harm:

- other staff – most people have their favourite story of chefs losing their temper
- customers – over half the incidents of violence in pubs occur around closing time
- criminals – this might be in the course of a robbery, or out of some act of vengeance.

Violence from other staff

This may be partly a question of management style. Some top chefs, for example, believe in a rough regime, and their staff put up with it for the sake of what they learn about cooking, and the career value of having worked at that establishment. Others deplore it and advise those subject to violence to get another job.

The ultimate course of action for any employee who is physically assaulted by a customer or a fellow member of staff is to take the case to the police and seek a prosecution. As in any court case, you will need strong evidence, such as doctors' reports and reliable witnesses.

Violence from customers

If violence breaks out, you should immediately contact the police using the emergency 999 service (see page 54). Never attempt to return violence with violence.

You and your staff (with appropriate training and guidance) can prevent violence from occurring by:

- spotting the warning signs – this means being out and about among your customers, observing, watching and listening for rowdy behaviour, arguments, aggressive gestures, etc.
- counteracting frustration – with a combination of good customer skills and good service. Where it is necessary to have rules, everyone should be quite clear what these are, and it must be seen that they are applied fairly
- intervening before problems develop into a serious conflict – tactfully introducing a new subject to distract from an argument, exercising firm control, taking the heat out of the situation by talking calmly, slowly and deliberately in your normal tone of voice.

Violence from criminals

This is largely a question of improving security, so that the opportunity for violence does not arise (covered in more detail in Section 6). You should certainly never seek confrontation, e.g. by resisting a request to hand over money, or by reaching for the alarm button.

Protecting your staff

Never leave one female staff member with a male customer: watch staffing levels and ensure a male/female balance, especially at night.

Make sure you know how your staff get home at night. Encourage them to park in safe areas under lights, or to use black cabs or well known mini-cab firms/drivers.

Consider issuing personal alarms to your staff.

If you do install warning instruments such as panic buttons, make sure they can be activated without endangering anyone. By trying to raise the alarm, you could agitate a violent robber. (Generally, the police do not advise the use of panic buttons.)

Some pubs have installed wider counters at the bar, and raised the height of the floor on the staff side of the counter to give serving staff more protection.

Mike Gillette, business crime officer, Scotland Yard, interviewed by Penny Wilson, *Caterer & Hotelkeeper*, 1 October 1992

 A booklet *Violence to Staff* is available from the Health and Safety Executive (see page 12) and more detailed information will be available in *Guidance on Preventing Violence to Staff in the Retail Sector*, to be published by HSE shortly.

Taking over a pub for the first time

The first 6 to 12 months of taking over a pub are the most difficult, particularly if the previous management have tolerated after-hours drinking, gambling, under-age drinking, etc., and if you don't know the area well. Problems include: barred customers returning and regulars trying it on to see how far you will let them go.

To establish order you need to have the respect of your customers. There is no simple formula for gaining this, but the following will help:

- establish clear and consistent standards
- combine firmness with fairness: the same rule for everyone, troublemakers dealt with decisively and appropriately
- create a sociable, friendly atmosphere in which aggressive behaviour will seem out of place (and therefore less likely to happen). Get to know your customers and make them feel welcome
- balance friendly involvement with a degree of professional detachment
- make sure your staff understand their roles and responsibilities in the prevention of trouble, but do not expect them to run the pub for you.

Safety with equipment

Contents guide

Work equipment .... this page

Dangerous machinery 36

Electrical equipment 37

Gas equipment 39

Play areas and equipment 40

In October 1991, a 21-year-old employee of a fast food / take-away restaurant was electrocuted while investigating a fault with filtering equipment for the fryers.

In 1991/92, 43 children aged between 1 and 16 years suffered major injury in play areas, and 35 children in the following year. Most of these involved falls from a height, others were the result of slipping, tripping or falling. However this probably only represents one-third of the number of accidents which occurred, due to the failure to report them under the RIDDOR regulations (see page 15).

Since January 1993, the safety of equipment used in the workplace has been covered by wide ranging and explicit regulations. There is great emphasis on safety in design and construction. There should be the minimum risk of an accident occurring because someone has used the equipment wrongly, or not known about a particular precaution.

Safe procedures for using equipment remain essential. Certain equipment will always have the potential to cause harm, because it has sharp cutting blades, for example.

Training, supervision, further training, regular checks and constant alertness provide vital back-up to the mechanical guards and other built-in safety design features which equipment used in the workplace must have.

Work equipment

The Provision and Use of Work Equipment Regulations 1992 (often shortened to PUWE or PUWER) require employers (and the self-employed) to:

- ensure that equipment is suitable for the purpose(s) for which, and the place in which it will be used

- ensure that equipment is used in accordance with the manufacturer's specifications and instructions

- ensure that equipment is in efficient working order and good repair, inspecting, testing and maintaining it as necessary, and keeping the maintenance records up to date

- where a specific health and safety risk is involved, restrict the use of the equipment to those who have had adequate training

- provide health and safety information and instructions to all those who use work equipment, and to their supervisors or managers

- train those using equipment, and their supervisors and managers.

All equipment provided for use on the premises for the first time (whether it is new, second-hand, hired or leased) must comply with legislation implementing any EC Directive relevant to the equipment. Check that the equipment bears a CE mark (see page 32), and ask the supplier for a copy of the EC Declaration of Conformity. If the equipment is not covered by a product Directive (likely during the transition period, up to 1 January 1997), it should meet very detailed safety requirements.

Dangerous machinery

Section 17 of the Offices, Shops and Railway Premises Act 1963, which required protective measures to prevent the operator coming into contact with any dangerous part of machinery, has been replaced by similar provisions in the 1992 work equipment regulations. The two sections of the Act which apply to young persons' use of equipment, and training continue in force:

- no person under the age of 18 may clean, lubricate or adjust *any* machine if doing so exposes that person to risk of injury

- no person may work on *prescribed dangerous machines* (see box) unless he or she has been properly instructed and trained or is directly supervised or in the process of being trained.

Prescribed dangerous machines

Such machines are specified in the Prescribed Dangerous Machines Order 1964. The following might be found in catering establishments:

power-driven
- machines of any type equipped with a circular saw blade
- vegetable slicing machines
- food mixing machines when used with attachments for mincing, slicing, chipping and any other cutting operation, or for crumbing
- worm-type mincing machines
- rotary knife bowl-type chopping machines
- pie and tart making machines
- dough mixers
- dough brakes
- wrapping and packing machines

power-driven or manual
- circular knife slicing machines
- potato chipping machines
- guillotine machines (e.g. for paper cutting)

Training plan for a mixing machine

– extracts only

Attention You will be trained to assemble and dismantle a mixing machine and taught how to use and clean the machine.

Interest What can the machine specifically be used for?

What would kitchen life be like without the machine?

Training will help in the achievement of an NVQ/SVQ.

Question	Why is it important that you are trained?
Answer	Law, own safety and safety of others.

Step 1 **Ensure the machine is switched off and unplugged.**

Question	Why is it important to ensure the machine is switched off and unplugged?
Answer	Avoids any chance of the machine starting whilst being cleaned.

Step 2 **Approach machine with attachment (e.g. whisk) inside the bowl. The bowl to be fitted with collar guard.**

Question	Why is the machine attachment inside the bowl?
Answer	More efficient and effective. It's also safer.

Steps 3 to 5 are: fitting bowl clamps, beater/whisker, and how the gearing works. Trainer then demonstrates steps and trainee practises.

Step 6 **Demonstration of mixer, e.g. crumble mix**

Question	Why must our hands be dry?
Answer	To avoid any electrical shocks when starting the machine.
Question	What could happen if we had loose items of clothing?
Answer	They could get caught up in the machine while it is running.
Question	Why do we switch off the machine before adding more ingredients?
Answer	To avoid splashes.
Question	Why do we never leave the machine running unsupervised?
Answer	To reduce the risk of accidents.
Question	Why would you never reach into the bowl whilst the machine is running?
Answer	It could result in a very serious injury.

Trainer demonstrates step 6 and trainee practises. Steps 7 to 9 cover dismantling, cleaning and reassembling. The session ends with a verbal recap and a practical check prior to recording the training.

With thanks to David McKown, Training Manager, Residential, Catering & Conference Services, The University of Sheffield

Accident with a dough machine

CASE STUDY

The young man started work at around 6 o'clock in the evening. The company had a policy that permitted staff to finish early if they had completed an agreed quota.

It was well known that the seals on the machine deteriorated over time to a point where dough could seep into the mechanical drive area. When this occurred it became accepted practice to take off a fixed guard at the rear of the machine, a time-consuming process, and remove the offending dough.

The fixed guard was interlocked with the machine controls, so that when it was removed the power to the machine was cut off.

On the day of the accident the young man was rushing to finish, so that he could join friends at a late night party. The seals had deteriorated to the point where he had to remove the rear guard every 20 minutes to extract the dough. Because of this, and his eagerness to finish, he decided to try and defeat the safety interlock switch so he could keep the machine running while he removed the dough. He was able to rig the machine without difficulty.

Unfortunately his loose clothing got caught in the gears, and dragged him into the machine, killing him.

Ian Pemberton in *The Safety & Health Practitioner* (edited with permission), March 1993

ANALYSIS

Identify as many of the causes/factors which led to the accident as you can. Who has responsibility for these?

Electrical equipment

Electrical equipment has particular hazards:

- contact with even the normal mains supply, through a faulty lead or equipment, can be fatal – and much catering equipment works off a higher voltage

- overheated cables to electrical equipment, current leakage due to poor or inadequate insulation, sparking or arcing of electrical equipment can start a fire.

Safety with electrical equipment

1 Only use equipment which conforms to relevant British Standards, and carries a BS kitemark or CE mark.

2 When additional or replacement electrical systems are installed, ensure the work is done in accordance with the Electricity at Work Regulations (see overleaf) and the *16th Edition of the IEE Regulations* (your contractors will be familiar with this document, which sets out the technical data and minimum standards of the Institution of Electrical Engineers).

3 Ensure that equipment which is faulty, or suspected of being faulty, is immediately taken out of use until repaired or replaced.

4 Train staff who use portable equipment to look out for the visual signs of damage.

5 Have equipment regularly maintained and checked. The frequency of safety/maintenance checks and who carries them out depends on the amount of risk in using the equipment.

Contractors or electricians may tell you it is the law to have all equipment checked every six months, or once a year. This is not the case. It is the employer's responsibility to decide how often there are checks.

Setting up a maintenance programme

Inspect your workplace, listing the location and type of every item of electrical equipment. When there is one, note the manufacturer's number. Alternatively, use your own numbering system, putting a label where it will not be defaced, or spoil the appearance of equipment in public view. Such a list will help you check that no items are missed from routine checks or inspections. It will also help identify items which are brought into the workplace without permission.

Decide what inspections are required, by whom and when:

- *type of inspection* – exterior visual check, or full test and inspection, or both (e.g. visual monthly, full annually)

- *by whom* – an electrical contractor, your maintenance engineer, yourself or a senior member of staff. In all cases, follow specific instructions from the manufacturer.

Portable electrical equipment

Get into the habit of regularly checking portable electrical equipment, i.e. equipment which has a lead (cable) and plug and which is normally moved around (e.g. vacuum cleaners, kettles, table lights, irons) or which could be moved (e.g. food mixers, rotary irons).

Before checking, always turn off the machine (at the controls and at the plug), then unplug.

Check for any of the following:

- cable damage – e.g. fraying, kinking, cracking or tearing on outer part (sheath), coloured insulation of inner cables visible

- plug damage – e.g. cover cracked, prongs loose or bent, prongs blackened (a sign of overheating)

- damage to external casing of equipment, loose parts, missing screws

- evidence of misuse – e.g. melted casing (suggesting overheating), moisture present (suggesting equipment has got wet).

If you find any faults, report the details/arrange for the equipment to be repaired. In the meantime withdraw it from service and label it clearly so that it will not be used.

When using portable electrical equipment

- keep the cable away from sharp edges. Make sure it is not constantly flexed or stretched near the point of entry to plug or equipment, or lying in such a way it might cause someone to trip

- make sure there are no knots in the cable

- ensure the equipment is stable and safely located, e.g. heaters not too close to flammable material, sockets not overloaded (use a proper distribution board, not an adaptor).

Checking a plug

With moulded plugs, check the fuse is correct for the equipment being used (according to the manufacturer's instructions).

With other plugs, remove the plug cover to check:

- fuse is correct (as above)

- cord grip holding the outer part (sheath) of the cable tightly

- wires, including the earth where fitted, attached to the correct terminals: green/yellow to E or earth, brown ('Mr Brown is a live wire') to L or live (this will be attached to the fuse holder), blue to N or neutral

- terminal screws are tight

- no sign of internal damage, overheating, corrosion, etc.

The person who does the check must be competent (see checklist). A visual check of cables and plugs on portable equipment is within the competence of someone who has been given basic training

- **when** – consider what equipment is used for, where it is located, and manufacturer's recommendations.

You will wish to have some equipment (e.g. refrigerators, microwave ovens) tested and inspected regularly (e.g. yearly), because breakdown would cause considerable inconvenience.

Some smaller items of equipment (e.g. irons) will need to be visually checked by you or a competent member of staff every 6 to 12 months, and tested/inspected every 1 to 2 years. More frequent visual inspections, e.g. quarterly, may be necessary for portable heaters which are moved from place to place, and used roughly, and equipment which has a lot of use by customers or guests (hair dryers, kettles, etc.).

Double insulated equipment (e.g. some desk-top computers, table lamps) will not normally require testing, but formal visual inspection must be made every 2–4 years.

Even small establishments have quite a number of items. A written record of safety checks will reduce the risk of a piece of equipment being overlooked, and help ensure continuity when there are changes of staff or responsibility.

 CHECKLIST

In-house inspection, maintenance or repair of electrical equipment

The person responsible for doing this should have adequate:

- knowledge of electricity
- experience of electrical work
- knowledge of the equipment/system to be worked on
- experience in making in-house inspections/ maintenance/repairs
- experience in recognising at all times whether it is safe for the work to continue

Selecting a contractor or consultant:

- are you clear what has to be done?
- what will count as a successful outcome?
- have you fully briefed the contractor/consultant?
- have you had experience of the contractor's/ consultant's previous work?
- are you satisfied as to the competence of the contractor/consultant?

Adapted from *Health & Safety in the Office*, Winter 1993, Mike Everley

---

 Electricity at Work Regulations 1989

The regulations require employers, the self-employed and employees in so far as they have a measure of control over the dangers of electric shock, burn, fire or explosion associated with electrical equipment used at work to ensure that equipment is suitable for the use for which it is provided, maintained in good condition and properly used.

Under this very wide ranging duty (which should also be seen in the context of the PUWE regulations), specific points that may need attention because the equipment is electrical are:

- equipment should not be put into use where its strength and capability may be exceeded in a way that may give rise to danger (e.g. overloading plug sockets)
- equipment should be of appropriate construction where it might be exposed to adverse or hazardous environments (e.g. extreme temperatures, wet, dirty or corrosive conditions, explosive or flammable substances)

- equipment should be covered with insulation material, earthed and protected as necessary
- joints and connections in an electrical system must be mechanically and electrically suitable for use
- efficient means, suitably located, must be provided for protecting from excess of electrical current (e.g. fuses and circuit breakers)
- suitable means should be available for cutting off the supply of electricity and securely disconnecting electrical equipment
- the electricity supply should be cut off – that is, isolated from the electricity supply, not just switched off – before any work (e.g. maintenance or repair) is done on or near equipment (unless there is a very good reason not to do so, and suitable precautions are taken)

- adequate precautions must be taken to protect the safety of anyone carrying out work on electrical equipment which has been made dead (i.e. so there is no risk of someone else turning the electric supply back on before the work is completed)
- adequate working space, means of access and lighting should be provided to protect anyone doing work on or near electric equipment
- anyone working on or near electrical equipment should possess the appropriate technical knowledge and experience, or be working under the supervision of someone who has.

All electrical equipment used at work is covered, whenever it was made. Equipment includes items which use, conduct, distribute, control, store, measure or generate electricity.

Gas equipment

Before asking anyone to install, service or repair gas appliances or fittings, you must make sure that the person is registered with The Council for Registered Gas Installers (CORGI). This is a requirement of the Gas Safety (Installation and Use) (Amendment) Regulations 1990.

Safety with gas equipment

1 All key personnel should know how to turn off the mains gas supply. If the only place this can be done is a room normally kept locked (e.g. a basement store), the key must be accessible in an emergency. Ideally, there should be a second gas valve which gives a quick way of turning off the supply to the kitchen.

2 After work has finished in the kitchen, make a final check that all equipment has been properly turned off.

3 When the gas supply has been off, all pilot lights will need to be re-lit. This should only be done by someone with the necessary training.

4 Have equipment regularly serviced. Ignition jets and pilot lights should be kept clean. Problems with self-ignition devices etc. must be fixed without delay .

If leaking gas is detected

What action you take will depend on the area where the gas smell is detected. In a kitchen, the fault might be quite simple to remedy, e.g. a pan has boiled over and put out the flame. There are three priorities:

- avoid doing anything that might cause the gas to ignite – e.g. using a naked light, or striking a match, or turning a light or other electrical equipment on or off (which can create sparks)

- turn off any gas appliances which are still on, and check that all others are properly turned off

- open windows (and exterior doors) to get rid of the gas and leave them open until the leak has been stopped and any build-up of gas has dispersed.

If this process (which should take very little time) fails to reveal the source of the problem, turn off the gas supply in the room itself, or if this is not possible at the meter. All pilot lights should then be turned off (otherwise they will leak gas when the supply is turned on again).

Call in a gas service engineer to trace and repair the fault.

If gas continues to escape after the supply has been turned off at the meter, call British Gas emergency services. You should have the number to hand.

Do not turn the gas supply back on until you are told it is safe to do so.

Buying gas equipment

All equipment must comply with various safety regulations. Buying from a reputable supplier should prevent any problem. Also, from 1 January 1996 many gas appliances and gas fittings will carry the CE mark. This means they satisfy the safety and efficiency requirements in the Gas Appliances (Safety) Regulations 1992.

 CHECKLIST

Instructions for using equipment

- readily accessible and understandable to everyone in the workplace

- provision made for special needs, e.g. employees with language difficulties

- explain the conditions in which the work equipment may be safely used

- clear step-by-step instructions for operating

- instructions for dealing with emergencies and dangers which might arise

- amended where experience in using the equipment enables certain steps to be more clearly expressed

Play areas and equipment

Play areas with slides, bouncy castles, climbing frames, swings and so forth, are a popular customer attraction at many restaurants, pubs and hotels. Unfortunately, they can lead to accidents when children run into equipment, trip or stumble, for example (see box).

Youngsters may not appreciate the dangers of using play equipment, or deliberately abuse it. You can help reduce the risks by:

1 Careful choice of site for outdoor areas. Factors to consider include: fire escape routes, quality of drainage (so the site does not get waterlogged), quality of soil (not toxic through previous usage), protection against adverse environmental conditions (e.g. strong winds) and local hazards (e.g. road traffic), located where parents or guardians can adequately supervise.

2 Careful location of equipment. Children should not have to cross in front of or behind swings to get to other items. Moving equipment should not be placed in the entrance area. Swing frames should not be sited east to west (to avoid users being dazzled by the sun) – for this reason, and to avoid heat build-up, slides should not face the sun.

3 Only installing equipment which has been purpose-built and designed for use in a public play area. The British Standard 5696 *Play Equipment for Permanent Installation Outdoors* provides guidance on installation, maintenance, construction, performance and testing of play equipment.

4 Fencing off outdoor play areas, or providing some other means of preventing access during closing times and on other occasions when its use would be a risk (e.g. if the area is covered in snow or ice).

5 Checking play areas at least daily for signs of damage, broken glass, etc.

6 Establishing a planned maintenance and inspection programme (e.g. on a six-monthly basis) by the equipment supplier or specialist contractor.

7 Reminding parents and guardians of their responsibilities to supervise their children while in the play area.

8 Reminding children of the safety rules.

9 Closing off the play area immediately any of the equipment becomes unsafe, or if there is a danger of over-crowding or rowdy behaviour.

With some equipment, e.g. inflatable bouncing devices, consider limiting access to the times when you can provide supervision. This will prevent over-crowding and rough horseplay, and prevent damage to the equipment, e.g. a child piercing the walls of a bouncy castle with a pen knife.

With thanks to John Forte, Allan Powers, Michael Hall and Jeff Dixon

---

Maintenance of play areas and equipment

Maintenance is the essential feature of a safe play area.

Daily inspections

To be carried out by the manager as part of his/her overall responsibilities for the safe operation of the business.

Check for obvious damage, vandalism, broken glass and the operation of any safety devices. Hazards or repairs should be dealt with immediately, and where necessary the area or equipment closed off.

Annual inspection

To be carried out by the company's area surveyor.

Check condition of surfaces, fencing, etc. and for each piece of equipment: signs of damage, wear, corrosion, loose fixing devices, condition of paintwork/finishes, lubrication of moving parts.

Notices

While it is accepted that children entering the play area will usually be under supervision of relatives, this does not absolve the company and/or manager from his/her supervisory role. However, parents should be reminded of their responsibilities and a warning notice must be displayed.

Construction of equipment

All equipment should be constructed to a minimum standard in line with British Standard 5696.

Therefore all play equipment provided to the company for use by the general public should be to a commercial standard and not a domestic type.

Access to private facilities

The general public should not have access to any equipment provided by/for use by the manager's family.

Accidents in play areas: 3 case studies

- An eight-year-old child was climbing on the outside wall of the slide. She fell a distance of about 5 metres, fracturing her left leg.

- A six-year-old boy came down the slide at great speed. Unable to stop at the bottom, he hit a log fixed to the ground close by, suffering a large swelling on the back of his head.

- A child was climbing on the frame and fell, breaking his left arm. A notice attached to the frame, which was situated in the children's play area of a pub said: FRAME IS FAULTY AND FALLING DOWN. CUSTOMERS USE FRAME AT OWN RISK.

From reports by environmental health departments to the Health and Safety Executive, published in *Health and Safety in Service Industries 1991–2*

ire needs heat, fuel (anything which will burn) and oxygen
in other words, air). Kitchens are one of the most dangerous
places. Carelessly discarded matches and cigarette ends are
another major hazard.

Open doors and windows encourage a fire to burn faster by
increasing the oxygen supply and fanning the flames. As the
fire develops, poisonous smoke and gases spread up
staircases, along corridors, through ventilation shafts, etc.

You can do much to limit the risk of fire starting by controlling
all potential sources of heat or fuel, or better still by removing
one or the other altogether. If, through circumstances not in
your control, a fire does start, then the damage will be much
reduced if fire doors are kept properly shut.

This is, of course, an over-simplification. But it's because
these simple facts are often ignored by staff (through lack of
training and supervision) that many fires lead to enormous
human and financial cost.

Fire prevention and safety

Contents guide

Getting a fire certificate 43

*Reducing the risk of fire
breaking out* 44

Preparing for an emergency 46

50 people die in fire at leisure centre

CASE STUDY

The general manager of the Summerland Entertainment Complex
on the Isle of Man told the enquiry that it was the height of the
season and the staff were very busy. 'In evidence he accepted
that if a fire occurred, he relied on members of the staff using their
own initiative as to what to do to get people out safely. He did not
think there was much of a fire risk at Summerland.'

The fire started in a disused kiosk on the mini-golf terrace at
7.40 p.m. Efforts to deal with it were made by members of the staff
for at least 20 minutes and were wholly ineffective.

During the fire a member of staff, in a 'regrettable act of
misguided zeal' switched off the main electricity supply to the
building. The emergency generator should automatically have
started and provided emergency lighting. The member of staff did
not notice that the generator had failed to start. This action left the
covered escape staircase in the north-east corner in darkness at
the height of the crisis.

The first call from Summerland to the brigade was at 8.01 p.m.
The entire automatic alarm system was overlooked, and a public
telephone box was used.

Geoff Penn, Guidance Notes to *The Human Factor*, a video on health, hygiene
and safety produced by The Walnut Partnership for HCTC.

ANALYSIS

1 Why did things go so wrong?

2 Would all your staff know what to do if a fire occurred?

*Every year several people die and hundreds
suffer serious injury because hotel and
catering managers had under-estimated the
risks of fire, had no plan for evacuation, no
system for calling the fire brigade, and
inadequate fire training. Are you confident
that everyone knows what to do if a fire breaks
out on your premises? It could happen at any
time of the day or night.*

Making alterations to the premises

If you are considering changing the use of your premises, or making alterations, you should get the advice of your fire authority. Even quite minor changes can affect fire safety and require a change to your fire certificate. Establish that your preferred options are practicable before you go to the expense of architect's plans etc.

At this stage, you should also check whether you need planning permission and building control authority. It is not unusual for the building control officer to insist on additional fire-related measures, and by changing a part of the building you may find you have to conform to standards that are more stringent than when the building was originally constructed.

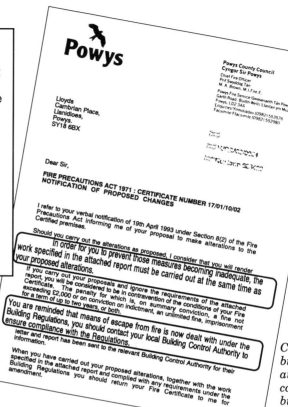

Even quite minor changes can affect fire safety.

Check with your local building control authority that you are complying with the building regulations.

Fire Precautions Act 1971 and related legislation

Fire precautions adequate and up-to-date?

The fire service will generally be consulted on the adequacy of your fire precautions when you apply for a liquor or entertainment licence (see box opposite), or for planning permission and building consent to make alterations or additions to your premises (see above).

Expect a visit from the fire officer before your application is considered, and a refusal if problems are found, e.g. inadequate fire escape routes.

Means of escape and means of fighting fire

Pubs and restaurants (regarded as shops, since their business is the sale to the public of food or drink for immediate consumption) and industrial and contract caterers (since they form part of offices or factory premises) have a duty under the Fire Precautions Act 1971 to provide adequate means of escape and means of fighting fire. Your local fire authority will give you advice on the practical implications of this.

Fire certificate

A fire certificate is necessary (imposing more specific requirements) where there are more than 20 persons at work at any one time, or more than ten persons at work elsewhere than on the ground floor.

Hotels, pubs and guesthouses must have a fire certificate if they provide sleeping accommodation for more than six persons (guests and/or staff), or if any guest/staff bedrooms are above the first floor, or below the ground floor. Such premises fall within the scope of the Fire Precautions (Hotels and Boarding Houses) Order 1972 (and comparable legislation in Scotland and Northern Ireland).

In establishing whether or not the premises are covered by the order:

- bedrooms used by the proprietor/resident manager/tenant or members of his/her family are ignored

- no conclusion can be drawn from the name of the establishment: carrying on the business of a hotel or boarding house keeper is open to many interpretations (e.g. it might include university or college halls of residence which offer accommodation to the general public during vacations).

Smaller establishments offering accommodation must, as a minimum:

- display a notice or other written instruction for guests outlining the fire procedures

- give staff instruction on the action to take in the event of fire, including walk over the escape routes

- carry out an evacuation drill at least once a year.

The fire authority has the power to prohibit or restrict the use of such premises if there is a serious risk to life.

Workplace safety

Employer's general obligations under the Health and Safety at Work etc. Act were to be made more specific under the Fire Precautions (Places of Work) Regulations, due to come into force on 1 January 1993, but subsequently postponed. Government will have to decide in due course how to implement EC requirements, as set out in the Workplace Directive and the Health and Safety Framework Directive.

Getting a fire certificate

1 Establish contact with your local fire authority. They will give you advice on how to apply and the requirements you have to meet.

2 Return the completed application form to the authority. From this stage until your application is approved, you can use the premises, provided you meet the requirements relating to means of escape, means for fighting fire, and fire training.

3 You may be asked to provide additional information, e.g. a plan of the premises, or to clarify certain aspects.

4 An officer from the fire authority will inspect your premises. If possible, accompany the officer, otherwise ask for a discussion at the end of the inspection. If there are aspects that the officer is not satisfied about, this is a good time to discuss how they can be resolved. A letter will confirm the additional requirements, and give a time limit.

5 Once the arrangements are satisfactory the fire certificate will be issued. This must be kept in the premises to which it relates.

6 If there is a problem which apparently cannot be resolved, the fire authority will normally issue a formal notice of refusal of a fire certificate. Your right of appeal will be explained. Pending the outcome of an appeal, it is an offence to use the premises for the purposes described in your application.

 CHECKLIST

What your fire certificate will specify

- use(s) of the premises
- maximum number of people on the premises at one time (in some cases)
- fire exits and emergency routes
- fire warning system
- testing and maintenance of fire warning system and its components, e.g. manual operating points, fire bells, emergency lights
- testing and maintenance of fire fighting equipment
- fire notices for customers/guests and staff
- fire instructions and drills for staff

Location of:

- fire doors
- emergency lights
- fire exit signs
- extinguishers (specifying type), fire hoses, water sprinklers, etc.
- automatic detection equipment, e.g. heat and smoke detectors
- fire bells or other warning devices
- manual operating or call points for sounding the alarm

Your fire certificate will specify the range of precautions and equipment which should be provided, and the frequency of tests, fire instructions and fire drills.

Some high risk factors

Any of the following will require special precautions against fire. These will be reflected in the requirements of your fire certificate, and whether or not an entertainment licence is issued (see box at right):

- complex escape routes, e.g. because of age or layout of building
- large number of persons present relative to size of building
- additional large number of persons present at a function or disco, say
- few staff so that little assistance is available to members of the public in an emergency
- kitchens
- oil-fired boiler rooms
- basements used as dining or bar area, kitchen or bedrooms
- individuals or small groups working in isolated parts of building
- high proportion of disabled persons
- presence of highly combustible products, e.g. paint in maintenance stores, products stocked in hotel shop, items on display in foyer or conference room

Entertainment licences

An entertainment licence is needed for any pub, restaurant or other place which publicly advertises entertainment with more than two performers, including karaoke, dancing to music or plays. Such licences are issued by the local authority and the officer concerned (usually the EHO) will advise on whether you need a licence and what the procedure is.

A licence will not be issued until the premises comply with the entertainment licensing technical regulations. These cover most aspects of building construction, but their main concern is with preventing fires and ensuring safe means of escape.

Conditions will be attached to each licence, including the maximum number of customers allowed on the premises at any time.

The local authority makes random inspections. If the officer finds fire exits blocked or locked, this may lead to a prosecution.

With thanks to Ronald Bolton

Reducing the risk of fire breaking out

What could start a fire? Where might the flames and smoke spread to? What would reduce the risk of fire? The activities that take place in your operation, and the layout of your premises are unique, so the starting-point has to be a careful inspection of every area and analysis of every activity.

You may find a detailed checklist helpful in making repeated inspections easier. But beware of the danger of treating the checklist as just a ticking exercise, with the result you fail to observe a new hazard.

A major cause of fire is equipment failure – because it is not regularly maintained, because a fault has been ignored or not reported, or because no action is taken by management when a fault is reported.

Another problem is poor working practices – waste allowed to accumulate, cleaning and maintenance materials stored in the wrong place, equipment left on when unattended, electric sockets overloaded. It is more difficult to prevent contractors being careless, but a tour of inspection each day after they have finished work will provide a safeguard against fire risks, as well as a way of monitoring their work.

Irresponsible or thoughtless behaviour by guests or staff, e.g. ignoring the safety notice and putting clothes to dry on top of an electric convector heater, are more difficult problems to tackle. Vigilance is the best defence – observing and correcting the problem – and notices, signs and information designed to raise safety awareness.

Do not invite potential problems by failing to empty ashtrays, providing too few ashtrays, or ashtrays of poor design, so the cigarette can easily fall out. Ban smoking in areas of high fire risk, e.g. store rooms. Waste bins in bedrooms and public rooms should be made of metal.

Security is another issue (see Section 6). Many fires are deliberately started (arson).

Furnishings and fittings should be fire-resistant. Check with your supplier that they meet the relevant British Standard. For beds and bedding, this substantially reduces the risk when, despite warnings, people smoke in bed.

The principal causes of fire in licensed premises are:
- cigarettes, matches, pipes, etc.
- rubbish, wastepaper, etc.
- electrical equipment
- room heating appliances
- cooking appliances
- vandalism (especially by children).

Fire prevention

Smoking
- provide sufficient large ashtrays
- empty regularly into metal container
- inspect premises after closing time
- look for discarded cigarette ends: under bench seats, behind curtains, in crevices of upholstery, on carpets

Rubbish, wastepaper
- remove all rubbish from building as soon as possible
- cartons, wood shavings and packaging materials are highly combustible, and should be kept in a safe place

Electrical equipment
- electric current is a source of heat – faults in wiring and fittings cause heat
- misuse of electrical appliances can easily cause fire

Room heating appliances
- portable heaters – oil, electric or gas – can easily start a fire if knocked over
- do not place near, or place upon them: clothes, cloths, books, papers or any combustible material
- take care that loose paper, e.g. Christmas decorations, does not fall on to any open fire, radiant heater or storage heater
- paraffin oil heaters should be filled outdoors, and **never** when alight

Fat or oil fires
If fat or oil in a pan or deep fryer catches alight:
- cover immediately with fire blanket or close fitting lid, to exclude air
- turn off heat
- do not move the pan for at least 30 minutes
- **never** use water to put out an oil or fat fire

Cooking appliances
- ensure that pilot jets on gas rings and ovens are properly fitted, clean and kept alight
- check that burners in gas ovens have ignited properly after turning on

Contractors
If welding equipment or blow torches have been used, inspect the area 30 minutes after the work has been completed and again 30 minutes later to ensure that materials are not smouldering.

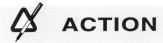 **ACTION**

The statistics on fires reveal some clear messages on where the main dangers lie. From the pie charts on this page, make up your own diagrams on flip chart paper or OHP slides, and use them in your next fire training session to encourage your staff to identify:

1   the most likely causes of fire in their workplace

2   measures which should be taken to reduce the risk.

Origin and location of fires in restaurants, cafés, pubs, etc., 1991

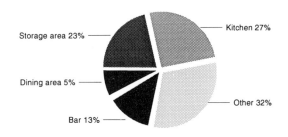

Source: Home Office, *UK Fire Statistics*, 1991

Based on fires attended by fire brigade: 3428.

Causes of all fires in hotels, 1984–88

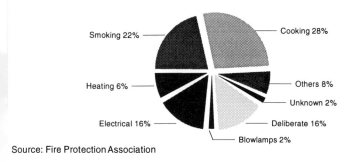

Source: Fire Protection Association

Causes of serious fires in hotels, 1990

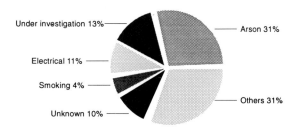

Source: Fire Protection Association

Serious fires were those costing £50,000 or more to the insurers, or involving death.

Safety with open fires

- Do not build up with large quantities of coke, coal or logs, which can fall on to the hearth and set fire to carpets.
- Never carry live coals from one room to another.
- Fit a spark guard wherever practicable. Always leave guard in position when fire is left unattended.
- Never rake out an open hearth and leave cinders burning on the hearth.
- Always remove hot ashes in a metal, lidded container.
- Never use petrol, paraffin or spirits for lighting or reviving open fires.
- Do not use a newspaper for drawing a fire into life.
- Have chimneys swept regularly.

FIRE PREVENTION is everybody's business

Fire exits and routes – are for your safety. Keep them free from obstruction at all times.

Extinguishers – are provided to tackle fires. Do you know where they are and how to operate them? Find out today – tomorrow may be too late. Never use them to prop open fire doors.

No smoking areas – are for your safety and comfort. Never try to beat the ban – that secret smoke could become embarrassingly public.

Security – protects against people who start fires for kicks. Lock all doors and windows at the end of the day.

Waste – is fuel for fire. Do not allow it to accumulate on the floor. Keep it in metal containers with lids. Clear it away regularly.

Stock (of food, cleaning materials, etc.) – is always on the move. Keep it away from heaters and lights, and at least ½ metre below sprinkler heads.

Storage areas – kept tidy help prevent fire and allow any outbreak to be tackled more easily.

Equipment servicing – and repair are jobs for the experts. Do not try and do them yourself. Report suspected faults, damaged cables, etc., to your manager at once.

Shut-down check

Power	off at mains.
Appliances	switched off and unplugged.
Smoking	check ashtrays and waste paper bins.
Keep tidy	get waste outside to a safe place.
Lock up	you don't know who your next visitor might be.

Preparing for an emergency

If your premises are covered by a fire certificate, make yourself familiar with the detailed requirements it makes for:

- ensuring that adequate means of escape are available for use at all times
- providing customers and guests with information on what they should do in an emergency
- giving instruction to staff and holding fire drills
- checking and maintaining fire detection and fire fighting equipment.

For independent operators, the log book available from your fire authority will provide a suitable reminder of what has to be done, and how frequently. This book will be inspected by the fire officer. If you belong to a group or large organisation, you will probably be given a supply of forms or books to record fire training etc. Both senior management and fire officers will check these records.

Someone (e.g. the proprietor or manager of a small business, the health and safety officer in a larger establishment) should have specific responsibility for fire safety, with a deputy to take charge when that person is not on duty. Many fires occur at night. In hotels and inns this is the time when the maximum number of guests will be in their rooms, and most or all of the management and staff have gone to bed:

- in small establishments, a senior member of staff, the manager or proprietor should sleep on the premises and be ready to take charge if the fire alarms ring
- in medium and larger establishments, the night staff and/ or the night manager should have sufficient training to respond competently in an emergency.

Means of escape

Escape routes allow people to get out quickly when there is an emergency. When an escape route is also the main corridor and staircase, it requires constant vigilance to ensure that cleaning trolleys, piles of soiled linen, equipment, etc. are not blocking the route. Escape routes not used regularly, e.g. the emergency staircase in a multi-storey building, should not be turned into storage places for spare mattresses and furniture.

If exterior fire escape doors are a security risk, install an approved locking system which allows them to be opened easily in an emergency. Do not use a chain and padlock – a dangerous practice, which cost 48 people their lives in the 1981 Dublin discotheque fire.

 CHECKLIST

Fire responsibilities

In the event of fire, who will
- alert the person in charge?
- call the fire brigade?
- attend to those requiring special help?
- check that everyone has been evacuated?

In hotels, inns and other residential establishments who will:
- identify the room numbers of the elderly, disabled, children and anyone else requiring special help?
- take the register/room list to the assembly point?

Information for the fire brigade

A plan of your premises should be displayed or kept in a place agreed with the fire authority, indicating the location of:
- control panel for fire detection and alarm system
- stairways and escape routes
- extinguishers and fire hoses
- shut-off devices for gas and electricity supply
- shut-off device for ventilation system
- installations and areas of particular risk.

An electric storm set off the fire alarm in a Brighton beachfront hotel. The small lobby was suddenly filled with guests (all foreign) in a panic. No one knew what to do and worse, no one could find a single member of staff or management to guide them. Half an hour later, in the small hours of the morning when the fire brigade arrived, no one could find a guest list and firemen discovered that the manager never stayed overnight at the hotel.

The elderly man who was left in charge slept through the commotion. So too did an elderly guest.

Caterer & Hotelkeeper, 13 August 1992

Lives will also be in danger if escape routes get cut off because smoke or fire has spread through a door left propped open, or because the smoke seal has become damaged, or a self-closing mechanism has not been adjusted.

If your premises are not covered by a fire certificate (which will detail what is required), install self-contained battery-operated emergency lights which come on automatically if the normal lighting fails. The aim is to provide sufficient light for people to see their way out of public areas and along escape routes.

Information for customers and guests

Customers and guests generally have two disadvantages if there is a fire. They do not know the building well, and they have not had the opportunity of practising the emergency drill.

Clear, prominently displayed notices and a simple plan can do much to help (see checklist). To prevent defacement, or because it looks much more professional, consider laminating or framing the notice. Check that you include all the information specified in the schedule to your fire certificate.

The needs and safety of all groups of people must be considered. Do your customers include non-English speaking visitors from abroad, the disabled, elderly or children? Will the hard of hearing hear the fire alarm? Do you need fire notices in braille, or French and German? Your tourist board, and trade or professional association will give you advice and put you in touch with experts.

The welcome letter or guest folder in rooms is also an effective way of reminding guests to be careful when smoking, and drawing their attention to the fire procedures, location of fire exits, alarm call points, etc. Stress that guests should alert management, who will call the fire brigade – otherwise some might believe they are doing the right thing by calling 999 on their room telephone or mobile phone.

Hudson's, like many pubs and restaurants, is located in a shopping complex. The fire procedure reflects this.

CHECKLIST

Fire notices for guests and staff

What to do if the fire alarm sounds:
- how to leave the building
- where to assemble

What not to do:
- do not stop to collect personal belongings
- do not run
- do not use the lift
- do not open a door if you suspect there is a fire on the other side
- do not re-enter the building until advised to do so by the manager/officer in charge

What to do on discovering a fire:
- raise the alarm by breaking the glass of the nearest fire alarm point (specify location)

FIRE ALARM PROCEDURE

HUDSON'S
A Tradition of Excellence

1 If you discover or suspect a fire, go immediately to one of the nearest fire call points, situated by every fire exit, and activate the alarm.

   If it is safe, contact telephone Control and inform them of the fire location.

2 On activation of the alarm, you will hear intermittent fire bells which are backed up by an alert message on the public address system.

   All staff should await further instructions. No evacuation is required at this stage.

3 If found to be a false activation, an all-clear message will be given over the PA system twice saying 'Please note the emergency has now been cleared'.

4 If it is a full alarm situation then the alarm system will proceed to continuously sounding bells. An evacuation message will be played through the PA system.

5 All members of staff must evacuate the building.

   The lifts should not be used.

   Staff should assemble at St Phillips Churchyard.

   The Emergency Coordinator will wear a yellow jacket for easy identification.

6 The Senior Fire Officer will only allow a return to the building when he is satisfied that it is safe.

   No attempt to return should be made until this assurance has been given.

Making sure staff know what to do

Fire training should be a top priority for anyone new to your team, including staff who work on the premises outside normal hours, such as cleaners. All staff should have refresher training at least once, and preferably twice a year. Those on duty at night should have training at three-monthly intervals.

Temporary or casual staff should be shown the means of escape and told about the fire routine: this might require a few minutes at the beginning of their work session, similar to the demonstration given to airline passengers shortly after take-off.

Everyone needs to be quite clear what they must and must not do in an emergency. Things can go badly wrong, when someone assumes responsibility e.g. to fight the fire, when the priority should be to sound the alarm. The checklist will help clarify what needs to be covered.

Fire drills

Once a year, more regularly for larger premises, all staff and any guests present at the time should rehearse the fire routine. Everyone should be informed that there will be a fire drill that day, and the time. This will minimise any disruption or anxiety when the fire alarms sound, and will help ensure the cooperation of guests. A member of management or staff will have to sound the fire alarm. There will be no smoke and flames, and no fire brigade, but in other respects the circumstances should be as close to reality as possible.

If there are alternative escape routes, one of them should be closed off immediately before the drill begins. Place notices at each entry point stating *Fire drill: due to fire and smoke this escape route cannot be used* (or similar words).

Added value can be given to the fire drill by:

- timing how long it takes to get everyone out of the building after the alarm has sounded

- placing observers at key points to note the behaviour of people

- asking staff and customers individually to comment on any difficulties or concerns they had (you might learn, for example, that the fire alarm is difficult to hear in a particular room, or that people are confused by the wording of the fire notice).

 **CHECKLIST**

Fire training

- who is responsible for fire safety
- calling the fire brigade
- how the fire alarm system works (particularly important if you have a two-stage alarm)
- the escape routes from each part of the building
- importance of fire doors and escape routes, especially those not in regular use (so they are not obstructed)
- where the assembly points are
- roll-call procedure for staff and guests
- procedure for contractors

On discovering a fire

- how to raise the alarm
- location of alarm call points
- location of indicator panels

On hearing the fire alarm

- turning off/unplugging appliances
- closing doors and windows
- not stopping to collect personal belongings

Evacuation procedure

- not using lifts
- special arrangements for the physically disabled
- special arrangements for those with difficulty seeing or hearing
- informing and reassuring guests/customers/new staff
- directing or escorting people to exits
- checking public areas

Fighting fire

- safety aspects
- location of fire fighting equipment
- use of fire fighting equipment

Specific workplace hazards/responsibilities

- supervisors/department heads: responsibilities for their staff
- kitchen staff: use of fire blankets, turning off gas and electric equipment
- reception staff: register of guests

Fire warning systems

For businesses which are covered by a fire certificate, this will set out the minimum requirements for automatic detection of fire, and fire warning systems. If you do not need a fire certificate, then at the very least you must have a way of warning people. In all but the smallest ground floor premises, this warning will normally be an electrically operated fire warning system with manually operated call points.

Your insurance company might insist on various precautions whether or not this is the case, you should seek the advice of the fire authority and/or a fire protection company. The cost will not seem so high when you compare it with the losses which would follow from a fire.

Barking Max saves landlady's life in fire drama

MAX the labrador was hailed a hero yesterday after he saved his owner's life.

His barking woke landlady in time to escape the fire, which gutted her first floor private lounge in the Piccadilly Inn.

Fire also got into the roof of the pub and part of the lounge floor was so badly damaged it collapsed into the pub below.

Thanks to Max, Mrs , who was in the pub alone when the fire started about 4.20am yesterday, was able to run across the road to part-time barmaid to use her telephone to summon help.

Trapped by fire or smoke

Your personal safety

If the escape route is filling with smoke:

- keep low, crawl along the floor if necessary
- breathe shallowly through the nose
- in large rooms, keep to side walls
- in passages, keep close to the wall
- feel your way with the back of your hand

If the escape route is not safe to use:

- go to the nearest room – feel the door and handle. If hot, proceed to the next room. If cool, open the door slightly – be ready to slam shut if you find smoke or flames – and enter if safe.

Trapped in a room:

- stay low if the room is smoky
- seal the room against smoke entering from the outside: stuff a blanket or rug under the door. Even more effective, if there is a bath or basin in the room, are wet sheets, towels, etc.
- signal for help: shouting out of window/waving sheet/flashing light, etc.
- if water is available, throw on to hot surfaces (e.g. door).

Smouldering cigarette end

A room attendant was working in a first floor bedroom of a small hotel. Just before going for a coffee break she vacuumed-up the contents of the ashtray.

While she was having her break, the bag of the vacuum cleaner ignited, and the fire spread to a pile of soiled linen which was nearby.

The door to the stairwell was held open magnetically. Thus the smoke spread upwards to the second floor, where it proceeded to spread along the corridor.

An alarm system was fitted and normally the detectors would have been activated, thus closing the fire doors. However, the service engineers had turned off the system while they were doing some maintenance on it.

A housekeeper on the third floor was the first to notice the smoke, and telephoned the receptionist. The receptionist alerted the manager, who went to the third floor to investigate. The manager then called the fire brigade.

Fortunately there was little damage, but the hotel was successfully prosecuted for various breaches of the Fire Precautions Act.

Andrew Ings, International Safety Media, Braintree

ANALYSIS

Several people were at fault in this incident. What should each of them have done and/ or not done?

Fire fighting equipment

You should have fire extinguishers of the appropriate type, preferably near exits and escape routes and in high risk areas, e.g. the kitchen. As a general rule, it should not be necessary to travel more than 30 metres from the site of a fire to reach an extinguisher. If you are covered by a fire certificate, this will specify locations and types of extinguisher, fire hoses, automatic sprinklers, etc.

There should be no delay in replacing an extinguisher which has been used – preferably with one held in reserve.

Guide to extinguishers likely to be used in catering areas

Type	Suitable for	Extinguishing action	Warnings	Method of use
Water (red)	Fires involving ordinary combustible materials, e.g. wood, cloth, paper.	Cools the burning material.	Do not use on live electrical equipment, burning fats or oils.	Direct the jet at the base of the flames and keep it moving across the area of the fire. After the main fire is out, re-spray any remaining hot spots.
				If fire is spreading vertically, attack it at the lowest point, then follow upwards.
Carbon dioxide (black)	Fires involving flammable liquids or liquefiable solids, e.g. oil, fat, paint, petrol, paraffin, grease. Safe and clean to use on live electrical equipment.	Smothers flames by displacing oxygen in the air.	Has a limited cooling effect. Take care that fire does not re-ignite. The fumes can be harmful. Ventilate the area as soon as fire has been extinguished.	Direct the discharge horn at the base of the flames and keep the jet moving across the area of the fire.
Foam (cream)	Fires involving paper, wood, etc. AFFF (aqueous film-forming foam) extinguishers also suitable for fires involving flammable liquids.	Smothers the fire. Some types also have cooling action.	Do not aim directly into liquid in case it splashes fire further. Some types not suitable for use on live electrical equipment.	Direct jet at inside edge if fire in container. Otherwise stand well back and sweep jet from side to side.
Powder (blue)	Fires involving flammable liquids or liquefiable solids, e.g. oil, fat, paint, petrol, paraffin, grease. Safe on electrical equipment, but does not readily penetrate spaces inside equipment, so fire may re-ignite.	Knocks down flames.	Limited cooling effect, so take care the fire does not re-ignite. Causes a considerable mess, so that it may require several hours work to clean up after extinguishing a small fire.	Direct the nozzle at the base of the flames and with a rapid sweeping motion drive the flame towards the far edge until the flames are out. Repeat as necessary (some extinguishers can be shut off). Electrical equipment: disconnect from the electricity. Direct the jet straight at the fire if possible, so that the powder can penetrate interior of equipment.
Fire blanket	Small fires involving burning liquids and burning clothing.	Smothers the fire.		Hold the blanket carefully so that it protects your body and hands from the fire, and place it over the flames. Take care not to waft the flames in your direction, or towards bystanders.
				For a fire involving clothing, wrap the blanket around the burning area, but not over the victim's nose and mouth. Roll the patient on the ground.

Footnote: Halon extinguishers (green) are not recommended because of the damage the gas causes to the ozone layer. If you have halon extinguishers, it will not be possible to re-fill them once discharged.

Security of property and people

Your property and well-being, and those of your employer, colleagues, customers and staff are at risk from the dishonest, the opportunist, and the deliberate troublemaker. Security equipment and procedures can do much to reduce the risks, but all too often the problem occurs because of inadequate training, poor supervision, or unwillingness to take action. For example:

- failure to observe suspicious behaviour – the person did not recognise it as suspicious, or was paying insufficient attention to notice, or because reporting similar matters in the past has resulted in a rebuff, or lack of acknowledgement

- not reporting an incident because it seems too trivial – not realising that even the smallest incident can give vital warnings or clues

    deviating from procedures – because they create more work, or seem pointless, or because sticking to the procedure would lead to a confrontation, which the person feels unable or unwilling to handle.

Contents guide

Basic rules of security .... this page

Cooperating with the police 54

Bomb threats and terrorism 55

Basic rules of security

People still get away with tricks that haven't changed for decades, like causing a disturbance in the bar or foyer to distract attention while accomplices steal wallets, bags and jewellery. Or conning a room attendant to let them into 'their' room using a master key. But the pattern of crime is changing. Violence and drugs are serious problems in some pubs, hotels and hospitals. The anonymity offered in some hotels makes them the ideal location to conduct drug transactions. Car thefts are a widespread problem.

A first step to greater security involves staff and management: increased awareness of the potential problems, and better procedures. Minor physical changes to the premises can also be very effective, e.g. window locks and grills, security chains and viewers on bedroom doors.

Review security arrangements regularly. The police will offer advice.

Keep a record of all crime incidents, whether or not they are reported to the police at the time. Apparently trivial incidents, or others not reported at the request of the customer or guest, may later provide valuable information for the police.

When management and staff act as a team in an emergency, each person setting about their duties calmly and efficiently, they generate a feeling of confidence. This helps everyone. It particularly helps customers, who do not have the advantage of being able to practise emergency procedures.

Entrances

Reduce the number of public entrances to the minimum. Install an automatic bell on the front door of small hotels where reception desks are unmanned. Control other entrances with locks or alarms acceptable to your fire service. External fire doors can be fitted with a warning sign and an audible sounder, to reduce the likelihood of unauthorised use.

A separate staff entrance may be appropriate, well away from those used by the public, and protected by a security system.

Try and vary the timings of any high-risk activities, such as the removal of cash by security van, or locking of the premises at closing time. This will make it more difficult for incidents to be planned.

Public areas and car parks

Arrange furniture etc. so that public areas can be easily observed. Mirrors at vantage points can help reception, barstaff, etc. to observe comings and goings discreetly.

Outdoor areas and car parks should be well lit. Avoid plants and trees which allow thieves to work unseen.

Put up warning signs or posters at strategic points in car parks, to remind customers to secure vehicles and remove property, or place it out of sight. Leaflets handed out with car parking tickets are another way of reinforcing the message.

Protecting customers and guests

Ensure overnight guests are properly registered (see box). Unless you only accept guests by prior arrangement, the notice limiting your liabilities under the Hotel Proprietors Act 1956 should be displayed at reception. Guests should be able to leave valuables in your safe or a personal security locker.

People enquiring about guests, in person or by telephone, should not be able to find out what room number the guest is occupying. Public announcements should never reveal both guest name and room number, e.g. 'Would Mr Jones of room 10 please contact reception'.

Establish a control system for guest keys, so there is minimum risk of someone else being able to get the key to an occupied room. A thief should not be able to see if the occupant of a room is out (e.g. because the key and/or message rack is easily visible, or returned keys are left lying on the reception desk). If key cards are used, staff should always insist that these are produced when guests collect their keys. Blank key cards must be kept secure.

While servicing bedrooms in which guest belongings have been left, staff should be aware of the opportunist thief. The room should be locked if unattended, and no one should be admitted without checking with reception or a manager that he or she is the genuine occupant.

Identity checks with a difference

Streets bursting with revellers mean tight security at the Chicago Hilton & Towers on New Year's Eve. Control is paramount. One colour of wristband is issued to guests and another colour of wristband to people only attending a function. Guests not wearing a wristband are turned back at checkpoints set up at entrances and the elevator access. Guests have taken well to the idea: the wristbands have become something of a status symbol.

Chris Baum, *Hotels*, September 1992

Registering guests staying overnight

Most accommodation providers keep details of the names and addresses of guests. After all, this provides you with a valuable marketing resource and a first line of enquiry if there is a problem paying the bill – although anyone with fraud in mind is not likely to give a useful address! – or you have to return lost property. If you prefer a more informal approach, welcoming guests as friends and being content to know them as 'Jim' or 'Helen', you must nevertheless ask them to give their full name and nationality.

The Immigration (Hotel Records) Order 1972 requires anyone offering accommodation for reward, to keep such details (and their date of arrival) for every person aged 16 years or over.

For non-British passport holders a record must also be kept of their passport number, certificate of registration or other document establishing identity and nationality. On or before their departure from the premises, aliens must inform you of their next destination and, if known, their full address there.

You must obtain the information for each person, even if they are sharing a room. Any member of the party can give it on behalf of the others, or a third party such as the travel agent who made the booking, or the courier accompanying the group.

The information must be kept for at least 12 months, and made available at any time to the police or the Home Office.

Foreign diplomats, their families and staff are exempted from the need to register by the Diplomatic Privileges Act 1964. But to establish their status, you will need some information, i.e. their name and that of their embassy.

Key control

Sign any keys issued to staff in and out. Strictly limit access to master keys. Use sub-masters where practicable, permitting access to one floor or area only.

Have locks changed if keys are lost. Keep a register of lost keys, when they were found missing and the circumstances.

Do not label or number keys so it is obvious to anyone who might find them what lock(s) they will open. Your postcode or PO box number will usually be sufficient to ensure that keys taken absent-mindedly by guests are returned.

If you are changing to an electronic key system, consider one that will tell you which cards have been used to open a particular lock and when. A useful security option is the sub-master card that only works at particular times or on certain days. Another is the card that gives selected users access to conference rooms or leisure facilities.

Staff employment

Always follow up references. Avoid taking on staff without a satisfactory reference from the most recent employer.

Make clear in staff conditions of service what action you will take where you have grounds for suspecting dishonesty, and if this is proven. Include the right to search staff lockers and the rooms of live-in staff.

Conditions of employment should also allow for random searches: this must be done in private, and may only include examination of bags, a request to turn out pockets and a search of outer garments. Anything more intensive, such as a strip-search, can only be carried out by police, after the person concerned has been arrested.

Lost property

Staff should be clear on the procedure for lost property, and what happens if the property is unclaimed. A lost property book or form provides a useful way of obtaining and recording appropriate details.

Anyone finding lost property has a duty to trace the owner. If you keep it for yourself, this is theft. If a customer has used a credit card or cheque, you may be able to make contact via the credit card company or bank. For an overnight guest, the reservation details will usually provide enough information.

If you are unable to establish contact with the finder, and the item is valuable, you should inform the police. They may ask for the property to be handed to them. Valuable items will be kept by them for six months. If the owner is not traced, the property is returned to the finder.

If the finder is one of your guests or customers, the unclaimed property should go to them.

 CHECKLIST

Cash security
- tills regularly emptied of excess cash
- cash kept secure, preferably in a safe
- large amounts of cash not kept on premises

Banking cash
- no regular routine and route varied
- colleague acts as lookout

If you are attacked
- do not provoke your attacker: your first concern must be your own safety and that of the innocent people and customers around you
- cooperate with the attacker, but give away as little information as possible
- never take a chance on a handgun not being the real thing
- note details about the attacker's physical appearance, manner of speech, any vehicle used, and the direction in which the attacker escapes – never attempt to follow
- alert the police and security immediately
- do not handle anything the attacker has touched, to preserve fingerprints

Right to search
The company reserves the right at any time to search any locker allocated to you and to request that you and/or your property be searched, should the need arise, at any reasonable time. During any searches you have the right to be accompanied by another member of staff chosen by you. Further you will not remove any item belonging to the company or our guests from company property, nor take such items into your control without the express prior permission of your senior manager.

A clause of this sort in contracts of employment provides a way of reinforcing workplace rules. If an employee refuses to allow the search, you would have to start the disciplinary process.

Counterfeit money
If you find a note has been forged after the customer has departed, give any details to the police (e.g. it was used to pay for a meal). The police will be able to warn other businesses, and this may eventually lead to an arrest.

To detect a forged note: feel the paper – it should not be limp, shiny or waxy. The print should be sharp and well-defined. Watch out for notes that are blurred or hazy. Check the note has a thread embedded in the paper, which will appear as a continuous line against the light.

Cooperating with the police

If your premises are unoccupied outside opening times, give the police a list of those people who have keys, and how they can be contacted in an emergency. If you are the only person with a key and you will be going away for the weekend, for example, consider what would happen if there was a fire or burglary while you were away. There is obviously a limit to the extra responsibilities you can ask neighbours, friends or relatives to accept, but the work of the police is much more difficult if they cannot contact anyone.

Business watch schemes

Neighbourhood watch schemes help reduce crime by encouraging householders to take more notice of what is going on in their area, and developing a feeling of shared responsibility. The business equivalent (e.g. Pub Watch and Hotel Secure) can have similar benefits, through the sharing of information with other publicans, restaurateurs and hoteliers, and increased cooperation with the police.

How the scheme works

Proprietors or managers get together, perhaps through the local branch of their trade association, to cooperate on security arrangements. A coordinator is appointed.

The coordinator contacts the local police to organise an introductory meeting between the committee and the police to establish full and open support for the scheme and to agree the basic responsibilities and objectives.

The police will usually host the launch meeting. They will nominate a permanent liaison officer and recommend ways of grouping members (more than 25 premises are unwieldy).

A communication system is then set up between members. Radiopaging devices have the advantage of circulating information correctly within seconds. Fax machines are valuable for transmission of photographs and detailed descriptions of suspects. Telephone links are a less suitable option, because of the tendency for messages to get distorted as they are passed along the chain, and the risk of the chain being broken when person D is unable to contact person E.

On a regular basis, the police provide relevant crime statistics, trends, patterns and monitoring information to assess the effectiveness of the scheme.

Members meet regularly to discuss mutual problems, exchange information on known criminals and get up-to-date advice on crime prevention techniques.

Contacting the police in an emergency

If you or your senior staff have to make a 999 emergency call to the police regarding a theft, violence, or any other sort of security problem, help the police respond effectively by being ready to tell them:

- the type of problem or potential trouble
- the type of assistance required
- as full a description as possible of the troublemakers and any vehicles involved
- if the problem has moved on, in which direction it was heading.

Crime watch in practice

The Manchester Hotels Security Group meets monthly. Each hotel is represented by a member of senior management whose job involves some responsibility for security. Initiatives so far have included:

- exclusion notices served on known local criminals, those strongly suspected of being involved in crime and nuisance visitors such as prostitutes. An exclusion order from one hotel applies to all
- circulating details of slow-paying customers and of those who cause damage or distress to other customers through unruly behaviour
- exchange of still photographs taken from security video cameras
- a verbal update on members of staff who have left or been dismissed because of suspected theft or other unacceptable behaviour – in view of the delicacy of this area, nothing is written down.

In one incident, a credit card check on a late booking from two people showed the card to be stolen. When challenged the two ran. Their description was transmitted to the other hotels, where they were refused service.

The value of sharing information at meetings was brought home when one member mentioned worrying levels of linen theft. Others, it seemed, were suffering from the same problem. After discussion, car boot sales were felt to be the most likely outlet for monogrammed linen. Through the group's police links, forces in outlying districts were alerted and within a short time, the thieves were apprehended and convicted.

Bob Gledhill , *Caterer & Hotelkeeper*, 9 September 1993

After starting a Pub Watch scheme, licensees in Basildon, Essex, saw an all-round fall in pub-related violence and crime: assaults down 30%, offences involving damage down 36%, burglaries down 20%, incidents involving deception down 43%. Over six months, 75% of reported crimes were detected, well above the country-wide average.

Dominic Roskrow, *Publican*, 16 November 1992

Bomb threats and terrorism

You may not consider yourself an obvious target, but terrorists use unpredictable ways to achieve their aims. And being close to the target can mean you suffer just as much from the damage and general havoc that a serious incident causes. Another threat is the terrorist copycat – a disgruntled ex-employee perhaps, who makes a hoax bomb threat, or leaves an incendiary device.

Managing the threat

The priority is always to safeguard life.

A lot of bomb threats turn out to be hoaxes. Anyone likely to answer incoming telephone calls should be trained in the procedure for dealing with bomb threats (see checklist overleaf). The more information they can get, the easier it will be to decide whether or not the call is genuine, and may assist police in subsequent enquiries. If in doubt, treat the call as genuine.

Be prepared to take decisions, according to your level of responsibility. If evacuation is necessary, carry it out quickly and calmly. Ensure staff do not leave handbags, attaché cases, etc. behind, to avoid wasting time having them searched.

The police stress that the decision to evacuate has to be made by whoever is in charge of the premises – proprietor, manager or someone appointed as security coordinator. Close liaison with the police will ensure that the decision-maker has all the known facts, as evacuation may actually increase the dangers, e.g. if the bomb has been planted outside the building in the knowledge that an evacuation will be ordered. In such circumstances, it may be considered safer to move everyone to an internal room, which has no external walls, or windows (in effect, a 'blast shelter').

There is much that you can do by:

being alert to anything which is out-of-place, or unusual

using your senses to the full – your eyes to observe, your nose to smell (the smell of petrol or marzipan may denote the presence of an incendiary or explosive device)

good housekeeping – rubbish cleared, everything in its proper place

having a good personal knowledge of the layout/organisation of your work area/premises, so that you are more likely to notice anything unusual, and in order to advise the police/security where to search

ensuring your staff know what to do and what not to do.

Covent Garden, London, 12 December 1992

City of London, 27 December 1993

 **CHECKLIST**

Role of a security coordinator

- in command and able to set pre-arranged plans into motion – to search/secure and/or evacuate premises
- in a position to make on-the-spot decisions
- liaise directly with local police
- in possession of floor plans to assist police and emergency services
- known to **all** staff
- able to coordinate any emergency or evacuation arrangements with police and other emergency services

Metropolitan Police, Hotel Intelligence Unit

Searching the premises

Consult the police and/or security consultants before drawing up detailed procedures. If management and staff will be involved in a search:

- develop a plan in advance, so that everyone is clear about their duties and responsibilities

- once key people have had the necessary training, hold a practice run

- alter the plan on the basis of this experience

- keep a high state of awareness with refresher training and practice runs.

The success of a search depends on spotting the unfamiliar, a package in the wrong place, or a piece of panelling which appears to have been tampered with. This will be easier to do if the premises are divided into as many sections as there are searchers, and each section is given to the person most familiar with it: the cellar and stores to the food and beverage manager etc. Once an area has been searched, it should be sealed off, to avoid repetition.

When a suspect package is found, keep everyone away until expert assistance arrives. On no account should the package be touched, or attempts made to defuse it from a distance, e.g. spraying it with water or a fire extinguisher.

Evacuating the premises

Evacuation procedures should deal with:

- how customers and guests are informed (an announcement over the public address system may lead to panic)

- what routes to use (the main entrance is often a prime target for bombers)

- how to prevent people re-entering the building before it is safe to do so

- where to locate meeting points, so there is minimum risk of injury if the bomb does explode

- checking that everyone has been evacuated

- remaining in communication with police control.

Remember:
- ☑ Keep calm
- ☑ Try to keep the caller talking, using excuses if necessary, e.g.: 'I'm sorry there's a lot of noise here, I can't hear you properly'.
- ☑ Obtain as much information as you can
- ☑ If possible, alert someone else without the caller being aware – so that your manager/security officer can be informed
- ☑ Do not put the handset down, or cut off the conversation
- ☑ When the call has finished, immediately alert your manager/security officer

CHECKLIST

Telephone bomb threats

Record as much of the following information as possible *(a real form should give more space)*
MESSAGE *exact words*

....

Code name used (if any) ....

If you are not told these details, ask the caller:
THE FIRST TWO QUESTIONS ARE THE REALLY IMPORTANT ONES

Where is the bomb? ....

What time will it go off? ....

What does it look like? ....

What kind of bomb is it? ....

How is the bomb fused? ....

Why are you doing this? ....

Who are you? ....

Which organisation do you represent? ....

Listen out for and note, any information about the caller, and where he or she is calling from:
Time of call ....

Details of caller

Man	☐	Woman	☐
Child	☐	Old	☐
Young	☐	Not known	☐

Speech of caller

Calm/rational	☐	Nervous/excited	☐
Rambling	☐	Drunk	☐
Speech defect	☐	Laughing	☐
Serious	☐	Message prepared	☐
Message unprepared	☐		
Natural accent	☐	Accent put on	☐

Type of accent ....

Background noises

Call box pay tone	☐	Talking	☐
Traffic	☐	Typing	☐
Music	☐	Aircraft	☐
Rail station	☐	Children	☐
Animals	☐		

Other details

Number of telephone on which call was received

....

Your name ....

With thanks to Metropolitan Police and RAF

The industry's record on food safety is not good. Every year thousands of customers and staff suffer food poisoning, and the numbers appear to go up relentlessly, year after year.

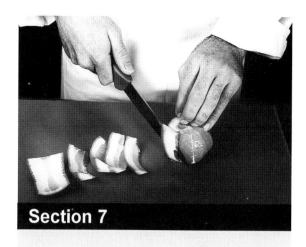

Managing food safety

Food safety legislation

This has led to tough action against caterers. The Food Safety Act 1990 (summarised on page 63) introduced an unlimited fine in the high courts, and up to two years' prison sentence. At the same time, the Act gave strong powers to environmental health officers (EHOs), who are responsible for enforcing much of the legislation.

These powers have been used. In just one year, 1992, over 40% of the catering establishments inspected by EHOs received a written warning. More than 27,000 improvement notices were served requiring action to be taken, and nearly 150 emergency prohibition notices, stopping activities for a time. There were 709 prosecutions and 411 businesses were closed.

There is, however, another side to the Food Safety Act – the defence of due diligence. This provides a powerful incentive to good practice, because if something does go wrong, you can claim in your defence that you took all reasonable steps to prevent the particular circumstance from occurring. These steps typically include showing that you have trained your staff, that temperatures of food are carefully monitored at all critical stages, and that food storage is properly controlled.

Now, as part of the process of harmonising food hygiene standards within Europe, a lot more changes are taking place, involving the regulations made under the Food Safety Act. By mid-1995 the 1970 food hygiene regulations, widely regarded as out-of-date and unnecessarily prescriptive, will have been replaced by similar but broader requirements relating to premises and equipment. There will also be an emphasis on setting up hygiene management systems – a new feature for food hygiene legislation in the UK – and applying appropriate controls. One of these controls concerns supervision and training.

In effect, the industry is being given greater responsibility for managing food safety, to ensure its customers can continue to enjoy their food and drink. But those who ignore this responsibility, or do not appear to take food safety seriously, can expect the full weight of the law. They might also find themselves on the caterer's blacklist, prohibited from running a food business.

Contents guide

Food safety legislation .... this page

Food safety management 66

Food hygiene inspections 74

Prosecutions under the Food Hygiene (General) Regulations 1970 reached their highest in recent years with 1739 food businesses affected. These led to 1556 convictions and more than £1.3 million in fines.

Yet EHOs were able to visit only 61% of restaurant and other caterers, and less than half the hotels and guesthouses.

Institution of Environmental Health Officers, 1990/91 Report

Regulations on food safety

The Food Safety Act prepared the way for various regulations, so that the law would keep pace with new techniques for processing food such as irradiation, and developments in the industry generally, such as the registration of food premises and the training of food handlers.

The 1994 food safety regulations put into effect the EC Directive on the *hygiene of foodstuffs* and replace (from mid-1995) the Food Hygiene (General) Regulations 1970, their Scottish equivalent, and the markets, stalls and delivery vehicles regulations.

The regulations themselves are very short. The schedules give guidelines on food premises, equipment, personal hygiene, etc. These *rules of hygiene* form the basis of the checklists on these pages, and on page 61. If you are familiar with the 1970 regulations, you will see a marked similarity in the general requirements relating to food premises and equipment. At the same time you will note the greater flexibility of the rules, with the use of 'where appropriate' and 'where necessary'. (The checklists in this book, intended to be a summary only, make frequent use of the words 'adequate' and 'generally' as a form of shorthand.)

Further clarification on what can be considered appropriate or necessary, and in what circumstances, will be given in industry guides to good hygiene practice. These will be drawn up for appropriate sectors of the industry, but there is no legal requirement for this to happen. Trade associations and other industry bodies will play the lead role, and government will assess them. Enforcement officers will give due consideration to the advice contained in any recognised guide when assessing compliance with the regulations.

For new kitchens, or reconstructions which involve building control approval, it is possible that you will have to meet specific requirements in the building regulations on such matters as ventilation, and floor, wall and ceiling surfaces.

The issue of temperature control had not been resolved at the time of writing. Government has announced that it will simplify the controls set out in the Food Hygiene (Amendment) Regulations 1990 and 1991 (see page 60). In the meantime, EHOs considering enforcement action on temperature control have been asked by government to be mindful of its intention to introduce simpler requirements.

You may have heard of proposals for the compulsory training of all food handlers (or even been told that this was already a legal requirement). The matter has indeed been much discussed and various sets of proposals have been issued by government. The outcome, which forms part of the Food Safety (General Food Hygiene) Regulations 1994, is that food businesses are required to train, instruct and supervise their staff as they consider necessary for them to do their job safely.

Food premises

☐ kept clean and maintained in good repair and condition
☐ adequate natural and/or artificial lighting
☐ suitable and sufficient means of natural or mechanical ventilation
☐ mechanical air flow from a contaminated area to a clean area avoided
☐ filters and other parts of ventilation systems requiring cleaning or replacement readily accessible
☐ adequate drainage facilities, with no risk of contaminating foodstuffs
☐ adequate changing facilities for personnel

Layout, design and construction of food premises

☐ permit adequate cleaning and/or disinfection
☐ protect against accumulation of dirt, contact with toxic materials, shredding of particles into food and the formation of condensation or undesirable mould on surfaces
☐ permit good food hygiene practices, including protection against cross-contamination between and during operations by foodstuffs, equipment, materials, water, air supply or personnel, and external sources of contamination such as pests

Hand-washing and toilet facilities

☐ provided with adequate natural or mechanical ventilation
☐ wash basins available, suitably located and designated for cleaning hands
☐ adequate number of flush lavatories available, connected to an effective drainage system (lavatories must not lead directly into rooms in which food is located)
☐ wash basins for cleaning hands provided with hot and cold running water, materials for cleaning hands and for hygienic drying; where necessary the provisions for washing food must be separate from the hand-washing facility

---

Food not of the substance (or quality) demanded

A sandwich bar in London's West End was fined £200 and ordered to pay £400 costs, after a nurse discovered the top of a thumb in a take-away salad. The court heard that while chewing what she thought was shredded cabbage, the nurse felt something resist her bite, felt it with her tongue and immediately spat it out.

Following the incident an EHO visited the sandwich bar and discovered an employee working in the basement with a bandage on his thumb. He explained that while slicing red cabbage he had become distracted and cut the top of his thumb. Although rushed to hospital, no one had checked to see if the missing part of his thumb was in the food.

Health & Safety at Work, September 1993

the only place for staff to wash in was a hand basin in the first floor toilets — and only cold water was available.

Other problems included inadequate working spaces for food preparers, raw chicken was stored on top of cooked foods and other food was stored on the floor.

The inspectors took the view that there was an immense risk to public health, said Mr ~~Moore~~.

"~~Khan~~ told the inspectors he was going to open that evening so he was served with an emergency prohibition which was stuck on the door for prospective customers to see."

After hearing the evidence, Judge Sir ~~David~~ ~~Kingston-Morgan~~ told ~~him~~ he was "putting the public in danger of being poisoned" and said he had escaped a prison sentence by "the thickness of a hair".

Food rooms

That is, rooms where food is prepared, treated or processed, but not dining areas.

- ❑ floors and wall surfaces easy to clean, and, where necessary, disinfect – generally this will require the use of impervious, non-absorbent, washable and non-toxic materials; walls should have a smooth surface up to a height appropriate for the operations
- ❑ floors allow adequate surface drainage, where appropriate
- ❑ ceilings and overhead fixtures designed, constructed and finished so as to prevent the accumulation of dirt and to reduce condensation, the growth of undesirable moulds and the shedding of particles
- ❑ windows and other openings do not allow accumulation of dirt
- ❑ windows which can be opened fitted where necessary with insect-proof screens which can be easily removed for cleaning. Where open windows would result in contamination of foodstuffs, windows must remain closed and fixed during production
- ❑ doors easy to clean and disinfect – generally this will require the use of smooth, non-absorbent surfaces
- ❑ surfaces (including surfaces of equipment) in contact with food easy to clean and, where necessary, disinfect – generally this will require the use of smooth, washable and non-toxic materials

Facilities for washing food and equipment

- ❑ adequate provision for any necessary washing of food
- ❑ every sink, or other such facility provided for the washing of food, has adequate supply of hot and/or cold drinkable water as required, and is kept clean
- ❑ adequate facilities for cleaning and disinfecting work tools and equipment, constructed of materials resistant to corrosion, easy to clean, with an adequate supply of hot and cold water

Other types of premises

That is, premises which are: movable/ and/or temporary (e.g. marquees, market stalls, mobile sales vehicles); used primarily as a private dwelling house; used occasionally for catering purposes; vending machines.

- ❑ sited, designed, constructed, kept clean and maintained in good repair and condition so as to avoid the risk of contaminating foodstuffs and harbouring pests
- ❑ appropriate facilities to maintain adequate personal hygiene (including washing and drying of hands, sanitary arrangements and changing facilities)
- ❑ surfaces in contact with food in sound condition, easy to clean and, where necessary, disinfect – generally this will require the use of smooth, washable and non-toxic materials
- ❑ adequate provision for the cleaning and, where necessary, disinfecting of work utensils and equipment
- ❑ adequate provision for the cleaning of foodstuffs
- ❑ adequate supply of hot and/or cold drinkable water
- ❑ adequate arrangements and/or facilities for the hygienic storage and disposal of hazardous and/or inedible substances and waste (whether liquid or solid)
- ❑ foodstuffs so placed as to avoid, so far as is reasonably practicable, the risk of contamination

Equipment and food containers

All articles, fittings and equipment with which food comes into contact:

- ❑ kept clean
- ❑ constructed of such materials and kept in such good order, repair and condition as to minimise any risk of contamination and (with the exception of non-returnable containers and packaging) to enable them to be kept thoroughly cleaned and, where necessary, disinfected
- ❑ fitted so as to allow adequate cleaning of the surrounding area

Food waste and other refuse

- ❑ not allowed to accumulate in food rooms, except so far as is unavoidable for the proper functioning of the business
- ❑ food waste and other refuse deposited in closable containers of appropriate construction, kept in sound condition, and easy to clean and disinfect
- ❑ adequate provision for the removal and storage of food waste and other refuse
- ❑ refuse stores designed and managed in such a way as to enable them to be kept clean and to protect against access by pests and against contamination of food, drinking water, equipment or premises

Water supply

- ❑ adequate supply of drinkable water (specified in the EC Directive relating to potable water: water intended for human consumption), used whenever necessary to ensure foodstuffs are not contaminated
- ❑ ice which might otherwise contaminate foodstuffs, made (from drinkable water), handled and stored under conditions which protect it from all contamination
- ❑ steam used directly in contact with food contains no substance which presents a hazard to health or is likely to contaminate the product
- ❑ water unfit for drinking used for the generation of steam, refrigeration, fire control, and other similar purposes not relating to food, conducted in separate systems, readily identifiable and having no connection with, nor any possibility of reflux into, the drinkable water systems

Registering your premises

Registration of food premises is required by law (see box below). The process is free, and the local authority cannot refuse your application. If you have outlets in more than one local authority area, you must register separately with each.

You should notify your local authority of any change:

- in the nature of the business
- in the addresses at which movable premises are kept
- of proprietor. The new proprietor will have to complete an application form.

The registration form (available from your environmental health department) is simple to complete.

Who has to register

The Food Premises (Registration) Regulations 1991 require everyone who runs any premises used for selling, distributing and preparing food to declare details of the premises and the business to the local environmental health department.

Businesses which operate less than five days in any five consecutive weeks do not have to register, nor do guesthouses with three bedrooms or fewer. Other exemptions include tents and marquees where catering is provided as part of an event.

New food businesses must be registered at least 28 days before they begin trading.

Temperature controls

The Food Hygiene (Amendment) Regulations 1990 and 1991 set out two temperatures for storing high-risk food: 8°C for desserts containing milk, cooked pies and similar perishable foods which will be further cooked before being eaten, and 5°C for soft cheeses, sandwiches and cooked products containing meat, fish, eggs and cheese, etc. which will not receive further cooking. At the time of writing the government was consulting with industry on several options for simplifying the requirements. It seemed likely that the UK would adopt a single temperature system (see box), and allow food manufacturers to vary this for particular products.

Food wrapping materials

Clingfilm, foil, greaseproof paper, freezer bags and trays – any wrapping or container which is intended to come into contact with food – must meet strict standards so that the quality and safety of the food are not harmed. Unless the wrapping or article is clearly intended to come into contact with food, it must be marked FOR FOOD USE. Any specific conditions or uses for which the item is intended must also be stated (Materials and Articles in Contact with Food Regulations 1987).

Temperature control regulations: the likely option

Applies to	All foods which support growth of pathogenic microorganisms or formation of toxins to be kept at temperatures which would not result in a risk to health and having regard to their intended use.
	Businesses to identify steps critical to ensuring food safety and ensure adequate safety procedures are identified, implemented, maintained and reviewed.
Temperature	Single maximum temperature of 7°C or 8°C.
Exceptions	Except where the label or other written instructions from the manufacturer specify a higher temperature in combination with shelf-life.
	Limited periods outside temperature controls to accommodate the practicalities of handling during preparation, transport, storage, delivery, display and service of food.

A CITY centre wine bar has been fined £11,500 after food safety inspectors found "mould, slime and dust-laden cobwebs" in its beer cellar.

Among the problems found, he added, were mould, slime and dust-laden cobwebs.

Dirt had fallen from a curtain onto the beer kegs during the inspection.

The total fine was made up of:
- £3,000 for not keeping the external surfaces of beer lines and connections clean.
- £2,500 for not keeping the beer cellar floor, walls and other parts of the structure clean.
- £2,500 for having an accumulation of filth in the cellar.
- £3,500 for not keeping the ice-making machine clean.

Protecting food from risk of contamination

☐ no raw material or ingredients accepted if they are known to be, or might reasonably be expected to be, contaminated so that after normal preparatory or processing procedures, they would still be unfit for human consumption

☐ raw materials and ingredients kept in appropriate conditions to prevent harmful deterioration and to protect them from contamination

☐ all food which is handled, stored, packaged, displayed and transported protected against any contamination

☐ food so placed and/or protected as to minimise any risk of contamination

☐ adequate procedures in place to ensure pests are controlled

☐ hazardous and/or inedible substances, including animal feedstuffs, adequately labelled and stored in separate and secure containers

Transport of food

☐ conveyances and/or containers used for transporting foodstuffs kept clean and maintained in good repair and condition, designed and constructed to permit adequate cleaning and/or disinfection

☐ receptacles in vehicles and/or containers not used for transporting anything other than foodstuffs where this may result in contamination of foodstuffs

☐ bulk foodstuffs transported in containers reserved for the transport of foodstuffs if otherwise there is a risk of contamination, with clear marking to this effect

☐ where conveyances and/or containers are used for transporting anything other than foodstuffs, or different foodstuffs at the same time, effective separation of products and effective cleaning between loads to avoid risk of contamination

☐ foodstuffs in conveyances and/or containers so placed and protected as to minimise the risk of contamination

Personal hygiene

☐ every person working in a food handling area maintains a high degree of personal cleanliness and wears suitable, clean and, where appropriate, protective clothing

☐ no person, known or suspected to be suffering from, or to be a carrier of, a disease likely to be transmitted through food or while afflicted, for example with infected wounds, skin infections, sores or with diarrhoea, permitted to work in any food handling area in any capacity in which there is any likelihood of directly or indirectly contaminating food with pathogenic microorganisms (see page 17)

The law and good practice

Statements such as 'wooden chopping boards are not allowed', 'cellars must have tiled floors', may reflect good practice and a standard you would wish to achieve. But when the business's resources are limited, it is sometimes necessary to look at what the law actually requires.

Misunderstandings should be less likely once the 1994 food hygiene regulations take effect (mid-1995), and industry guides to good hygiene practice have been published. In the changeover period, guidance from LACOTS, the Local Authorities Coordinating Body on Food and Trading Standards, provides clarification of many of these issues. The guidance also gives a valuable insight into the new approach of both government and local authority environmental health departments:

wooden chopping blocks and cutting boards – acceptable provided they are made of hardwood, properly designed and constructed, kept in a good state of repair, and maintained in a clean condition

insect screens – before they can be required on openable windows or doors, there must be evidence of insect infestation and/or risk of contamination

nail brushes at wash hand basins – their provision should not be enforced by means of improvement notices (the 1994 regulations make no mention of nail brushes)

hand washing – the provision of bactericidal soaps is not required, nor can hot air dryers be deemed 'unsuitable' hand drying equipment

public area of bars and restaurants – in general it is inappropriate to apply the 1970 regulations to such areas (the 1994 regulations have a separate set of requirements for rooms where foodstuffs are prepared, treated or processed – excluding dining areas)

disinfecting articles and equipment – this can only be required if it is relevant to food safety

waterproof dressings – there is no requirement to provide coloured dressings or dressings containing metal strips for easy detection as foreign bodies

smoking during breaks – this does not pose a risk to food safety provided the smoker observes good personal hygiene practice before resuming food handling activities

staff overclothing – the regulations do not prohibit buttons or pockets on such garments

cellars – structure clean and in good order, repair and condition to enable effective cleaning: painted wall surfaces and ceilings generally acceptable, sealed concrete floor generally acceptable. Tiled walls and floors are not required. Brick stillages do not have to be painted

dry goods storage – structure clean and in good order, repair and condition to enable effective cleaning: sealed concrete floor may be acceptable, block, brick or rendered walls may be acceptable, bare wooden shelving/racking may be acceptable. There is no legal requirement for separate stores for raw vegetables and dry goods

bar servery – general requirement for cleanliness etc. as above. There should be suitable and sufficient sinks/washing facilities in premises for glass washing – in general, either a double bowl sink and drainer, or a mechanical glass washing machine with a separate sink. Sealed (e.g. painted or varnished) wooden shelving is acceptable for the storage of glasses. Glasses can be kept on racks or hooks.

Use-by and best-before labelling

The *use-by* date is the date up to and including which the foodstuff may be used safely, e.g. cooked, processed or consumed, provided it has been stored safely. The *best-before* date is the date up until which the foodstuff will retain its optimum condition, e.g. it will not be stale.

Food producers/suppliers are responsible for deciding which type of date marking to use. The Ministry of Agriculture, Fisheries and Food (MAFF) guidelines indicate that use-by labels should be put on all foodstuffs which need to be stored at low temperatures (below 8°C) to maintain their safety rather than their quality and have a relatively short product life after manufacture, after which they would be likely to carry dangerous numbers of food poisoning organisms. Virtually all other foodstuffs require a best-before date.

You should find the date mark is followed by simple and clear storage instructions and conditions of use. If a strict storage temperature is required, the instructions will tell you the maximum temperature at or below which the food should be stored to maintain its safety and quality.

You commit an offence if you sell or have in possession for sale food that has passed its use-by date. Food frozen before this date has been reached, for use as an ingredient or a compound foodstuff or as part of a meal in a catering establishment, is an exception (see first box).

Food labelling and menu descriptions

Customers who are unable to eat certain foods for reasons of health, or who simply do not want to eat meat products, for example, rely on the accuracy of your menu descriptions and drink lists, and informed answers to any questions they might ask you or your staff before ordering.

The Food Labelling Regulations 1984 help ensure that useful information is available to you and to your customers. For your part, you must display the name of the food, dish or drink, either on a menu, or by a notice near the point of sale. The alcoholic content of beers, wines, spirits and similar drinks should be stated, and there are detailed requirements on how this should be done, and when it is unnecessary.

Organic food from plant products has to conform to detailed EC standards (legislation on animal products is expected to follow). Trading standards officers may wish to satisfy themselves that dishes described on your menu as organically produced do comply with the EC rules.

This symbol can be used on labels or menus, but it must be accompanied by the words 'irradiated' or 'treated with ionising radiation'. However it is unlikely to be a common sight, while the British remain wary of the acceptability of irradiated foods.

Restaurant owner fined over kitchen

A Shrewsbury restaurant owner was today fined £1,100 after a court heard how environmental health officers found his kitchen encrusted with grease and food scraps.

Freezing food before use-by expiry date

If the frozen food is further processed within a catering business then no offence is committed, provided the food remains fit to eat.

However, if the food is frozen and then sold to the consumer in its original wrapper after the use-by date is expired, then an offence is committed regardless of the condition of the food.

LACOTS, the Local Authorities Coordinating Body on Food and Trading Standards

---

Forewarned is forearmed

Following the report in *The Times* of 4 February 1992 that a peanut allergy had killed a 17-year-old girl in a leading boarding school, *Caterer & Hotelkeeper* published this advice in its letter page from Duncan Holloway, head chef at Eton College:

On enrolment most institutions ensure that students or their parents are asked for details of any history of allergies. But are the necessary steps taken to ensure that the caterer is notified, and does the caterer maintain good records to ensure that staff know the situation? Similar considerations apply to students attending the short courses which any institution runs.

The MAFF (see text) have issued guidance on peanut allergies.

Irradiated food

If a dish or food item menu has been irradiated, or an irradiated ingredient represents 25% or more of the total product, your customers should be informed of this. To comply with the Food Labelling (Amendment) (Irradiated Food) Regulations 1990, the menu or dish description must use the words 'irradiated' or 'treated with ionising radiation'. A more general statement that dishes 'may contain irradiated food and/or ingredients' is acceptable, and avoids the need constantly to change notices and menus.

So far only one operator (Isotron plc of Swindon) has been given approval in the UK to treat food using this process. The licence allows the irradiation of a range of herbs and spices.

Food Safety Act 1990

The Act's scope is wide. Most catering and food businesses are covered, as are those operated by public or local authorities and those that are non-profit making. It applies to most stages of processing including preparing food, storing or transporting it for the purpose of sale, delivering or serving, selling, possessing for sale and offering, exposing or advertising for sale.

The term 'food' refers to almost anything that is eaten, drunk or chewed, including water, articles and substances used as ingredients in the preparation of food, even if they are of no nutritional value. Any food on the premises is presumed to be intended for human consumption, until the contrary is proved.

Rendering food injurious to health

It is an offence to make food harmful by:

adding or using any article or substance as an ingredient in its preparation

removing any constituent

subjecting it to any other process or treatment.

Food safety requirements

It is an offence to sell, offer, expose or advertise for sale, or have in your possession for the purpose of such sale or of preparation for such sale, any food which fails to comply with food safety requirements, i.e. food:

which has been rendered harmful

is unfit for human consumption

is so contaminated (whether by extraneous matter or otherwise) that it would not be reasonable to expect it to be used for human consumption.

Consumer protection

An offence is committed if the food is sold and not of the nature, substance and quality demanded by the customer:

the nature – different food from that specified, e.g. pork fillet sold as veal

the substance – contains non-food material, e.g. a piece of broken glass

the quality – e.g. the food is stale.

It is also an offence to label, present, or advertise food in a way which falsely describes the food or is likely to mislead as to its nature, substance or quality.

Enforcing authorities

Local authorities (district councils in Scotland) enforce the Act. Environmental health officers (EHOs) enforce food safety aspects. Trading standards officers enforce labelling, food composition and contamination issues which do not pose an imminent risk to health.

Officers have the power to:

- enter your premises at all reasonable hours, without notice. If admission is refused, or the premises are unoccupied or the occupier temporarily absent, the authority can issue a warrant for entry, by force if need be

- inspect your premises, processes and records, and to seize and detain any records which might be required as evidence

- inspect food to see if it is safe

- take samples of any article or substance which may be required as evidence in legal proceedings

- take samples of food or any article or substance intended to come into contact with food, and submit these to a public analyst or food examiner.

It is an offence intentionally to obstruct an officer during the course of his or her duties, to fail to give any assistance or information which may reasonably be required, or to give information which is false or misleading. But you are not required to answer any question or give any information if to do so might incriminate you.

Where any food fails to comply with food safety requirements, the officer may:

- order that it is not to be used for human consumption, and that it is not to be removed, or is to be removed to some specified place

- detain or seize suspect food in order to have it condemned.

If any unfit food is part of a larger batch, it will be taken that the whole batch is unfit unless the contrary can be proved.

The officer may be accompanied by anyone else felt to be necessary for the inspection.

Improvement notices and prohibition orders

If a significant breach of the Food Safety Act or regulations made under the Act is found, the officer can serve an *improvement notice* on the proprietor (explained in greater detail on page 75).

If there is imminent risk to health, an *emergency prohibition notice* can be issued with immediate effect. Within 3 days, the officers must make an application to court for an *emergency prohibition order*. You must be given at least one day's notice of the intention to go to court.

The court may then impose a *prohibition order* if there is a risk of injury to health and the proprietor is convicted of a food safety offence. This can be limited to specified processes or treatments, or to the use of the premises or equipment for particular purposes, or, more generally, for the purposes of any food business. It can be imposed on the proprietor or manager of the premises personally, prohibiting him or her from managing any food business, or a particular type of food business.

A copy of the order must be displayed in a conspicuous place on the premises. The order remains in force until the authority certifies that the risk no longer exists, or a court lifts the order.

Permitted defences

It is a defence for the person charged to prove that:

- he or she took all reasonable precautions and exercised all due diligence, including proper supervision of food handling staff. The defendant must prove that all reasonable checks were made on the food and that he or she could not have known that an offence was being committed

- the offence was due to the act, or default of a person not under his or her control (e.g. the supplier), or to misinformation supplied by another person. The defendant may have to prove there has been no complicity with the other person.

Due diligence

This is only applicable in the event of legal proceedings, if the defendant voluntarily uses the defence that he or she took all reasonable precautions and exercised all due diligence. While good procedures, carefully supported by records (e.g. of temperatures and training) would be invaluable in such a defence, they are not of themselves a legal requirement.

Training of food handlers

The guides to good practice which the industry's trade and professional associations will be developing jointly, are likely to provide more detailed guidance on training. Until then, EHOs will follow the code of practice for improvement notices (see also page 75). In summary, the code says:

- a person handling open foods which are susceptible to contamination would be expected to have been given the equivalent of training contained in the basic or certificate food hygiene course run by national organisations such as the Institution of Environmental Health Officers, Royal Society of Health and Royal Institute of Public Health and Hygiene

- in low-risk situations (e.g. handling prepacked foods), the provision of suitable written or oral advice to a food handler, with active supervision, may be sufficient.

While the hygiene courses referred to above provide a guide to training content, there is no requirement to attend one or other of them, nor to pass an examination or gain a certificate. However, if there is no certificate, an EHO might wish to assess the level of food hygiene awareness during an inspection (by a combination of observation and questioning).

Other hygiene regulations

The 1994 general food hygiene regulations provide the general baseline hygiene standard applicable to any food business. Stricter controls cover areas of higher risk, such as manufacturers and producers of products of animal origin: meat of all types including game, poultry and rabbit, meat products, fish, eggs, milk (including goats' milk) and milk-based products.

These more detailed controls do not generally apply to caterers supplying the final consumer. Two possible exceptions are:

live bivalve molluscs including oysters, mussels, cockles, farmed scallops, whelks and winkles: any business or operator dealing with these must comply with the hygiene standards contained in the Food Safety (Live Bivalve Molluscs and Other Shellfish) Regulations 1992

ice-cream – if you make your own ice-cream, it must be pasteurised (i.e. heated to kill bacteria). As the Ice-Cream (Heat Treatment, etc.) Regulations 1959 are likely to be amended by the forthcoming Dairy Products (Hygiene) Regulations, you should check with your EHO before you attempt to make your own ice-cream.

Advice on personal hygiene is more effective when it is written to have an impact on the reader.

Caterer's blacklist

Before employing someone in a managerial role it is possible to check whether that person has been prohibited from working in a food business by contacting the Institution of Environmental Health Officers (IEHO) on 071 928 6006. Details are also published in *Food Forum*, the IEHO's quarterly food safety bulletin.

The Office of Fair Trading maintains a computer database of those convicted under a wide range of safety regulations. This is accessible by enforcement authorities.

Those owning or entrusted with the day-to-day running of a food business can be served a prohibition order under the Food Safety Act 1990. The order lasts for at least six months.

The judge also ma… order banning … taking part in the ma… ment of any food con…

Afterwards, … vironmental Health … cer, … …, said: … have a duty to protect public and we will … shirk from carrying it ou… Only 22 people throug… out the country have be… banned from running … restaurant since the A… came into force.

Smoking

It is forbidden to smoke in food rooms or whilst handling open food. Not only is this to prevent cigarette ends and ash from contaminating food but also because:

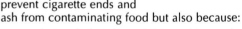

- people touch their lips whilst smoking and they may transfer harmful bacteria to food
- smoking encourages coughing and droplet infection
- cigarette ends contaminated with saliva are placed on working surfaces.

Nose, mouth and ears

Up to 40% of adults carry staphylococci in the nose and mouth. Coughs and sneezes can carry droplet infection for a considerable distance and persons with bad colds should not handle open food. Disposable single-use paper tissues are preferable to handkerchiefs. Picking or scratching the nose is not acceptable.

As the mouth is likely to harbour staphylococci, food handlers should not eat sweets, chew gum, taste food with the fingers or an unwashed spoon, or blow into glasses to polish them.

CASE STUDY

The inspection that led to a £45,000 fine

After we had identified ourselves to a woman in the reception area of the restaurant, she went into the private quarters to summon the proprietor. My colleague and I went into the kitchen. A man arrived smoking a cigarette which he extinguished in the sink. He was the manager. I said we were here to inspect the premises and he agreed to accompany us. We then went to each part of the premises to assess its general structure and check for signs of pest infestation. At my request the manager produced the log book left by his pest control contractor. It showed one treatment 5 weeks and another 4 days prior to our inspection.

Continuing the inspection, I found in the large rear store room several rat droppings and several trays of poison which had been consumed, disturbed and overturned.

Having established several serious contraventions of the Food Hygiene (General) Regulations 1970 and the Food Safety Act 1990, I cautioned the manager and asked him if he understood the caution, to which he replied 'Yes'. I then asked him if the pest contractor had filled the bait trays in the rear store room on his last visit and the manager answered 'Yes'.

From this time, I decided that conditions were sufficiently serious to warrant legal proceedings and my colleague and I gathered evidence in the form of scrapings, samples and photographs.

During the course of our inspection we saw the cook preparing pre-cooked chickens on a cutting board that was filthy, deeply cut and scored. When asked about the apparent undercooking of the chicken quarters and the dirtiness of the cutting board, the manager replied that all the meat would be recooked after it had been shredded. I reminded the manager that he was still under caution and asked when the cutting boards had last been cleaned. The manager answered that the chef scrapes them with a cleaver. I asked 'How else does he clean them?' and he replied 'With Fairy Liquid in the sink'. I asked if he used a sanitiser or similar product. He answered 'Yes' and showed me the product. Asked when they were last cleaned with bleach, he answered 'One week ago'. We then asked whether he had separate cutting boards for raw and cooked meat and he said he used one board for all meat and one board for all vegetables.

On the work surface was an electrical slow cooker full of cooked boiled rice. Probed in several places, the rice gave an even temperature on each probe of 17.9°C. The ambient temperature in the kitchen was found to be 18.3°C. When asked, under caution, the manager at first said that the rice had been cooked that morning, but questioned closer, he admitted that it had been cooked the day previously and left out unrefrigerated. I asked the manager if he intended to use this rice for his customers and after a short while the manager said that he would not. I then asked the manager what rice would be used if a customer came into the premises and asked for a dish that included boiled or fried rice. He considered his answer for a short while and said 'I would sell them chips'. So I repeated the question and asked if it was correct that if a customer came into the restaurant and wanted a dish that included rice he would not sell them rice this lunch time and he replied 'That's right, I would sell them chips'.

I asked him to show me the bathroom that was used by the food handlers. We went upstairs. The first floor toilet was in the bath-room. The room was untidy, strewn with soiled clothing, and a soiled baby's disposable nappy was lying on a wicker chair. The wash hand basin had no soap nor nail brush and there were no clean towels. Although the ground floor toilets were allegedly not used, the urinal smelt strongly of urine. In both WCs there were part-used rolls of toilet paper and newspapers.

Grant Courteney, Environmental Health Officer, Newbury

ANALYSIS

While you are unlikely to come across conditions as poor as those described, you will have to deal with inspection visits by EHOs.

1　What would you say about the way the manager reacted to the visit of the EHOs, and the answers he gave to their questions? In similar circumstances what would you have done and said?

2　What contraventions to the food safety legislation did the EHO observe early on in the inspection?

3　What hazards can you identify in each of the photographs?

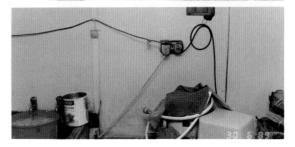

Food safety management

Food poisoning in any circumstances is potentially serious. For astronauts on a space flight it would be catastrophic. In the 1970s, NASA played a leading role in developing a management control system known as HACCP to ensure there were no risks of food poisoning affecting American space missions. Said as 'hassap', the initials stand for *Hazard Analysis and Critical Control Points*.

The value of a HACCP-type approach has been increasingly recognised by caterers. The Food Safety (General Food Hygiene) Regulations 1994 require you to have a food safety control or management system in place. This involves:

1 Identifying hazards (i.e. things with the potential to cause harm), and at what point they may occur.

2 Identifying which of these points are critical to food safety: the critical control points.

3 Establishing effective control and monitoring procedures at critical points.

In this way you will be able to have more assurance that attention and resources are being focused in the right areas for food safety.

The regulations require you to assess your operation, be aware of, and control any step which is critical to food safety. There is no obligation to have a formally documented system, although for some establishments, especially the larger ones, this will be advisable.

HACCP is one type of assessment system. ASC or Assured Safe Catering is another, gearing the HACCP procedures to the catering industry. The principles are similar.

Consider a small take-away restaurant with a menu of hamburgers, a selection of dressings and French fries. The main hazards would be associated with the hamburgers, since they could be contaminated with food poisoning organisms on arrival, or at any stage up to the time they are served. So the investigation would focus on how they are purchased, stored, handled, cooked and held before service. Besides the hazards arising from the nature of the hamburgers (uncooked beef), other areas to look at will include equipment, personnel and premises. You can explore this example further with the activity on page 69.

How the text headings relate to the 3 steps

The text on pages 67 to 70 explains these three steps under the following headings:

⇒ **1 What hazards exist?**

⇒ **2 Where can they be controlled?**

⇒ **3 How can they be controlled?**

If your operation is fairly complex, a flow diagram may help clarify what stages are involved, and how they interact.

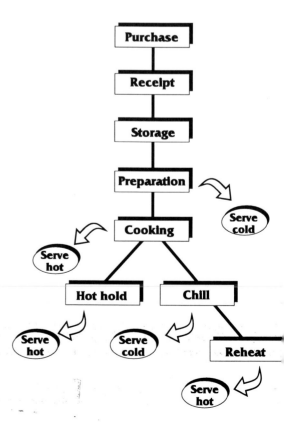

 Further information is available in the Department of Health's booklet *Assured Safe Catering*, HMSO, 1993, ISBN 0 11 321688 2, from which this flow chart has been adapted.

Step 1: What hazards exist?

You need to take a very wide perspective here, and be as open-minded as possible. The aim is to identify all hazards, not just those which are obvious at first glance. A brainstorming session with your colleagues and staff may help to do this. Questions you could ask include:

- what uncooked foods might contain food poisoning bacteria or toxins when they come into the premises? – e.g. chicken and eggs (salmonella), meat (clostridium perfringens), vegetables and rice (bacillus cereus), red kidney beans (various toxic substances)

- what other sources of harmful bacteria are there? – e.g. food handler ill, or failing to wash hands after using toilet or smoking, equipment not properly cleaned, pests

- how can harmful bacteria spread from one product to another? – e.g. cross-contamination through using the same chopping board for raw and cooked foods

- are there any other substances which might make the food harmful? – e.g. contact with cleaning agents, chemical reaction from being stored or cooked in wrong container, glass or china breakages in kitchen

- are there any conditions which would encourage harmful bacteria to multiply to dangerous levels?– e.g. food remaining at room temperature for a long time

- is there sometimes a long delay between cooking a hot dish and serving it?

- is there sometimes a problem because food has not defrosted in time?

- is appropriate equipment available for day-to-day operational requirements, e.g. a blast chiller to chill food quickly, a blast freezer to freeze food, a thawing cabinet to defrost food?

- are some dishes reheated before service?

- are there particular problems because of the nature of the operation? – e.g. hard-to-predict demand (motorway service area), long distances for the food to travel (hospitals)

- are there any procedures which are not working? – e.g. stock rotation of frozen foods (hard-to-read labels, capacity of freezer), meals forecasting (so that too much is regularly prepared)

- what conditions would allow harmful bacteria to survive cooking? – e.g. food not cooked to safe temperature.

If ways of eliminating or reducing the likelihood of these hazards occurring emerge from these discussions, make a note of them. This will help when you come to consider controlling and monitoring measures.

Food poisoning outbreak at buffet

On the evening of 17 May 1990 over 150 people attended a trade exhibition at a local hotel. A buffet was provided between about 5.30 p.m. and 8.30 p.m. This consisted mainly of chicken drumsticks, sausage rolls, vol-au-vents, pizzas and sandwiches.

Over the course of the following 3 days at least two GPs had independently realised that an outbreak of food poisoning had occurred and notified the Environmental Health Department of Kerrier District Council.

The senior EHO inspected the hotel kitchens and interviewed the proprietor and head chef under formal caution. No food samples from the function remained.

Faecal specimens were collected from catering staff and most of the people who had attended the function and who had been ill. Fortunately, two independent people who had attended the function had taken home some chicken drumsticks and were able to submit these for examination.

Results of the investigation

310 raw partially frozen chicken drumsticks were delivered in an unrefrigerated van to the hotel on 14 May at mid-day. 50 were removed for a separate function and the remainder put into a large pan and placed in the refrigerator at about 1 p.m. to defrost.

The following morning they were put single depth into clean trays and heated in a fan-assisted oven at 200°C for about 30 minutes. They were cooled in the kitchen until about 11 a.m., when they were rolled in flour, dipped in fresh egg wash and rolled into breadcrumbs. They were then laid on to clean trays, possibly two-deep, covered with clingfilm and placed in a chest freezer.

On 17 May, they were removed from the freezer at about 9.30 a.m. and left to defrost in the kitchen. At about 1 p.m. the drumsticks were deep fried for 3–4 minutes to brown them and placed on clean trays to cool. At about 2 to 2.30 p.m. the drumsticks were put on to stainless steel serving flats and refrigerated until 5 p.m. when they were heated in 4 batches and served over the 3 hours or so during which the buffet lasted.

W B Trevena, Senior EHO (Food), Kerrier District Council, in *IEHO Food Forum*, September 1992

ANALYSIS

From the details given in the case study:

1 What practices do you think might have led to the outbreak of food poisoning?

2 How would you approach the preparation of food for a function such as this?

Step 2: Where can they be controlled?

You could personally supervise every stage and every activity in your kitchen, temperature probe, clipboard and stopwatch in hand. But so long would be spent controlling, that the food would not be ready in time. Quite rightly, you might ask: is all this effort worthwhile? Isn't there a better system?

There is, and that is why the term 'critical control point' or CCP has come to join the catering language. The concept helps you focus on the stages where control is most effective. Consider first, where control would *not* be effective:

- you can't do anything to prevent dangers at that stage, e.g. the delivery of fresh vegetables – you can check the quality but you cannot detect harmful bacteria

- there is nothing that needs controlling from the food hazard point of view, e.g. how customers' food orders are received in the kitchen.

So these are not critical control points. If a later step will make the food safe, e.g. boiling vegetables, then that is not a CCP. But if no later step will make the food safe, e.g. grilling a steak to order, then that step is definitely a CCP.

Many foods contain harmful bacteria in their raw state. But when the food is cooked most of the bacteria are killed, so that the food at that point is safe to eat. In this situation, purchasing is not a critical control point with regard to food safety, but the cooking is.

If the food is not served immediately, then depending on the conditions in which it is held it may be contaminated by:

- harmful bacteria from other sources, e.g. contact with raw foods, equipment which is not clean, poor personal hygiene

- spores formed by some bacteria, e.g. clostridium perfringens in raw meat and poultry, bacillus cereus in vegetables, cereals, rice and dehydrated products. These can survive cooking, and if given the right conditions, will germinate and multiply to large numbers.

In these situations there may be one or more critical control points, covering how the food is handled, at what temperature it is kept and for how long.

When prepared foods are purchased that are stored then served (e.g. ready-made cream cakes), purchasing would be a critical control point. The delivery and storage temperatures and possibly the length of time in storage would also be CCPs.

Try to avoid CCPs which clash with peak service or preparation periods: if they do, there is a risk they won't be carried out properly.

Training, instruction and supervision, backed by workplace instructions and reminders, are the only way that some hazards can be controlled.

Food preparation

Use separate areas within the kitchen for preparing raw meat and cooked foods. A work flow system could be devised for your own particular kitchen which ensures that there is no preparation of raw meats adjacent to cooked meats, sandwich or salad preparation.

Use one sink for vegetables and salad washing only. If a separate food sink is not provided, then ensure one sink is kept for food washing during preparation time and then the sink is thoroughly cleaned prior to it being used for equipment and utensil washing, etc., and vice versa.

Under no circumstances should a sink be used for washing equipment and utensils and then used for food washing unless it has been thoroughly sterilised between uses.

A well-understood system of colour-coding for chopping boards, knives, items of cleaning equipment and even areas of the kitchen, is a powerful defence against cross-contamination.

⚡ ACTION

the two scenarios below, the operation has been broken down into three ...ages: receipt, storage, and preparation and cooking. Go through ...cenario One, then read the box where the hazards at each stage are ...entified before considering the suggested control points.

...en turn to Scenario Two. Assume you have taken over the take-away ...staurant described. Your priority is to introduce a food safety manage-...ent programme. Make some notes on what this will involve, including:

  what hazards exist

  where they can be controlled, and which are critical control points.

Hazards in Scenario One

Receipt   As the hamburgers come from a central supply point in refrigerated delivery vehicles, and there are rigorous controls at all stages, there are unlikely to be any significant hazards for the take-away manager to worry about. The ACTION on page 73 lists some of the hazards that might otherwise be present.

Storage   Here also, most of the hazards you would expect to find (e.g. temperature variation, products kept beyond use-by date, etc.) seem to have been anticipated and avoided.

Preparation & cooking   Personal hygiene standards and preparation procedures remain potential hazards. If the automatic cooking control on the grills does not work as it should, the burgers might not be sufficiently cooked, so that bacteria survive. If, perhaps because too many burgers had been cooked ahead of demand, some are kept for a time, the bacteria might multiply to dangerous numbers.

Stage	Scenario One	Scenario Two
Receipt	Take-away unit belonging to a medium-sized company: the hamburgers come from the company's own central production unit, and are delivered in the company's refrigerated vehicles. Rigorous quality control systems are in place at all stages.	Take-away purchases from a local supplier: detailed purchase specification covers quality and origin of the meat used, fat content, additional ingredients (e.g. seasoning, colouring), weight and dimensions of each burger, etc., burgers chilled to 3°C on delivery.
	Control point *outside packaging and quantity checked on delivery* (assumption is that quality has been controlled by supplier)	
Storage	Immediately after delivery burgers are transferred to the cold room in their packaging, with use-by date visible. No other products are stored in the cold room, and there is a well-established procedure for using older stock first. Automatic temperature monitoring equipment with printout and alarm system. Maintenance contract on cold room with 2 hour emergency call-out.	Some burgers unpacked after delivery, trayed-up and placed in under-counter refrigerators, others left in packaging and placed in cold room.
	Control points *temperature printouts checked periodically* *maintenance occurs at scheduled intervals* *supervisors/staff know what action to take if alarm sounds*	
Preparation and cooking	Garnishes and dressings closely specified, with minimum of on-site preparation (e.g. pickles pre-sliced, lettuce shredded). Pattern of business predictable, with well-established system for ensuring stock available of popular items. Staff all have food hygiene qualifications, with regular refresher training. Rota provides for adequate staffing at all times including peak periods. Burgers cooked on automatic grills, to consistent degree of doneness. Packaged then placed in appropriate rack of hot-holding display equipment, so that older stock moves forward. Counter staff collect from front of hot display when customer orders.	Garnish prepared in advance of service, and as necessary during opening hours. Pattern of business can be unpredictable. High staff turnover, some have basic hygiene certificate, but guidance from more experienced staff and supervisor main method of training. At peak times staffing level sometimes inadequate. Burgers char-grilled, staff controlling length of cooking.
	Critical control points *core temperature of burgers at completion of cooking (+75°C)* *core temperature of burgers during hot display (+63°C)*	
	Other control points *length of time burgers remain in hot display before sold* *training records* *quality control of products* *maintenance checks on grills and hot-holding equipment*	

Step 3: How can they be controlled?

Now that you have decided where the critical control points exist, how can you use them to greatest effectiveness? What needs to be measured? There is a range of questions which need to be considered, and the answers to some will depend on the answers to other questions.

When does control happen? For a continuous process, e.g. the fridge temperature control, is once or twice a day sufficient? Or should the equipment have an automatic temperature monitoring and recording system?

Who will act? This person must have the knowledge and authority to take corrective action if the target levels are exceeded.

How are they to act? Precise instructions may be needed, e.g. whether to record the air temperature in the cold room, or insert a temperature probe into the centre of food, in which case the probe must be sanitised before and after each use.

What action should be taken if target levels are exceeded? Bring the situation back under control (return food to oven to cook some more). Inform the manager. Dispose of the food.

Are tolerances appropriate? For example, that reheated dishes reach 75°C at the centre for 3 minutes, but a temperature in the range 73°C to 77°C, for between 2 and 4 minutes, would be acceptable.

What types of control are appropriate? Such as:

- checks on suppliers, e.g. visiting their premises

- purchase specifications – drawing up detailed criteria such as the origin and quality of the meat for burgers, and roast joints less than 2½ kg in weight, and not more than 10 cm in thickness or height (if they are not served immediately, above these limits they take too long to cool after cooking)

- work procedures – e.g. that temperatures of chilled and frozen food items are checked on delivery, vegetables are examined for signs of spoilage, all salad vegetables are rinsed in an appropriate sanitiser, glass serving dishes (or use of any other glass) in the kitchen are forbidden (because of the danger of breakages leading to contamination of food)

- supervision – e.g. that food handlers use different coloured chopping boards in accordance with instructions, checking use-by or best-before dates on packaging, and checking equipment is clean before use

- record-keeping systems: time food put in hot display cabinets, temperature when cooking completed

- audits by management or outside consultants (some industry examples are given).

McDonald

CCP3: HYGIENE CONTROL –15%	OK	Not OK	Commen
Hand sanitation equipment available (soap, nailbrush, hand-drying, etc.)			
Hand-hot water			
Crew in kitchen wash hands every 30 minutes			
Evidence of good hygiene practice			
Cuts and wounds covered with blue plaster			
No crew/managers working with colds/flu			
No jewellery worn			
Protective equipment v			
Gloves worn for salad preparation			
Gloves worn for all mix re-run handling			
TOTAL			

CCP3 Hygiene control

When washing your hands c first entering the kitchen, cl that all the materials are available. Whilst completing audit, watch for good hand-washing practice. Is regular handwashing taking place? the managers leading by example?

Extract from the guidelines for completion of the McDonald's audit

CCP5: TIME CONTROL –15%	OK	Not OK	Comment
All frozen products within shelf-life			
All chilled products within shelf-life			
All secondary shelf-lives controlled by timers or labelling:			
In chiller			
On dress table			
In reach-in chiller			
In reach-in freezer			
In front counter chill display cabinet			
10 minute transfer bi holding time adhered			
10 minute chicken cabinet holding time adhered to			
TOTAL			

CCP5 Time control

Check the primary shelf-live all frozen and chilled produc If any of these shelf-lives ha been exceeded then the audi an automatic F grade.

Check for secondary shelf-li

- dress table: sauces 6 ho condiments 2 hours, che 30 minutes

- reach-in chiller/freezer: hours

Check the individual times c products in the front counte chilled display cabinet. Are cards used correctly in the transfer bin?

Extract from the guidelines for completion of the McDonald's audi

At McDonald's sheets like these are used to audit critical control points. An overall score of less tha 90% results in a failure.

xample of a control procedure.

Food deliveries

★★★
★★

IND COOPE RETAIL

1 Canned and bottled products should be examined and any dented, rusted or swollen cans returned. Bottled products with an abnormal colour are also to be returned. Vacuum packed products should not show loss of volume.

2 Frozen foods to be examined for signs of thawing. Items that are thawing or where ice has formed in the bottom of the packaging are to be returned.

3 Refrigerated foods should be rejected if the temperature on delivery is warmer than 8°C.

4 Examine joints of meat and meat products for quality and colour. Fresh meat deliveries should arrive below 8°C. No raw and cooked foods should be transported together.

5 Reject dry goods of unusual colours or with punctured or torn packaging.

6 Any product, the odour or appearance of which is unusual or causes concern, should not be accepted, nor should any product delivered in an unhygienic manner.

7 Examine use-by and best-before dates to ensure the product has sufficient life for your needs, and taking into account stock levels.

8 Immediately place foods in a designated storage area. Ensure that raw and cooked foods are kept separate. Place new deliveries in date sequence, to ensure adequate rotation.

Food handling practices

- [ ] evidence of recognition of high and low risk products in the preparation chain
- [ ] careful use of boards and equipment to avoid cross-contamination
- [ ] minimal unnecessary food mess during preparation
- [ ] clean as you go in practice
- [ ] products stored correctly throughout production process
- [ ] correct and suitable dishes and containers utilised for food products

Food temperature control

- [ ] daily written record maintained of temperature checks
- [ ] food temperature checked and recorded throughout production
- [ ] food checked on the service counter before service and at each sitting
- [ ] in holding and on service, hot food between 63°C and 70°C
- [ ] reheated dishes achieve a minimum 82°C
- [ ] salad and rolls and other chilled products held at between 0°C to 3°C

Extract from the audit relating to kitchen organisation.

The audit procedure used by contract caterers CCG Services Limited provides a point of reference for the area manager, the client if appropriate, and the unit management team every day. The manual spells out the type of recognisable physical standards by which an overall workplace standard can be judged.

An OK score is given when all the appropriate performance indicators are observed, IMPROVE when one indicator is missing, and FAIL if two or more are missing.

FOOD TEMPERATURES

Week commencing 7 FEB 94

Day	Food	Temp
MON	Chilli con carne (microwave)	78
	Tuna pie ''	74
TUE	Tagliatelle (- microwave)	82
WED	Coleslaw (in fridge)	5
	Chilled chilli mix	4
	Chilled steak & kidney mix	3
		8
THUR	Sausage hot pot	
	Vegetable chilli	
FRI	Chicken & leek pie	
	Coleslaw	
SAT	Coleslaw (in fridge)	
	Chopped ham	
	Defrosted chicken casserole	
SUN		

Comments ✱ All food temperatures Satis... air temp. high for part
A = All food thrown away. Equip...

AIR TEMPERATURES

Week commencing 7 FEB 94   Equipment Type Large fridge

	Temp.	Int.	Temp.	Int.	Temp.	Int.
MON	3		4		3	
	Time 8.30am		Time 1.20pm		Time 8.00pm	
TUE	2		5		3	
	Time 8.45am		Time 1.45pm		Time 9.00pm	
WED	8°C		8°C		4C	
	Time 8.30am	TW	Time 12.00pm	TW	Time 8.30pm	
THUR	2°C		4°C		2°C	
	Time 8.30am		Time 1.00pm		Time 8.00pm	
FRI	3°C		3°C		3°C	
	Time 8.30am		Time 12.40pm		Time 8.15pm	
SAT	15°C		—		—	
	Time 8.30am		Time Equipment out of action until repaired		Time	
SUN	2°C		3°C		3°C	
	Time		Time		Time	

Comments ✱ Food temperatures taken -see next page.
✱✱ Engineer called. Food temps. taken.

Using the temperature log book

The log book is designed to make the recording of refrigerator temperatures easy and simple.

Each page of the book represents one week. For those pubs that have several refrigerators they can be numbered and a separate page used for each.

The log book is set out to allow for up to three recordings per day. All that is required is the air temperature of the piece of equipment, the time the reading was taken and the initials of the person taking the reading.

The page designed for recording food temperatures allows for up to four entries per day. Both hot and cold food temperatures can be recorded.

STAKIS

Reviewing the process

From time to time, you need to check that the system is functioning effectively by asking questions such as:

- have any new hazards been introduced, e.g. using more part-time staff who have not had hygiene training?
- are the critical control points the right ones?
- are monitoring systems working as they should?
- is the record-keeping appropriate?

Separate from this, you or a senior colleague should carry out spot checks. These should be done in such a way that staff cannot anticipate when they will happen, but know that they do happen. For example:

- checking records of time–temperature readings
- observing operations at critical control points
- interviewing staff about the way they monitor.

Formalising the system

For small operations, food safety management is always likely to remain informal, even instinctive. It is similar to cash and stock control – when the only person handling money is the proprietor, a simple system works best.

In the larger operations, more is required if the approach is to be successful:

- commitment of directors and senior management – a food safety policy statement is a useful way of demonstrating and communicating this
- a director or senior manager given overall responsibility for all food safety matters
- organisational arrangements set up for implementing the policy, clearly setting out the responsibilities of all those concerned
- procedures and systems documented, e.g. in a company food safety manual.

Do not be over-ambitious when you get to the stage of introducing a formal system. Consider a phased approach, starting with one or two stages. The first stage could involve some people only. Subsequent stages could involve everyone to some extent. This gives your staff a chance to get used to the new systems, and you the opportunity to fine-tune procedures before they become too established.

Receipt, storage and use of frozen foods

1 Delivery of frozen foods must be checked to ensure that: temperature is no higher than – 10°C: use a probe thermometer, but do not pierce packaging; product specifications and quantities accord with what was ordered; packaging is in good condition: damaged packaging may lead to 'freezer burn'.

2 New supplies of frozen food must be placed into deep freeze storage (at –18°C) at once, unless intended for immediate use.

3 Deliveries must be date marked and used in rotation. Goods must be placed on shelves with sufficient gap to allow easy circulation of cold air. In chest freezers, new stock must be placed underneath existing stock. In walk-in units, food must be placed on shelves.

4 There is no provision for freezing foods on the premises, and this practice is therefore strictly prohibited.

5 Deep freeze cabinets may not be used for rapid chilling of food. Neither may hot food be placed into the freezer as this will raise the temperature of the unit and adversely affect other foods.

6 Frozen raw meat joints and poultry should be thawed out slowly and thoroughly in refrigerators or using rapid thaw equipment. Crash thawing by immersion in sinks of water (e.g. poultry) is **not** permitted. Crash thawing of foods using the defrost cycle of a microwave oven is permitted, provided the product is used or processed immediately afterwards, or held in a chill cabinet for not longer than 24 hours before consumption.

7 Thawed or partially thawed food must be stored in refrigerators, and should be used within 24 hours.

8 It is permissible to partially use the contents of a frozen food package (e.g. peas), provided that the remainder is returned unthawed to the freezer immediately and that the package is completely resealed.

How the activity relates to the 3 steps

The activity opposite takes you through *step 1*, helping you to identify hazards and at what point they occur. It encourages you to consider what control measures are appropriate – part of *step 2*, and how they can be monitored – *step 3*. The decision on what control points are critical – the other part of *step 2* – will depend on the characteristics of your operation.

> 1 **What hazards exist?**

> 2 **Where can they be controlled?**

> 3 **How can they be controlled?**

⚡ ACTION

ome of the stages in a typical catering operation are given in the table below, with examples of hazards, control measures and monitoring rocedures. (To keep the table simple, bacteria means food poisoning acteria and includes toxins, the poisons produced by bacteria.)

repare a similar table for the steps that apply in your establishment. Give areful thought to how you complete each column, so that the information s as comprehensive and useful as possible. Decide which control easures are critical. Done thoroughly, the exercise could form the basis f your own food safety management system.

Have your staff got the equipment they need? Boards should be replaced before they get badly stained and gashed like this one.

STAGE	HAZARDS	CONTROL MEASURES	MONITORING PROCEDURES
urchasing	Food from unsafe sources. Contains harmful substances. Contaminated with bacteria.	Buy from reputable suppliers. Authority to purchase restricted to those with knowledge of quality.	Draw up purchase specifications. Check suppliers on-site. Keep records of suppliers' performance.
elivery	Food not kept adequately chilled/ frozen during transportation. Food not adequately protected from contamination during transportation.	Use reputable suppliers. Buy from local suppliers. Use cold boxes when buying from cash and carry.	Check temperature, appearance, smell, wrapping.
rozen storage	Temperature variation leading to bacterial growth, premature thawing with juices/blood from one product contaminating another. Products kept beyond best-before date.	Maintain freezer temperatures. Label foods. Rotate stock. Have equipment serviced regularly.	Check temperatures/use temperature monitoring equipment. Check date labels. Check maintenance log.
hilled storage	Temperature variation. Cross-contamination from raw to cooked foods. Products kept beyond safe life.	Maintain safe chilled temperature. Separate storage for raw and cooked. Label foods, rotate stock. Equipment serviced regularly. Cleaning/defrosting schedule.	Check temperatures/use temperature monitoring equipment. Check stock rotation. Check cleanliness of interior.
ry storage	Attack by pests, vermin, etc. Contaminated by non-food products. Food past best-before date.	Adequate shelving, storage bins, etc. Separate storage for cleaning agents. Stock rotation.	Regular/spot checks on stores. Pest control contractor log checked.
hawing	Bacterial growth. Incomplete thawing. Defrosting juices contaminate other foods.	Safe thawing procedures. Production planning (so adequate time is allowed for thawing). Use thawing cabinet.	Supervise thawing. Checks on product before cooking.
reparation	Cross-contamination from raw to cooked foods. Bacteria have time/conditions to grow. Poor personal hygiene. Flies, pests spreading bacteria. Contact with cleaning agents. Foreign substances in food. Equipment contaminated.	Separate equipment for raw and cooked foods. Strict cleaning/personal hygiene rules. Use of sanitisers, colour-coded cleaning cloths. Clean protective clothing daily. Ban on glass or packing materials in food preparation areas.	Supervision, regular and spot checks of cleaning, working procedures, personal hygiene, wearing of jewellery, protective clothing, etc.
ooking	Bacteria survive. Spores survive.	Safe cooking times and temperatures established. Weights/size of joints restricted.	Temperature at centre of food checked. Supervision/observation.
ot-holding	Bacteria grow/produce poisons.	Equipment set at safe temperature. Set holding times/temperatures.	Temperatures and time held checked. Record when food put on hot display.
ooling	Bacteria grow/produce poisons. Cross-contamination.	Safe procedures established. Chilling equipment used.	Supervision/spot checks. Times and temperatures checked.
eheating	Bacteria survive.	Reheated to above 75°C.	Temperature at centre checked.
ervice	Cross-contamination. Bacteria grow.	Chilled/heated display cabinets. Maximum time on display.	Check temperatures and times.

Food hygiene inspections

Environmental health officers (EHOs) can inspect your premises at any reasonable time. They will usually come without notice, especially if their visit follows a complaint.

It is possible that the EHO's visit will be combined with that of the trading standards officer, or that the visit will serve more than one purpose, e.g. because you have asked for advice. Follow-up visits can be expected if problems arise.

The frequency of routine inspections (these may or may not be by appointment) will depend on the risk posed by your business, and its previous record. There is a scoring system for determining the minimum frequency (see box). Ask your EHO to tell you what inspection rating has been allocated to your operation, and explain how this has been arrived at.

Purpose of inspections

The emphasis of inspections is on identifying actual and potential hazards, and making an assessment of the risk they represent to public health. The overall aim is to encourage you to adopt good food hygiene practice.

The other purpose of inspections is, of course, to identify contraventions of food safety legislation, and seek to have them corrected. Where this happens, you should be given clear advice on the nature of the contravention, and what you must do to comply with the law (see checklist opposite).

Focus of the inspection

If you have a food safety management system in place, the discussion of this is likely to take up the major part of the inspection. After this, the EHO will proceed with the visual inspection, to confirm that you have correctly identified the critical points, and that controls (including the training and/or supervision of staff) are operating satisfactorily.

In a small business, the inspector will expect to see adequate controls in place, rather than a formal, documented hazard analysis system.

If you do not yet have a system in place, or you fit into the small business, lower risk category but do not have adequate controls, the EHO will carry out a fuller visual and physical examination. In this case, the inspection will usually start with a quick tour of the kitchens, stores, etc. This helps the officer assess the areas which require closer scrutiny.

At the end of the inspection, the EHO will usually give advice on how your systems and procedures could be improved, and discuss any matters where you are going wrong. If there are serious problems, you must be told what action the EHO intends to take. If there is sufficient evidence and prosecution is intended, the EHO may formally caution you. You have the right to remain silent (see case study on page 65).

Inspection rating scheme

Potential hazard of premises   *Points*

Type of food and method of handling ....min. 5, max. 40

Example: day-to-day handling or preparation (including cooking) of open high risk foods, e.g. restaurants, staff canteens, pubs, take-aways serving more than 20 consumers each day 30

Consumers at risk .... min. 0, max. 35
20 points of which apply to vulnerable groups, e.g. the elderly

Example: premises supplying essentially local trade .. 5

Compliance   *Points*

Food hygiene and safety .... very good 0, very bad 25

Example: high standard of compliance with statutory obligations and industry codes of practice, some improvements still possible 5

Structural condition of premises .... very good 0, very bad 25

Example: some non-compliance with statutory obligations and industry codes of practice, premises are in the top 50% of premises and standards are being maintained or improved 10

Confidence in management/control systems ... highly confident 0, no confidence 30

Example: reasonable record of compliance, technical advice available, have documented procedures and systems 5

Score

A score of between 91 and 175 means a visit every six months at least, between 71 and 90 every year, between 41 and 70 (as for the example above) every 18 months.

Confidence in management/control systems

What influences the inspector's judgement?

- track record of the company, its willingness to act on previous advice and enforcement, and the complaint history of the company

- attitude of management towards hygiene and food safety and food hygiene training

- technical knowledge within or available to the company on hygiene and food safety matters, including hazard analysis and the control of critical points

- existence of external quality assurance accreditation or satisfactory documented procedures and systems.

Use of improvement notices

The *Code of Practice on the Use of Improvement Notices* was revised in 1994 to reflect the government's preference for more informal enforcement of food safety legislation as a first resort, and when circumstances permit.

If defects are found on inspection, informal procedures will be used where the EHO believes they will lead to an improvement within a reasonable timescale. But you can expect formal action where:

the risk to public health is considered serious

you have a bad record for not complying with the food hygiene regulations

the officer believes an informal approach will fail.

Improvement notices or other legal action are unlikely to be used before summer 1996 to enforce the requirements of the 1994 general food hygiene regulations which relate to food safety management systems and the training and/or supervision of food handlers. A more advisory approach can be expected on these new requirements in the first instance.

After this transition period, a formal approach to their enforcement is still likely to be restricted to those instances where:

there are other, significant breaches of the food hygiene requirements

the food business involves high risk operations, there are clear breaches of the requirements relating to food safety management or training, and there has been no response to informal approaches.

Serving of an improvement notice

Improvement notices are served against the proprietor, but the officer should ensure whenever possible that the person responsible for taking action (e.g. the local manager) receives a copy of the notice. The wording of the notice should be clear and easily understood. It will state the legal provisions which have been contravened, the measures to be taken, and by when.

The period of time given for completion of work should be a realistic one, taking into consideration the nature of the problem, the risk to health and the availability of solutions. The EHO should discuss with the proprietor or the proprietor's representative what would be reasonable, although agreement is not necessary.

If the EHO intends to prosecute in addition to serving an improvement notice, this should be made clear at the time the notice is served.

 CHECKLIST

Inspection by an EHO

If you do not have the authority to deal with the inspection, immediately contact your manager or proprietor, and politely ask the officer to wait.

What you should do

- show courtesy throughout
- ask the officer if there is anything specific he or she wants to do – it may not be a full inspection, simply a spot check on product date codes
- arrange time to be with the officer for the inspection – if necessary, ask the officer to wait while you put other commitments on hold
- discuss any significant findings as they arise
- take careful note of any suggestions, observations or advice

What you are entitled to expect

- a courteous manner throughout
- on arrival, to be shown identification and told the purpose of the inspection
- where appropriate, opportunity to discuss matters relating to hygiene systems and procedures
- confidentiality with respect to trade secrets
- adherence to reasonable food safety precautions (the officer will normally wear his or her own protective clothing)
- accurate advice or interpretation of requirements which are given to you in any word-processed document or pre-printed letter, circular or advisory booklet (whether or not issued as part of the inspection)

On completion of the inspection

If the officer finds that there are problems, you are entitled to be told what these are.

If the officer decides on an informal approach:

- summary of the matters which, in the opinion of the officer, breach legal requirements
- clear distinction between what the EHO is recommending you do because it is good practice and what you must do to comply with the law
- reasons (in writing) for any action you are asked to take
- where there is an apparent breach of law, a statement of what that law is
- reasonable time to meet requirements, except where there is an immediate risk to public health

If the officer decides on formal action:

- that any improvement notices, informal written advice or inspection report following an inspection, are sent together, whenever possible.

For an emergency prohibition order, see page 63.

Meeting the requirements of the improvement notice

If you (or your proprietor) wish to carry out alternative measures to those specified in the improvement notice, you should discuss these with the EHO as soon as possible. Do not proceed until you have confirmation in writing that the alternative work has been approved. Ideally, try and talk through any requirements including timescales for work, before the EHO leaves your premises.

If it is likely to take longer than you have been allowed to complete the improvements, and there are good reasons, you should make a formal request for an extension of the time limit. Do this as soon as possible and certainly before the expiry date of the notice. Such requests must be in writing and you are entitled to be advised of the decision in writing.

As soon as the work has been completed, let the EHO know. A visit will follow to see that everything is now satisfactory. In all probability, your next routine inspection will be sooner than it might have been otherwise.

If you think the outcome is not fair

Contact your local authority's head of environmental health to see if the problem can be resolved informally. If disagreement remains, approach your local councillor.

If you think your local authority is applying the law in a different way from other authorities, seek advice from the Local Authorities Coordinating Body on Food and Trading Standards (LACOTS) or, in Scotland, the Scottish Food Coordinating Committee. Do this through your trade association or through your local authority by writing to the Chief Environmental Officer.

You have the right to appeal to a Magistrate's (or, in Scotland, the Sheriff's) court. The details of how you can do this will be included on the improvement notice.

This is a typical follow-up letter, where the EHO found a number of problems, but did not consider it appropriate to take more formal action. The regulation numbers, and some of the wording, would be different under the 1994 regulations, but none of the problems identified are the sort that any food operator should tolerate.

I write in connection with my recent visit to your premises on 21.02.1994. Listed below are those items that were found to be contravening the Food Hygiene General Regulations and should be attended to to ensure compliance. To assist you in prioritising these works, I have marked certain items with an asterisk. These should be dealt with immediately since they are likely to affect the safety of the food produced. I have also included advisory comments that if you were to follow would help you to ensure that the requirements of the legislation are being satisfied.

Sanitary accommodation

Regulation 16 requires you to maintain the sanitary accommodation in a clean and efficient order. To enable you to comply you must:

a) Carry out all necessary repair works to ensure that the structure can be effectively cleaned.
b) Thoroughly clean all surfaces including the toilet and wash hand basin.*
c) Provide soap, nailbrush and means of drying hands at the wash hand basin.*

Washing-up area

Regulation 25 requires that all parts of the structure should be clean and maintained in good repair. In order to comply with this regulation you **must** carry out the following:

a) Remove the mould growth from the walls and ceiling and thoroughly clean.*
b) Remove the pockets of dirt and debris that had collected on the floor.*
c) Repair or replace the partly collapsing sink base unit to enable it to be effectively cleaned.

In addition you are **advised** to:

a) Repaint the surfaces.
b) Remove the large number of miscellaneous items kept in
cle

2/..

Food preparation/storage rooms and servery

Regulation 25 requires that all parts of the structure must be clean and maintained in good repair. To enable you to comply with this regulation you **must**:

a) Clean the painted plaster walls that were dirty and chipped throughout.*
b) Clean the floor coverings throughout as they were dirty and had accumulations of debris at the edges.*
c) Replace the worn floor tiles in the servery to enable the floor to be kept clean.

In addition you are **advised** to:

a) Consider a suitable alternative wall coating such as ceramic wall tiles or proprietary catering cladding in the food preparation areas.

Regulation 9 requires that all reasonable steps are taken to prevent the risk of contamination. In order to comply it is recommended that you carry out the following:

a) Cease the practice of cooking kebabs from frozen. It is recommended that they are thoroughly defrosted in a refrigerator before cooking. Partly cooked kebabs should not be re-frozen and used again for cooking as this increases the risk of contamination to the food. Once used the remains of kebabs should be disposed of.
b) Food which is unfit or not intended for human consumption must be kept apart from food which is intended for sale. It is suggested that such food is kept in a suitable container with a close fitting lid clearly marked 'waste'.
c) The practice of using cotton cloths for wiping surfaces down is discouraged since cloths tend to provide ideal conditions for bacterial growth, i.e. damp, warmth, and most likely food from the food residues being wiped up. It would be advisable to use a disposable cloth such as 'J' cloths.

General comments

The following matters are examples of good practice which you are **advised** to consider implementing to raise general standards further:

a) It is advisable to take regular checks of all refrigerators and freezers to ensure that they are working within acceptable temperature parameters, e.g. refrigerators 5°C and freezers −18°C. You would also be advised to keep a written record which can be used for future reference of the temperatures actually achieved on a daily basis.
b) It is recommended that you employ a reputable pest control contractor to carry out regular surveys of the property. This is known to be a cost effective way of identifying early stages of pest infestation which with prompt treatment can save long term expense and complications.
c) The basic food hygiene course is strongly recommended, and as a minimum requirement the manager should attend.

Some of the general comments from the letter

... and how the letter ended.

I trust that those items marked with an asterisk will be completed by the time of our next visit on 3.03.94. The remaining items should be scheduled to be completed over a period of three months. If you would like to discuss any of these matters further, please contact me on the above telephone number. However if you feel aggrieved by the contents of this letter or any other matter relating to this inspection then you should contact the Assistant Head of Environmental Health, who will be happy to discuss any concerns you may have.

With thanks to Rushmoor Borough Council

Your workplace has its own particular hazards, which demand their own safety measures. Earlier sections of the book should have helped you get an overall picture of what these hazards are, your legal responsibilities in relation to them, and how safety procedures can be established. This section takes each of the main areas of operation in turn.

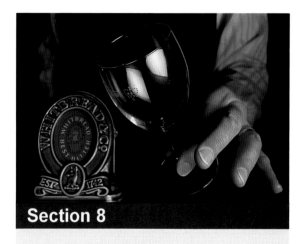

Workplace safety by area of operation

In the bar

Falls, cuts from broken glass, and injuries from manual handling are among the most common accidents behind the bar. Other dangers, which have also been covered elsewhere, arise from hazardous cleaning agents, particularly those used for glass washers (page 29), equipment, much of which is electrical, some of which has very hot surfaces (e.g. coffee machines) (Section 4), fire, where one of the greatest risks is from cigarette ends which get behind cushions or on to the carpet and are not found until too late (Section 5), security, including the threat of bombs (Section 6), and contact with the HIV virus (page 98).

Preventing violence

Staff provide essential back-up to the licensee's overall approach. They should know what will and will not be tolerated, and how to deal with customers who complain or are merely awkward. But staff should not be expected to deal with seriously aggressive customers, or fights, or have to get difficult people to leave the bar.

Spotting the warning signs

Violence rarely comes 'out of thin air'. Changes in the atmosphere and mood can signal danger. Is the broken glass the result of an accident, or a gesture of anger? While experience is important, it never replaces the signs you and your staff can observe from being out among the customers, watching and listening while collecting glasses, wiping tables, etc.

Any unusual behaviour can be a clue: sudden silences, everyone looking in the same direction, higher-pitched voices, aggressive gestures, rowdy or silly behaviour.

You should also make a point of monitoring toilets, corridors, car parks, and any other areas where troublemakers think they will not be noticed.

Contents guide

In the bar .... *this page*

In the cellar 80

In the kitchen 82

In the restaurant 86

In housekeeping 88

In reception, portering and administration 89

In leisure 90

Section 9 deals with those issues that affect some of the industry or some styles of establishment more than others: fraud and other security issues, safety with display screen equipment, precautions against Aids and legionnaires' disease, and building services.

Counteracting frustration

Slow service, being served out of turn, nowhere to sit, being jostled by other customers, no toilet paper, machines that don't work, loud music, too much or too little heating – these can all build up customers' feeling of frustration. Frustration can quite suddenly turn into aggression.

If you couldn't predict that the pub would be so busy or illness has left you short-staffed, there is not much to be done about jostling and slow service. But by acknowledging waiting customers, serving in strict rotation, and apologising for the delays and over-crowding, you can win most customers over.

Don't let your frustration lead to an unguarded remark, or a misdirected humorous comment. Like surly or unhelpful behaviour from your staff, these can trigger aggression.

Pool tables provide many opportunities for provocation, argument and conflict. You can reduce possible problems by establishing clear house rules (with a fair system for turn-taking), only having two cues (potential weapons) available at a time. If possible locate the table where you can keep a close eye on it at all times, and where players won't be jostled.

Managing closing time

Over half of violent incidents occur around closing time. You can reduce the risks with a clear, consistent method of calling last orders, and clearing the pub (see checklist).

When to intervene

Small problems, if ignored, can develop into serious ones. Generally, tactful intervention is never too soon. This can be as simple as asking if everything is all right, or steering the conversation on to a different topic. Standing near a group can be sufficient to defuse a potential problem.

Stopping known troublemakers at the door, or politely refusing to serve an aggressive group are other techniques. Show that you understand the customers' point of view.

The calming-down process

Take the heat out of the situation by talking calmly, slowly and deliberately in your normal tone of voice. Control your body language so you appear relaxed. Avoid prolonged eye-contact or aggressive gestures. Maintain a careful distance. If possible, move the offender away from his or her audience.

Exercising control

Make it clear what you want to happen: for the person to behave, to stop drinking, to leave. Through firmness, you give no room for argument.

De-personalise the encounter by emphasising your obligations to the law and to other customers, e.g. 'I know you're not a bad lad, but your behaviour tonight has really

 The text on violence and drugs has drawn on:

No Trouble! – published by The Portman Group, a video-based training package on the prevention and management of conflict and violence in pubs

Drugs and Pubs – published by Brewing Publications, a video-based training package for licensees and their staff

Order from Brewing Publications Ltd, 42 Portman Square, London, W1H 0BB, or through HCTC.

 CHECKLIST

Managing closing time

- clocks always tell the right time
- last orders and time are called exactly on time
- everyone can hear (or see) the signals, e.g. ringing bell, announcement by the publican, flashing lights
- staff are organised to cope with the rush of last orders
- music or juke box is turned down
- at closing time, lights are switched off behind the bar, towels hung over the pumps, staff moved from behind the counter – anything to help make it clear that serving has finished
- customers are acknowledged as they leave with a friendly goodbye
- while clearing glasses, wiping tables, etc., staff quietly remind remaining customers that it is nearly the end of drinking-up time
- last stragglers are cajoled to leave in a friendly, but firm manner: the licensee should personally deal with any really stubborn customers, emphasising the requirements of the law if necessary

been out of order', or 'I know this seems unfair, but I could lose my licence for serving someone who is over the limit'. If your action appears to make the person look silly in front of colleagues, you risk further aggression.

Don't announce an immediate barring order. If you think such a course is necessary, invite the person to come back the next day – hopefully in a calmer, more sober frame of mind. Failing that, you can always stop the person coming into the pub on a future occasion.

Do not hesitate to call the police if you need help. Do this via the 999 emergency service (so that there is proof that you have called).

If you belong to a Pub Watch scheme (see page 54) you will also want to alert other publicans.

Preventing drug use and dealing

High standards of cleanliness, service and vigilance – by management and staff – are powerful deterrents to drug dealers and drug users. They show that you care about your pub and your customers, and will not tolerate illegal activity.

The techniques that are so useful in managing violence (see above) are also important for drug prevention:

- high profile management – being there, knowing your customers, making your presence felt

- observing and listening while collecting glasses, emptying ashtrays, wiping tables, etc.

- regular checks on toilets (ladies and gents), car park, garden, etc.

- ensuring that staff inform you immediately, but discreetly, if they see or hear anything suspicious. There are well-established signs of drug abuse (see checklist), but remember that dealers are not always identifiable by appearance. They may be very respectable-looking.

If you have to deal with a problem:

- stay calm, to avoid provoking anger or aggression

- tell minor offenders firmly but politely that such activities are not allowed in your pub

- de-personalise the situation by emphasising your legal obligations – give facts, not opinions or moral judgements

- allow offenders the opportunity to back down without losing face

- maintain close cooperation with the police – if you suspect extensive drug use or dealing, ring the local police station and speak to your usual police contact. Keep a record of all such calls, including the time, the date, the person you spoke to and what you spoke about. In an emergency (e.g. violence, disorder), use the 999 service.

 CHECKLIST

Clues to drug abuse

- torn-up beer mats/cigarette packets/bits of cardboard left on table or in ashtrays
- foam stuffing taken from seats/left around
- roaches (home-made filter tips from cannabis cigarettes)
- small packets made of folded paper, card or foil
- pieces of burnt tinfoil
- any of the following left in toilets: drinking straws, empty sweet wrappings, spoons
- traces of powder on toilet seats or other surfaces in toilets – or obviously wiped-clean surfaces
- syringes – danger of infection, see page 98
- payment with tightly rolled banknotes, or notes that have been tightly rolled
- traces of blood or powder on banknotes

Physical symptoms

- very dilated pupils
- excessive sniffing, dripping nose, watering or red eyes
- sudden severe cold symptoms following trip to toilet/garden/car park
- white mark/traces of powder around nostrils

Behavioural signs

- excessive giggling/laughing/ talking
- vacant staring, sleepy euphoria, dopey
- non-stop movement, jiggling about, dancing
- gagging or retching actions
- excessive consumption of soft drinks
- sudden, inexplicable tearfulness or fright
- any marked alteration in behaviour following trip to toilet/garden/car park

Signs of dealing

- a person holding court, with succession of 'visitors' who only remain a short time
- a person making frequent trips to toilet (or garden or car park), followed by a different person/people each time
- people exchanging small packages or cash, often done in a secretive manner, but may be quite open
- furtive, conspiratorial behaviour – huddling in corners and whispering
- conversation includes frequent references to drugs

Brewers and Licensed Retailers Association

Drugs and their slang names

Ecstasy – 'E'
Amphetamines – speed, sulph, uppers, whiz
LSD – acid, tabs
Cocaine – coke, snow, Charlie, 'C'
Crack – stone, base, rock, wash
Cannabis – dope, hash, pot, weed, ganga, tac, bush, tarry, skunk, draw, grass, marijuana
Heroin – 'H', smack, horse, scag, gear, junk

In the cellar

References have been made in earlier sections to safety in the cellar, particularly in relation to manual handling and hazardous substances.

The rules of good cellar management

1 Keep cellar clean, tidy and well ventilated.

2 Clean pipes and equipment at least once a week with company-approved detergent steriliser. Keep detergents out of reach of children.

3 Pump beer out of line using water before cleaning: the sequence is beer, water, detergent solution, water, beer. Before serving always test that the lines are clear of water.

4 Clean utensils immediately after use.

5 Take care to avoid electrical equipment when hosing down. Motors should be disconnected.

6 Follow manufacturer's safety and maintenance instructions for compressed air dispense systems. This will usually include daily removal of water from the drain cocks, and weekly checks on the oil level of the compressor.

7 Use safety signs/strips to warn of low beams.

8 Turn off CO_2 cylinder valves between hours of service.

9 Ventilate cellar by leaving doors open for about five minutes each morning and evening.

Carbon dioxide (CO_2) – the dangers

CO_2 cylinders are designed, and are regularly tested, to withstand very high pressures. At normal cellar temperatures there is no likelihood of accidental excessive pressures as the on/off valve has a safety disc which will burst if the pressure does become excessive. This might occur if the cylinders are left for long periods in the sun or are damaged.

If the disc does rupture there will be a sudden noisy release of gas which may propel the cylinder around in a dangerous manner if not properly secured. Once the disc has ruptured, discharge cannot be stopped and the release of gas will continue until the cylinder is empty, with the casing becoming frosted up.

CO_2 has no characteristic smell. It is heavier than air so will tend to concentrate at floor level, travel down steps, etc. and lie in the lowest possible areas.

It can be very dangerous to inhale a high concentration of CO_2. Everyone who has access to areas where the gas is stored and used should know the precautions:

- if the symptoms of having inhaled CO_2 occur (see page 29), leave the area at once – notify the brewery or fire brigade

Beer pipe cleaner is corrosive, as you will note from the symbol on this product. For guidance on the use of hazardous substances see pages 29–31.

CHECKLIST

Pre-delivery check

- cellar lights all working
- ropes, ramps, hooks, chains, etc. used to control the delivery of barrels checked on a weekly basis
- mechanical hoist, if fitted, checked
- delivery area clear of obstructions
- returns separated from working stock
- area cleared for new deliveries

During delivery

- cellar flaps properly secured in open position
- while flaps/hatchways are open, someone in attendance and safety barrier in place to warn passers-by/the public/other members of staff (see industry training example on page 2)
- barrels not allowed to free-fall into the cellar – if the drop is less than 2 metres, a controlled free-fall system may be acceptable, using pads or cushions to absorb the impact and prevent the barrels from bouncing across the cellar. Only experienced, trained delivery crew should be allowed to drop barrels in this way

After delivery

- cellar hatches properly closed and secured

open all doors, the cellar flaps and any windows which are accessible without going into the cellar. No one should enter the cellar until it has been thoroughly ventilated, and even then, a second person should be within signalling distance, ready to help the person back to a safe zone if pockets of the gas have remained

spray the cellar floor with water, using a fine attachment on the hose. This will help absorb and dispel remaining CO_2.

Correct handling of carbon dioxide cylinders

Handle cylinders with care and keep away from heat source or direct rays of the sun.

Store cylinders not in use upright, strapped or chained securely to the cellar wall. (If cylinders have to be stored horizontally for some reason when they are not connected to the pressure system, they must be wedged.)

If the cylinder has to be moved before connecting to the pressure system, secure it properly. It must be upright.

Use only the correct reducing valve and connections between cylinder and dispense system, and to beer cleaning containers.

Shut off cylinder valve before disconnecting.

Remove empty cylinders from the cellar and return them to the brewery.

Inform the brewery should the cylinder frost up. If this happens, leave the cylinder to thaw out naturally.

Dispensing from two-part kegs

These have their own, integral gas chambers. Never attempt to refill with gas, or connect the beer chamber to a high pressure supply such as CO_2 or mixed gas cylinder.

If for some reason, the supply of gas in the internal chamber is insufficient to dispense all the beer in the keg, contact the brewery for advice.

If you suspect the contents of a keg or cask have frozen

Considerable pressure will build up inside the container, as a result of CO_2 being forced out of the frozen beer. Depending on the speed of freezing, and whether the container is moved or knocked:

- the shive (or plug) of a cask might shoot out, or the sides split
- the spear (or extractor) of a keg might be expelled, or the container become distorted.

To reduce the dangers:

- cover the cask or keg completely with sacking, a canvas sheet, tarpaulin or old blanket – do this as gently as possible
- warn everyone of the danger, and place safety signs to keep people away
- do not attempt to move the container until you can be sure the beer has thawed: this might take several days of mild temperatures, if the container has been exposed to severe conditions for a long time
- contact your brewery or supplier for advice on how the quality of the beer might have been affected
- label the container FROST DAMAGE: TEST, so that the brewery knows it must be tested before re-use: this should be done before there is any confusion as to which container had the problem.

The
BODDINGTON
Group plc

All the advice on these pages has been drawn from industry training material, and from guidance published by the Brewers and Licensed Retailers Association.

Scottish & Newcastle plc

Practices to be forbidden in the cellar

- ☒ Using a detergent at a dilution stronger than necessary or recommended, or mixing with hot water (unless instructions specifically allow this).
- ☒ Measuring or storing detergents in drinking glasses.
- ☒ Keeping detergent in a container intended for other purposes.
- ☒ Attempting to remove spears from kegs.
- ☒ Tampering with pressure equipment.
- ☒ Smoking in the cellar.
- ☒ Allowing animals in any part of the cellar.
- ☒ Lending out the CO_2 equipment.
- ☒ Using any equipment or CO_2 cylinders which have been exposed to fire, explosion or flood, until inspected by brewery technical services.
- ☒ Stacking kegs or cases above normal shoulder height.

Unsafe practices – carbon dioxide cylinders

- ☒ Standing up cylinders, unless secured.
- ☒ 'Snifting out' cylinders in the direction of the eyes.
- ☒ Forcing open a jammed valve.
- ☒ Connecting cylinders to unauthorised equipment.
- ☒ Attempting to interchange fixed equipment.
- ☒ Removing fixed installations.
- ☒ Altering or adapting equipment.
- ☒ Dismantling reducing valves.
- ☒ Altering or adjusting settings of reducing valves.
- ☒ Using the cylinder valve as a means of controlling the flow of CO_2.
- ☒ Touching frosted cylinders with bare hands.
- ☒ Carrying CO_2 cylinders inside a car or its boot, a closed van or a lorry cab.
- ☒ Using CO_2 cylinders to blow-clean grills etc.

In the kitchen

Few people would not put the kitchen near the top of the list of hazardous work areas in the industry.

Fire safety in the kitchen

1 Extinguishers and fire blankets readily available (page 50).

2 Staff trained in procedure for turning off equipment, and using fire blankets and extinguishers.

3 Equipment never left unattended when in use.

4 Extraction hoods, grease traps and filters kept clean, regularly inspected and maintained.

Precautions relating to fryers

1 Thermostats regularly tested and maintained.

2 Fill the fryer to the correct level. Pans should not be more than half full/two-thirds full when the food is immersed.

3 Never heat the oil or fat beyond the temperature recommended by the manufacturer. Some oils smoke and burst into flames at lower temperatures than others.

4 Never plunge wet foods into hot fat. The water will cause the oil to foam and greatly expand in volume.

5 Drain fryers and filter the oil regularly. Wait until the oil has cooled before you do this, and turn the equipment off at the mains supply. Make sure the container you are draining the oil into is large enough.

6 Change oil regularly (see page 33 for disposal). Oil which is old will smoke and burst into flame at a lower temperature than when new.

7 Do not rest trays or pans on the edge of the fryer. If they, or something on them get knocked into the oil, the splash of hot oil will cause a serious burn.

8 Free-standing fryers should be located between other equipment so they cannot get knocked over.

9 Never use bratt pans for deep frying.

Dangerous machines

1 Never operate without safety guard in position. Display safety notice near machine (available from supplier).

2 Strictly control who uses and cleans the machine: no one under 18, and no one who has not been thoroughly trained or is in the process of being trained and under supervision (see page 36).

3 Always disconnect from the power supply before cleaning: never rely on the on/off switch on the machine.

4 Follow manufacturer's instructions for cleaning.

5 Do not reconnect to the power supply until machine has been fully assembled.

Kitchen fire safety

According to the Fire Protection Association, between January 1992 and July 1993 there were 22 serious fires and two fatalities in commercial kitchens ('serious' defined as more than a £50,000 insurance loss). The total loss came to over £10 million.

Looking after pots and pans

Never allow pans to stand empty on hot stoves.

Aluminium – can be affected by certain food acids and become discoloured. Unsuitable for storing food. Never use washing/caustic soda or similar substances. Remove stains by boiling in weak solution of vinegar/water. Don't put in dishwasher. Use fine steel wool pads (except on non-stick surfaces).

Stainless steel – avoid using bleaches, undiluted detergent and coarse abrasive cleaners. Make sure food is stirred well when adding salt, which should be fully dissolved and not allowed to settle on the pan base. Do not use to store salty foods.

Copperware – do not use steel wool scourers.

Safety with ovens, grills and steamers

1 Take care when reaching into ovens.

2 Use dry oven cloths of a suitable thickness.

3 Do not rest foods on drop-down oven doors.

4 When opening oven doors (or steamers), do not stand directly in front of, or over the opening – steam from an oven can scald. Vent steamers before opening.

5 Remove lids from hot pans and dishes with care – use a cloth to protect your wrists and hands – steam can scald.

6 Do not leave oven doors open.

7 Switch grills and griddles off immediately after use.

8 Watch steamer gauges. Report any unusual increases and check water supply.

Stove work

1 Do not overcrowd the stove area – preferably one person at a time at each stove or cooking appliance (fryer, grill, etc.). Avoid jostling or distracting your fellow chefs.

2 Do not leave metal spoons in boiling liquids.

3 Avoid leaving handles of cooking pans over gas flames or electric radiants, or sticking out over the edge of the stove. If a pan handle or dish is hot (i.e. after removal from the oven) sprinkle it with flour to warn others.

4 For economy as well as safety, all gas and electrical appliances must be turned off when not in use.

5 Do not reach over naked burning gas appliances or glowing electrical radiants.

6 Don't overfill pans – allow for boiling over.

Knife safety and preventing cuts

1 Always cut or chop on a board – never on a stainless steel table or in the hand.

2 To stop a board slipping, put a damp cloth between the table and the board.

3 Never attempt to catch a falling knife.

4 Knives not in use should be put safely away – particularly don't leave them on the table, blade pointing upwards.

5 Never fool around with knives or use them as screwdrivers or can openers.

6 Keep knives sharp. Always use the correct knife for the task.

7 When passing knives to others, pass with handles towards the other person. When wiping, wipe from the blunt to the sharp end.

8 Do not leave sharp objects (e.g. knives) in sinks. Wash immediately and remove.

 More detailed information on catering equipment safety is available from the Health and Safety Executive (page 12), in:
Food preparation machinery
ISBN 0 11 883910 1

Health and safety in kitchens and food preparation areas
ISBN 0 11 885427 5

Washing-up

IND COOPE RETAIL

1 Care must be taken to ensure that crockery, cutlery, utensils and equipment, having been washed, are clean and free from traces of food, grease, stains and water marks. Washing-up may be done either by hand or machine.

2 Washing-up by hand should be done in a double sink, the first sink being filled with very hot water and detergent to clean articles. The water should be hot enough just to permit a person wearing rubber gloves to put their hands in the water. The second sink is also filled with very hot water and a sanitiser to rinse articles thoroughly. Thereafter they should be stacked in a basket to air-dry. Tea towels must not be used. Disposable towels are acceptable.

3 To achieve the best results, scrape food debris from the plates into a waste container before immersion in the first sink. Keep water very hot and use the correct mix of detergent. Use clean cloths and scouring pads, and protect hands by wearing rubber gloves.

4 Washing-up by machine first requires that the user checks and understands its operation and that the machine is functioning properly.

5 Having removed any food debris into a waste container, rinse or soak the articles, hand-washing to remove difficult particles. Once the machine has achieved its correct working temperature, check the supply of detergent and rinse additive. After the wash cycle, remove articles to air-dry.

6 Before stacking and storing, check that all articles are completely clean and dry.

7 Never mix stainless steel and crockery in the same rack.

8 Washing-up machines should be emptied, stripped and cleaned in accordance with manufacturers' instructions.

DE VERE HOTELS

The safety rules on pages 82–84 are based on the training guides published by De Vere Hotels.

Storage

1 Packages and tins on racks should be stored with the heaviest and largest on the bottom shelf.

2 Use proper stepladders for reaching high shelves. Do not climb on shelves, boxes or chairs.

3 With walk-in cold rooms/freezers, always check that no one is inside before locking the doors.

Waste disposal units

1 Turn on the water supply before operating, to ensure that the waste is flushed away effectively.

2 Do not feed with unsuitable materials – paper, metal, plastic, bones (except small ones), etc.

3 Feed the waste at an even rate, all the while running the water.

4 Never use your hands, or any hand-held instrument, to feed in the rubbish: allow the waste to feed through at its own pace, helped by the force of the water.

5 If a blockage occurs, always turn off the machine at the controls and unplug or isolate from the power supply. Follow manufacturer's instructions for clearing.

 ACTION

You are on the shortlist for a new job which will include responsibility for health and safety training to the kitchen staff. In advance of the interview you are sent the following, apparently extracted from your potential employer's accident records. You are asked to prepare some ideas to present to the interview panel on what you would do to prevent similar accidents occurring in the future.

1 The kitchen porter was pouring dishwasher detergent into a small tub when it splashed into his eye – causing severe irritation.

2 Cleaning a shelf under the dishwasher which contained drums of detergents, an employee tried to remove one of the drums. The weight caused her to drop it on the floor. Detergent splashed out of the top inlet hole on to her face.

3 While cleaning the inside of the dishwasher, he was splashed in the face by dishwash detergent. Goggles and gloves were supplied but not worn.

4 Two waiters were carrying a two-gallon pot of hot soup to the main kitchen, when one slipped. The soup splashed over him, causing severe scalds to his right hand and arms.

5 A kitchen assistant was cleaning behind units adjacent to the fryer. He slipped and grabbed the fryer, causing it to topple. The hot oil caused severe burns on his back and legs.

6 A young chef was draining the fryer, pouring the hot oil into a plastic container. It melted, oil ran out, causing serious burns to legs and feet.

7 A commis chef leaned over a work surface, not noticing the knife lying there. He received a severe wound in his stomach.

8 Two chefs were cleaning up at the end of their shift, one turned round with a knife in his hand to speak to a third colleague. This chef received a cut to the base of two fingers on his right hand.

9 Coming out of the kitchen, a waitress opened the door into a colleague's path. This person had her wrist broken in two places.

Safety with hazardous substances

Cleaning an oven: as this involves working in a confined space, training has to be very specific and rigorous. Ideally, only selected staff should be assigned to this type of task. Appropriate eye and respiratory protective equipment is needed, hand and arm protection, overalls and protective aprons. Gloves need to perform well against the chemical ingredients of the oven cleaner itself, and because of the need to stretch into the oven, should be long enough to protect the whole arm.

Dishwasher descaling agents and rinse aids: these are extremely corrosive. Problems arise because 25 litre containers of rinse-aid look like 25 litre containers of much less hazardous substances. A safe system should be established so that containers are never moved with the tops off. Replacement should be possible by moving the pump connection at the dishwasher, rather than the containers themselves. Avoid stacking containers on each other. Return empty containers to the supplier.

Aerosol and powder products: avoid these for general use (except for purpose-designed detergent and sanitisers for which a system of work has been established). It is all too easy for food to become contaminated by accident, e.g. powdered bleaches can easily be mistaken for sugar and flour.

General cleaners, sanitisers and detergents: use a dispensing system which gives controlled dosing and minimises splashing and spillage.

John Norton Doyle, *Health & Safety at Work*, August 1991

Knowing the right thing to do for the sort of minor accidents that might occur in a particular part of the workplace is an important aspect of first-aid provision (see page 24).

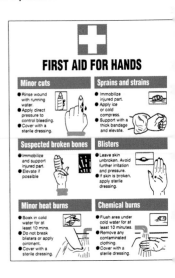

FIRST AID FOR HANDS

Minor cuts	Sprains and strains
● Rinse wound with running water. ● Apply direct pressure to control bleeding. ● Cover with a sterile dressing.	● Immobilize injured part. ● Apply ice or cold compress. ● Support with a thick bandage and elevate.

Suspected broken bones	Blisters
● Immobilize and support injured part. ● Elevate if possible	● Leave skin unbroken. Avoid further irritation and pressure. ● If skin is broken, apply sterile dressing.

Minor heat burns	Chemical burns
● Soak in cold water for at least 10 mins. ● Do not break blisters or apply ointment. ● Cover with a sterile dressing.	● Flush area under cold water for at least 10 minutes. ● Remove any contaminated clothing. ● Cover with a sterile dressing.

Microwave ovens

Position of oven

on a surface which is level, strong and stable

enough clearance for the door to operate freely

minimum 50 mm clearance at the rear and both sides of the oven for the air to circulate

away from major heat sources

electricity supply not overloaded, correct fuse

Containers/food coverings

do not put metal items or containers in the oven, e.g. crockery with metallic decoration, foil container

pierce plastic pouches and boil-in-bag type products unless package instructions state otherwise

check clingfilm is suitable for microwave use

General rules

never operate an oven which is empty

avoid misuse, e.g. to dry linen or warm plates

adjust packet or recipe instructions for reheating, defrosting, etc. to suit the power of your microwave: a 2000-watt oven will heat its contents much faster than a 1000-watt oven

make adjustments for number of items in oven; two items will generally take twice as long to cook as one item

do not overcook items: if food is left cooking in the oven too long, it will burn and may eventually catch fire

food which has a skin (e.g. tomatoes, potatoes, apples, egg yolks and whole trout) should be pierced before microwaving. Never try to boil an egg in a microwave.

Defrosting food

keep food covered or in original packing if possible, but remove metal twist ties

brush off visible ice crystals (these reflect microwaves)

allow time for the food to rest after or between bursts of defrosting so the heat can equalise

never completely defrost frozen foods: the edges may start to cook or dry and the centre will still be frozen

split up packs of sausages, chops, fish fillets, etc. as soon as they start to thaw

Reheating food

do not serve food that is just warm. Use a probe to test it has reached at least 70°C throughout: test every corner and several central points of large dishes

remove wrapping with care, to avoid escaping steam

stir liquids or products in sauces to distribute the heat evenly. Allow a short standing time for products which cannot be stirred to allow the temperature to equalise

Cleaning and servicing

follow manufacturer's cleaning and service instructions carefully, especially regarding: air filter, door, oven cavity, removing stubborn stains

Work instructions

reduce the risk of staff mistakes by setting the timings and power levels for particular dishes into the oven's memory

make regular tests to ensure the information is still correct

update the information if you change the menu

With thanks to Helen Stephens, Merrychef

Pest control

Check all dry goods at the time of delivery for pest infestation or damage before being placed into any store area or on to shelving, etc.

Check all equipment being brought from storage or new equipment for pest infestation.

Once original packaging has been opened, transfer dry foods (e.g. flour, rice, pulses) to pest-proof containers with close fitting lids. Ensure the lids are replaced after use.

Ensure all stored goods are kept off the ground and clear of walls, with adequate space between stock to enable regular inspection and cleaning.

Clear up all spillages immediately.

Refuse containers in the kitchen should have close fitting lids. Refuse receptacles outside the kitchen must be on hard ground, capable of being cleaned, away from vegetation and fitted with close fitting pest-proof lids.

Pay particular attention to crevices, e.g. around beer line pipes and between panelling. Cockroaches thrive in this type of environment.

Report any signs of a problem (see checklist) to the pest control contractor immediately. Check for any instructions about keeping evidence to help identify the pest.

Signs to look for: rodents and mice

- gnaw marks on packaging, food containers, stored equipment and building fabric
- droppings – these are small, oval shaped black pellet-like substances
- smear marks from the grease in the animals' coats left on the building fabric along runs
- runs in adjacent undergrowth
- holes and nesting sites
- footprints, tail marks in dust, etc.
- damage to the food itself
- the animals themselves
- offensive odours may indicate an infestation

Insect infestations in food

- webbing on food packaging, in the food itself or storage shelves or equipment
- small tunnels or holes in food packaging
- moulted skins, faecal pellets, egg or egg pouches – may indicate a severe infestation of cockroaches
- offensive odour
- layer of very fine crumbs/dust on shelves or surfaces or food

The text on pest control and this checklist is based on training guidance used by J D Wetherspoon plc

In the restaurant

Trips, falls and burns are the main hazards in the restaurant. Lifting is another. Some equipment and cleaning agents are a fire danger, as are discarded cigarettes and matches which go unnoticed, and burning candles left unattended.

Restaurant safety

1 Do not stack crockery or service dishes too high, or overload shelves.

2 Avoid over-filling service stations (dumb waiters). Pull cutlery drawer out slowly and carefully.

3 Do not stack chairs and tables above chest height. Check that the stack is secure before leaving it. Never stack furniture behind doors, in corridors or fire escape routes.

4 Take special care with flammable or potentially explosive materials, e.g. methylated spirits, gas cylinder aerosols. These should be away from heat and direct sunlight.

5 Follow instructions for using silver dip and other cleaning agents. Always wear gloves. Always rinse serviceware after cleaning and polish with a clean cloth.

6 Distribute the weight evenly on trays, and load only what you can carry safely and comfortably. Put hot foods in the centre, and liquids where small spills will be caught in the tray rather than spill on to you or the floor.

7 Never carry anything over the head of a customer or colleague. Take extra care near boisterous customers.

8 Do not overfill soup tureens/dishes, coffee or teapots.

9 Take care when using matches, and with lighted candles on tables and buffet displays.

10 Turn off flambé lamps when not in use.

11 Use a clean, dry serving cloth to carry hot dishes.

12 Warn customers when plates are very hot.

13 When opening sparkling wine, keep the cork covered with a service cloth while opening, and ease it out gently.

14 When serving at table, be aware that a guest may move the chair backwards or make other, sudden movements. Do not lean over a guest's shoulder. If space is tight, politely ask the guest to move to one side when you serve.

15 Watch out for guests' handbags, briefcases, etc. They present a tripping hazard. It's also likely that the guest will move them during the course of the meal, so check each time you approach the table.

16 Before cleaning floors during service, close off that area of the restaurant.

17 Remove used tableware to the wash-up area as soon as possible. Never let dirty items pile up in customer or service areas. Do not overload trolleys.

The text on restaurant safety (pages 86 and 87) has been largely drawn from this training aid, published by De Vere Hotels.

Some pages of McDonald's Restaurants comprehensive safety audit. Each section has a different points total and weighting depending on its relative importance.

The person doing the audit does not have to make subjective judgements: a question is either given full marks (a yes answer) or no marks (a no answer).

ood in display cabinets

Check food is chilled before it goes out (or adequately hot in the case of a heated display case).

Arrange food in cabinets carefully, so that nothing is above the load line, and the airflow not restricted.

oom service

When carrying items up staircases, always ensure that your view of the stair is not obstructed. Watch out for items left on stairways or loose/ripped carpets.

Before leaving the lift, check it has stopped level with the floor. Report faulty lifts immediately.

Don't forget your service cloth. The tray may be cool but the dishes you have to remove may be very hot.

Report any suspicious persons encountered in corridors or rooms thought to be unoccupied. A simple 'May I help you?' draws their attention to the fact that you have noted their presence.

n the leisure centre

On no account should glassware or china be used in the leisure area. If a guest carries a glass or plate through from another part of the hotel, politely offer to transfer the drink to a plastic tumbler, and the food to a plastic plate.

Take particular care not to slip. Wear suitable rubber-soled footwear.

Flambé lamps

Whether these use butane gas from a disposable cartridge, or methylated spirits (meths), they are a safety risk from fire or explosion:

- refuel or change the cartridge outdoors, in a well ventilated area – to avoid having to do this in a rush, or at night, have a spare, fuelled lamp available. Lamps should never be refuelled in the kitchen or restaurant
- store meths/spare gas cartridges in a safe place away from any source of heat (your fire officer will advise).

Butane-fuelled lamps

- check the washer in the adaptor regularly (it's on the underside of the lamp, where the cartridge is connected), and replace if cracked or deformed
- hold lamp upright when changing the cartridge, and do not over-tighten.

Meths-fuelled lamps

- the wick should be cool before you attempt to refill (this should not be a problem if you have a lamp on stand-by)
- wipe up any spills with absorbent paper or a cloth – dispose of this carefully, in a place where there is no fire risk.

Liquefied petroleum gas (LPG) cylinders

Your fire brigade will give advice, and should be made aware that you are using LPG cylinders.

Store spare cylinders in a secure outdoor area, where possible. Keep the area free from weeds, grass and other combustible materials. The cylinders should not stand or lie in water.

Changing cylinders

1 Avoid dropping or knocking.
2 Keep upright, valve uppermost.
3 Check that the valve is closed, and there are no leaks (LPG has a noticeable smell – if you are not sure, brush soapy water on the connection: bubbles indicate a leak).
4 Extinguish any flame, including pilot lights, while you are changing cylinders.
5 Close off the valve on the empty cylinder before disconnecting.
6 Use the correct spanner to ensure that the new cylinder is tightly connected.
7 Re-light pilot lights etc., and test that equipment is working satisfactorily.

LPG cylinders may be used in the kitchen, or outdoors for barbecues, or to operate room heaters.

Safety Audit

Part C - Management Systems			
Maximum Possible Score			
Maximum Score Adjusted for N/As	1000		
Actual Score			
Percentage			

Area	Points	Scoring	Comments/Action Required

Policy
- company and local policies displayed
- restaurant policy exists, signed + up to date
- Maximum Section Score
- Total available points adjusted for N/As
- Actual Subtotal for section

Organisation
- "safety manager" appointed
- restaurant safety circle active
- reward system in place
- H+S file set up and active
- Maximum Section Score
- Total available points adjusted for N/As
- Actual Subtotal for section

Planning and Implementation
- safety circle minutes kept on file
- safety circle meeting every 2 months
- safety circle action plans documented
- proof that action plans are implemented
- restaurant H+S objectives exist
- evidence on target for meeting objectives
- Maximum Section Score
- available points adjusted for N/As
- Actual Subtotal for section

- Maximum possible page score
- maximum page score adjusted for N/As
- Actual Subtotal for section

Safety Audit

Area	Points Available	Scoring Yes	No	N/A	Comments/Action Required
5. Hypodermic Disposal					
- area closed off					
- protective equipment is worn	20				
- sample person aware of risks/procedures	30				
- secure containers available if appropriate	30				
Maximum Score per Area	20				
Total available points adjusted for N/As	100				
Actual Score for section					
Kitchen Areas					
6. Grill cleaning					
- protective equipment worn					
- procedures followed	30				
- sachet opened away from face - no teeth!	40				
Maximum Score per Area	30				
Total available points adjusted for N/As	100				
Actual Score for section					
7. Smog Hog cleaning					
- vats covered if appropriate					
- asks for help with lifting if needed	20				
- ladders used if appropriate	20				
- follows cleaning procedures	30				
Maximum Score per Area	30				
Total available points adjusted for N/As	100				
Actual Score for section					
8. Filtering					
- person over 18 years of age					
- all protective equipment worn	10				
- area kept clear	15				
- machine never left unattended	10				
- machine in good working order	10				
- procedures followed	15				
- person understands risks/procedures	20				
Maximum Score per Area	20				
Total available points adjusted for N/As	100				

In housekeeping

Housekeeping staff have key roles to play in security and fire safety. Carefully established work procedures are needed to protect them from the virus which causes Aids, and to protect themselves and your guests from legionnaires' disease (pages 98 and 99). Other safety issues include manual handling, the use of hazardous substances, and preventing trips and falls.

Safety in housekeeping

1 All working areas should be kept in good order. This includes offices, storerooms, pantries, etc. Lighting should at all times be ample and effective.

2 Cleaning agents must be kept in their proper containers, clearly labelled and properly sealed when not in use. Store only in well ventilated areas, not beside hot pipes etc., nor in soft drinks bottles or any other type of container which could be mistaken for a consumable item.

3 Machinery and equipment should be properly cleaned and stored when not in use. All electrical flexible cables to cleaning appliances should be inspected regularly to ensure they are in good condition and properly connected to the appliance. Electrical equipment should never be interfered with or power points overloaded.

4 Where equipment is found to be faulty it must be appropriately labelled, and reported immediately to the person supervising. Put the equipment out of use until it has been repaired.

5 Trip hazards, e.g. flexes running across a work area, must be avoided at all costs.

6 Radiators, heaters, etc. should never be used as storage shelves.

7 Correct protective clothing and sensible working shoes must be worn at all times. Protective gloves must be worn when handling hazardous cleaning materials.

8 Long hair should be tied back off the face. Loose jewellery should be avoided. Attention should be given at all times to personal hygiene, and overalls should be maintained in a clean and orderly fashion.

Text based on training material developed by the University of Edinburgh.

Room cleaning

- Do not leave cleaning solutions or equipment unattended (particularly where children could be present).
- Do not overload trolleys.
- Do not empty broken glass or crockery in the plastic waste bag.
- Take care when disposing of smoking waste. Do not empty ashtrays into plastic bags or cardboard boxes.
- Do not leave linen where it will obstruct corridors and fire escape routes.
- Allow light bulbs to cool before touching.
- Report loose light fittings.
- Do not put a high wattage bulb in a lampshade designed for a lower rating.
- Clean the far side of the bath first, so you don't have to lean over a slippery surface.
- Wet bathroom floors can be slippery. Leave them as dry as possible, and take special care.
- Wash your hands after cleaning the toilet.
- Don't reach into waste bins. They may contain broken glass or used razor blades, etc.
- Close all the windows when leaving guest rooms. Open windows present a fire and security hazard.
- Check there are enough ashtrays available for guests' use.
- Unplug or switch off wall sockets to appliances not in use, e.g. TV, hairdryers. Make sure your hands are dry.
- Changing the bed: remove sheets carefully. Inspect bed for sharp objects/cigarettes. Get help when turning a mattress.
- Furniture should not block corridors or fire exits, even temporarily.
- Do not stack armchairs or occasional tables on top of chairs when cleaning rooms.

Signs of pest infestation

Small golden brown grubs with hairy tufts on edges of carpets or linen rooms where blankets are stored – larvae of carpet beetles.

Small holes in furniture – a sign of woodworm.

Holes in blankets which have been stored – a sign of moths.

In reception, portering and administration

Reception staff need to know what their role is in the event of a fire, or bomb alert. They require the instincts of a detective – to become aware of the comings and goings, to recognise faces, to have a good memory, to have a nose for suspicious circumstances, to be good at communicating with people.

Safety in the office

1 All solvents, e.g. typewriter cleaner, correction fluid thinner, should be correctly stored.

2 Filing cabinets should be positioned safely and only one drawer opened at a time. The heaviest items should be at the bottom of the cabinet. Close filing cabinet drawers as soon as you have found what you want.

3 When carrying files, do not carry so many that your vision is obscured.

4 Electrical appliances should be positioned where no accidents can be caused. If socket strips are used, these should be fixed to the wall, where practicable, and not left lying on the floor.

5 Tables, desks and shelves should not be overloaded.

6 Telephone cables should not be stretched across floors.

7 Do not use wastepaper bins as ashtrays. Outdoor clothing should not be hung over electric fires or heaters.

8 Never stand on stools or chairs.

9 Paper can cause cuts, as can wire and staples on boxes and packages: always check for protruding staples and pins when opening mail and packages.

10 Never place liquids on or near electrical equipment, e.g. photocopiers, computers, etc. Apart from damage to the equipment, accidental spillage could cause you to be electrocuted.

11 Turn off the power supply when changing typewriter ribbons/cartridges, photocopier toner or unblocking photocopiers or shredding machines.

Security procedures

Incoming mail – all suspicious incoming mail and packages to be checked before being sorted for distribution.

Delivery of parcels – check the contents with the person delivering. Only accept if fully satisfied. Ask chauffeurs leaving luggage for proof of their identity.

Items left for safekeeping or collection – only accept suitcases, hand luggage, parcels, packages, briefcases, etc. if they have been opened by the client for you to inspect.

Safe deposit – before granting facilities, confirm the identity of the person and that there are no grounds for suspicion.

Suspected letter and parcel bombs

The following points make unfamiliar material suspect:

- foreign and unfamiliar postmark
- the writing – unEnglish, lacking literacy or crudely printed
- letter labelled 'Personal' or 'Private' and addressed not to a named person, but a job title, e.g. 'The General Manager'
- address of the sender does not tally with the postmark
- excessive weight for size of parcel and apparent contents
- uneven weight distribution – may indicate presence of batteries
- grease marks – may indicate 'sweating' explosives
- smell – some explosives have a smell of marzipan or almonds
- abnormal fastening for the type of package – the outer envelope may contain an inner wrapping in the form of a booby-trap
- parcels or envelopes that rattle, feel springy or are damaged, giving a sight of wire, batteries or fluid-filled sachets

These are cumulative points which give rise to increasing degrees of suspicion. If this cannot be resolved:

- do not try to open or tamper with it, nor place in water nor put anything on top of it
- isolate it where it can do no harm, preferably on a table. Use minimum handling: it should be placed away from public areas, but where it can be inspected with ease
- open windows and doors in the vicinity: keep people away from it
- inform the police, giving them full details of the letter/parcel, and the markings and peculiarities which have led to suspicion

The text on security procedures by De Vere Hotels

 CHECKLIST

Portering staff training checklist

- procedure for releasing persons trapped in lifts
- methods of lifting, use of trolleys, ladders, etc.
- correct use of electrical equipment
- how to change various types of light bulbs such as fluorescent tubes, etc.
- if expected at any time to do minor repairs that require tools to be used, to ensure that they are in good order and used correctly
- protective clothing supplied for dirty work, particularly where caustic substances and paints are being used

Safety in the office text and this checklist by the University of Edinburgh

In leisure

In considering the safety of leisure facilities, the key concern becomes the user. This is because the user is particularly vulnerable to a whole range of risks. Some arise because of the nature of the activity, some because of the equipment that is used, some because of the unpredictable behaviour of other people using the facility, others because of the hygiene risks.

Plant room

1 Should be kept locked.

2 Must be kept scrupulously clean and all spillages cleaned up immediately.

3 All pipes, valves, etc. properly labelled.

4 Chemicals kept in clearly labelled containers. Separate, clearly labelled scoops provided for each chemical.

5 Staff handling chemicals to wear protective clothing (e.g. boots, apron, rubber gloves, goggles and face mask).

Changing rooms

1 Kept clean, and floor and surfaces treated with recommended disinfectant.

2 Temperature of showers regularly checked to ensure that scalding will not occur.

3 Checked on a regular basis for security reasons, and to monitor levels of cleanliness.

4 Lockers checked regularly, including locking mechanism.

5 Cubicles checked daily to ensure doors lock and seats are secure, and that there are no sharp edges or splinters.

6 Notices in place to remind guests not to leave valuables unattended.

Saunas

1 Alarm call facility, warning and information lights checked daily.

2 Staff on call with first-aid and resuscitation skills.

3 Sauna stove element and stones checked periodically during the day. Timer and thermostat monitored.

4 Doors checked for ease of opening.

5 Cleaned regularly and seating checked for splinters etc.

Sunbeds

1 Fitted with an alarm so that, in case of difficulty, users can call for assistance. Door to the sunbed room, if lockable, can be easily opened by an attendant from the outside (in an emergency).

2 Cleaned after each use with the recommended cleaner.

3 Lamps and timer regularly checked.

The text on pages 90–92 has drawn on training guidance produced by De Vere Hotels.

Rules for using sauna

Do not use if you are:
- ☒ six months or more pregnant
- ☒ suffering from a skin complaint
- ☒ suffering from circulatory disorders such as stroke, angina, heart disease or high blood pressure
- ☒ epileptic or prone to dizziness or blackouts

Guidance for use of sauna
- ☑ before use remove all items of jewellery
- ☑ maintain a sitting or lying position in the sauna area with legs at the same level (and therefore the same body temperature) as the body
- ☑ sit upright for 2 minutes prior to leaving the cabin, in order for the blood circulation to adjust (fainting may occur if this advice is not followed)
- ☑ take fresh air after leaving the cabin and walk around slowly in order that body temperature can adjust
- ☑ drink no alcohol before or just after taking a sauna

All prospective users advised of the precautions (e.g. do not use if you have a heart condition or are taking antibiotics), and risks (e.g. effects of ultra-violet radiation on the skin, risk of eye injury). Warning notices checked daily.

Suitable goggles provided for sunbed users.

Fitness suite/gymnasium

Equipment inspected daily and serviced regularly. Defective equipment taken out of use until repaired.

Staff with appropriate qualifications available to give instruction/advice on use of exercise equipment, and deal with an emergency.

Supervision at swimming pools

Constant poolside supervision by lifeguards provides the best assurance of pool users' safety. It must be provided if:

the pool is used by unaccompanied children aged under 15

crowded conditions are expected

food or alcohol is available to pool users

activities are taking place which generate excitement.

Constant supervision may not be necessary if the pool is quite small, used by a limited number of people, those people are likely to behave responsibly and there is no diving or other poolside facility which poses a particular risk.

If supervision is not provided, there must be a poolside alarm or telephone to summon help. A member of staff (with appropriate water-based rescue and first-aid skills) should be on call to deal with any emergency.

Swimming pools

Area well lit to prevent accidents. External windows kept clean. No glare/reflections on surface of water which prevent seeing into water.

Floors, passageways, ramps, stairs, etc. kept free from slipping or tripping hazards.

Broken or missing tiles and sharp edges where people walk barefoot repaired promptly. Drainage gulleys kept clean and unblocked.

Regular maintenance checks of all fittings (the combination of high humidity and chemicals encourages corrosion). Emergency lights tested daily.

Ban on glass and crockery in the pool area.

Warning signs, depth notices, NO DIVING signs, etc. in place and unobstructed.

Limit on maximum number of users (and staff know what to do when that point is reached).

Pool rules clearly displayed (e.g. no unaccompanied children, no unruly behaviour, no facemasks or snorkels, swimming costumes to be worn).

Fitness suites

If the facility is unsupervised:

- easily accessible alarm bell to attract staff attention
- clear diagrams/instructions to indicate how each piece of equipment should be used and any precautions that should be taken
- staff on call know correct procedure for dealing with heart attack, torn or strained muscles or fatigue due to over-exercise (the most likely types of emergency or accident).

Suggested house rules

- limit on number of users at any one time
- no users under 16 years of age
- appropriate clothing and footwear to be worn at all times.

STAKIS

Health and safety audit: pool area

- ☐ pool/spa test results satisfactory (results for last 3 months to be available)
- ☐ clarity of pool/spa water satisfactory (also check scumline)
- ☐ temperature of pool water relative to the air
- ☐ cleanliness of pool surround (tiles, walls, etc.)
- ☐ pool vacuumed (state last date)
- ☐ hand rails to pool and spa
- ☐ overshoes available for guests
- ☐ showerheads (state date last removed for cleaning)
- ☐ safety equipment available (e.g. reach pole, life saving ring, goggles, gas masks, etc.)
- ☐ emergency procedure training (state last date)
- ☐ panic button tested (state date and result of last test)
- ☐ fire instruction plan displayed, extinguishers in position, fire safety training (state last date)
- ☐ first-aid equipment available
- ☐ portable electric equipment checked (state last date)

Extracts from the health and safety audit used by Stakis hotels. The original form has a column for noting what requires attention, and the person responsible for taking action.

9 Pool users reminded of safety precautions where necessary, e.g. if they ignore NO DIVING sign. Notice listing basic points of action to help guests deal with an emergency.

10 If lone bathing is permitted in an unsupervised pool, it is advisable to control entering and leaving, so that you are aware at all times who is using the pool.

11 Rescue equipment in place, means of calling for help fully operational (e.g. poolside alarm, emergency telephone).

12 Staff trained to respond effectively in any emergency situation including: serious injury, discovery of a casualty in the water, lack of water clarity, smell of gas, complaints of sore eyes or skin irritation, broken glass in water, overcrowding, disorderly behaviour, alcohol abuse, fire or security alert.

Pool/spa water

1 Adequate pre-cleansing facilities provided (e.g. warm showers and foot baths) and pool users reminded of the importance of using them.

2 Filtration system properly cleaned and maintained. Floating debris removed from surface regularly. Build-up of body fats on the waterline removed regularly.

3 Water regularly tested to ensure necessary level of disinfection is maintained: for pools this may be as often as every two hours, for spas every 20 minutes.

Lifeguards

1 Possess appropriate skills and knowledge of observation, rescue, resuscitation and first aid.

2 Able to carry out rescues and take emergency action as required, including resuscitation and first aid.

3 Able to summon attention of pool users when necessary (a whistle may be appropriate).

4 Easily recognised for who they are (e.g. with a distinctive uniform).

5 Duties organised so that they can maintain a high level of vigilance. Regular breaks are important and a variety of duties can prevent boredom.

 Further information: *Safety in Swimming Pools*, Health and Safety Commission/Sports Council, ISBN 0 906577 83 7, available from the Sports Council, 16 Upper Woburn Place, London WC1H 0QP

The rapidly moving, warm water of spas, jacuzzis and whirlpools can cause the build-up of dangerous levels of body oils, skin debris and organic wastes. Cleaning and filtration procedures need to be very thorough, and water changes frequent, e.g. every two or three days.

Major causes of accidents in swimming pools

- unclear pool water (preventing casualties from being seen)
- absence of, or inadequate response by lifeguards/pool attendants in an emergency
- people swimming a short time after drinking alcohol or eating a heavy meal
- unruly behaviour such as running on the side of the pool, people ducking other swimmers, performing acrobatics in the water, shouting and screaming (this can distract attention in an emergency)
- poor or inexperienced swimmers straying out of their depth (half of those who drown are aged under 15)
- people diving into insufficient depth of water
- people using pools intended to be out of use
- people who have a medical condition, such as epilepsy, asthma, diabetes or a heart condition, not taking sufficient care.

Other issues of security and safety

Fraud and other security issues

If you handle every transaction yourself, you cut out the risk of deception, trickery or cheating by employees. But you could still be caught out by a supplier, a supplier's employee or a customer. From this base line, the risks of fraud increase with the number of employees, the number and value of cash and stock transactions, and number of customers. Insurance gives some protection. A reputation of successfully identifying fraud and prosecuting offenders is a powerful deterrent. Control measures are the third ingredient.

Get the balance right – between detection and prevention, between convenience and watertight control. It may seem sensible to require two managers' signatures before a bottle of Napoleon brandy can be issued, and wise to keep only one bottle in the bar stock. But what happens if it runs out and one of your best customers has to switch half-way through the evening to 3-star house brandy, because nobody can be found to authorise the issue of more Napoleon?

Accounting systems

It's when the figures don't add up that you know you've got a problem. Stock consumption has increased, yet sales are down. There seem to be more customers, and they appear to be spending more, yet there is less cash going into the bank.

This could mean that you need a different accounting system. Or you may have to invest in new equipment for tracking sales and stock movements. Neither of these decisions may be within your control. Whether they are or not, start by checking that you are making the best use of what you have:

- are suppliers' invoices always checked against delivery notes and order books?

- if pre-numbered stationery is used for taking customer orders, requisitioning stocks, billing customers, etc., are missing numbers identified and enquiries made?

- is access to accounts records strictly controlled, e.g. with passwords for computers?

- are spot checks made of physical stocks as well as regular stocktakes?

Contents guide

Fraud and other
security issues .... this page

Safety with display screen
equipment 96

Precautions against Aids 98

Precautions against
legionnaires' disease 99

Building services 99

'When we check the hotel's paperwork,' says Peter Smith, EHO Crawley, West Sussex, 'we expect to see in the records that shower heads have been removed, descaled, and soaked in sanitiser for 24 hours every three months or so. In between, the water should be turned up to 50°C and run for five minutes every two weeks.'

Pam Legate, *Hotel & Restaurant Magazine*, May 1993

Staff supervision

Spotting fraud isn't necessarily difficult, but it can require patience, perseverence, and strength of character. It's no fun catching out a long-serving employee who you know is having all sorts of personal difficulties, or confronting someone you have recently commended and promoted for their efforts.

It's important that everyone knows where they stand. Have a clear policy on the grey areas of when staff can accept drinks from customers, or take food home. Identify the weak points in the movement of stock and cash, limit the number of people involved, tighten up procedures and do spot checks more often. The activity and checklists expand on these themes.

Perform surprise checks frequently so they become expected. The element of surprise will be the timing and location of the check. That they are made frequently and written into job descriptions and standard operating procedures are what turns a detective endeavour into a preventive one.

If there are some checks, e.g. stocktaking the linen, which you cannot do yourself on a particular occasion, get them done by someone who has no responsibility for the area being checked, otherwise you present an opportunity for a cover-up.

Information security

A flood or fire could mean the loss of all your computer-based information, unless back-up disks or tapes are stored off the premises or in a fire-proof, flood-proof safe.

Establish a strict back-up discipline for all computer-users. Whether back-ups are done on a daily or more frequent basis will depend on how easy it is to re-enter or recreate data.

Protecting vulnerable customers and guests

Women on their own, the elderly and the physically disabled will appreciate extra care given to their security, e.g. reserved space in a well-lit area of the car park, close to the entrance; for overnight stays, a room which they can get to easily, without going down long, dark corridors; single women guests allocated to a particular floor; in restaurants, a table where they will feel comfortable and safe; loan of a personal alarm so that women can feel safe when out alone, particularly at night.

Giving advice to customers about security

You may need to train your staff on how to answer particular requests, e.g. where it's safe to go jogging or park the car. Helpful information should be provided, wherever possible, but make clear that the final responsibility rests with the person asking.

Remind your staff that the wrong advice can lead to a liability action. It is better to be honest and admit you don't know the answer, than make up information which subsequently proves to be unfortunate (e.g. because that night, for the first time ever, someone is mugged in the high street), or misleading.

Some basic rules about fraud

The easier the opportunity to commit fraud, the more likely it is to be exploited.

When considering fraud, put yourself in the position of the fraudster.

Never assume that a dishonest employee will wait around to be caught.

Try always to think of fraud in simple accounting terms.

Never seek the most complex solution to a fraud.

Failure by management to supervise their staff properly and/or weak systems of internal control inevitably lead to dishonest employees seizing the opportunity to commit theft or fraud.

Practically all jobs have some potential for fraud depending upon the ease of access and the degree of skill of the individual.

Usually the fraud will require some form of motivation, e.g. greed, an unsolvable financial problem or domestic crisis or perhaps someone is passed over for promotion and his/her attitude and loyalty change.

Use of CCTV protection

If you are considering installing a system, get advice first from your local crime prevention officer. The siting of cameras is particularly important: consider what crime you are trying to prevent and what each camera needs to do. Visible security is a valuable deterrent, and provides reassurance to customers and staff.

Carefully thought through, the system can produce other side-benefits. In hotels, for example, recording entry of guest arrivals may help resolve a claim for missing property by providing proof that the guest did not arrive with a suitcase or an umbrella (e.g. it was left at home or elsewhere).

Getting the best from CCTV

Set up a system for:

- identifying tapes – so it is clear from the outside of the box what period the tape covers
- reviewing them – to identify suspicious behaviour, e.g. someone 'casing' the building in preparation for a break-in
- keeping them for a sufficiently long period to cover previous incidents: 25 days is the recommended period
- maintaining and checking equipment – camera lenses must be kept clean; static dust will distort the picture on monitors, if allowed to accumulate.

Death on the premises

Discovering that someone has died may be a traumatic experience. Whatever the cause of death – through illness, accident or perhaps suicide – it is an emotional time.

Preparing for such an eventuality helps you and your staff cope. The priorities will depend on the size and nature of your business – the box gives some points to consider.

Prostitutes

Prostitutes might use your premises to conduct their business if you let them. It is easier to turn a blind eye to the problem, especially if the prostitute's customer is one of your regular and valued customers. But the risks are considerable:

- most people find prostitution deeply offensive and will avoid any pub, restaurant or hotel where they suspect it is going on

- these same people will tell their friends and colleagues

- even people who take advantage of a tolerant policy to prostitutes will not recommend the place to others who know them

- prostitutes tend to attract drug-related problems

- violence may follow a dispute over money, or be used as a threat to get more money

- some prostitutes have a male accomplice who will burst in on the proceedings, pretending to be an enraged husband, making threats and demanding money

- guests who have been robbed by prostitutes may try and blame hotel staff for the theft

- your staff can get involved, in securing the services of prostitutes, or acting as prostitutes themselves.

Prevention is certainly easier than the cure, but both can be difficult. It takes considerable experience and a fine sense of judgement to know when to challenge a guest. If you are right and the guest has already paid the prostitute, an ugly scene could ensue. If you are wrong, it will be extremely embarrassing. The box gives some suggestions.

Procedure in the event of death

1 Immediately notify the manager or security officer, who will inform the police and your head office, where appropriate.

2 Make sure the body, contents of the room etc. are not touched until the police arrive.

3 Extend comfort and assistance to any companion or relative of the deceased (this may require knowledge of and sensitivity to different religious or cultural traditions).

4 Assist the police with information so that the circumstances can be established and the next of kin informed.

5 Offer assistance to gather the deceased's belongings (it may be appropriate to have a witness present, and to make a record of each item, to avoid uncertainty later).

6 For foreign nationals, inform their embassy (or check that the police will do this).

7 Arrange for discreet removal of the body, so that other people are not alarmed.

8 Arrange counselling, if necessary, for the person who first discovered the death.

A policy on prostitutes

Based on his experience of waging an on-going battle to keep prostitutes out, the manager of one of London's leading hotels offered this advice to *Caterer* readers:

Devise a clear strategy with senior department heads about how a situation should be dealt with. This should involve a series of questions to the suspect and the guest, devised to expose the true nature of the situation.

Challenge suspects politely, but immediately. If they say they are a friend, colleague or relative of a guest, check with the guest and also check to see if the room was booked for single or double occupancy.

If it is night time and the guest supports the claim, point out that for safety (e.g. in the case of fire) unregistered guests are not allowed in guest rooms after a particular time.

If the guest attempts to register the suspect, point out that it will be entered on the account, with the guest's name and address and at the full rate. In the case of the business traveller, this would be seen by the guest's company.

Alternatively, point out that it is policy not to register additional occupants after a certain time.

Bear in mind that the guest may be excitable, perhaps because of alcohol.

Note of caution

In a case in the USA, a hotel was successfully sued for £4 million after challenging a young woman on the arm of an ageing executive. It transpired that, despite age and ethnic differences, the woman was the man's wife.

Bob Gledhill, *Caterer & Hotelkeeper*, 14 May 1992

Safety with display screen equipment

If the use of computers, word processors and other display screen equipment forms a significant part of a person's normal work (see caption to photograph), then the employer is required to take certain steps under the Health and Safety (Display Screen Equipment) Regulations 1992:

1 Carry out a risk assessment, and when necessary review or update it. The process involves a survey of the user's general working environment and equipment, including software (i.e. the programs) and hardware (central processing unit, keyboard, display screen, printer, etc.), the desk or work surface, chair, etc., and the pattern of use (not just hours and days, but to what extent other activities such as answering the phone or dealing with arrivals provide breaks from work at the screen).

2 Take steps to reduce the risk. Often the action required is quite straightforward (the checklist gives some measures).

3 Ensure that workstations meet certain minimum requirements regarding lighting, noise, furniture, etc. (summarised on page 97). For workstations already in use at 1 January 1993, employers have until 31 December 1996 to meet the requirements. If new equipment is put into use at a workstation, the whole of the workstation is regarded as new and must meet all the requirements.

4 Pay for eyesight tests for users who wish to have them, and if necessary for spectacles required as a result of the employee's work. Someone who is about to become a user may request a test, in which case this should be arranged before the person spends prolonged periods at the screen.

The employer is not responsible for problems or examinations unrelated to display screen work. Only the cost of basic corrective appliances need be met, i.e. of a type and quality adequate to correct vision defects at the viewing distances used for display screen work. The employer can contribute an equivalent amount to the cost of a designer frame, for example.

5 Provide users with health and safety training and information relating to their display screen activities. Topics this might cover include the hazards and risks (e.g. screen glare, lack of desk space), problems these can lead to (e.g. fatigue and stress, upper limb discomfort), measures to improve the situation (e.g. correct posture, adjusting height of chair, organising work to give breaks and changes of activity), who to tell if problems are experienced, and arrangements for eyesight tests.

Users employed by other employers (e.g. temps) and freelance people using workstations on your premises must be provided with health and safety information but not necessarily training. Users employed by other employers must also be provided with information on breaks and activity changes and training when their workstation is modified.

Receptionists, reservations assistants, secretaries, control clerks and other office-based staff who typically use computers for around two or three hours or more daily, will be considered 'users' under the regulations.

 **CHECKLIST**

Overcoming postural problems

- reposition equipment
- adjust the chair (height and back support)
- provide footrest
- provide document holder
- provide training in correct hand position and/o posture
- show user how to adjust equipment

Overcoming visual problems

- ensure the screen is kept clean
- reposition screen to avoid glare
- fit blinds on window to avoid glare
- place the screen at a more comfortable positic for the user

Overcoming fatigue and stress

- improve the workstation
- redesign the task
- provide new software
- provide the user with a degree of personal contr over the pace and nature of the work
- provide training, advice and information

Daily work routine of users

In many tasks, breaks or pauses occur naturally, e.g. in the work of a receptionist (to speak to guests), or a reservations assistant (between calls and enquiries). But if data or text entry requires continuous attention (e.g. a control clerk entering invoice details), then the supervisor should organise the work in such a way that suitable breaks or pauses are taken:

- short, frequent breaks (e.g. 5 to 10 minutes every hour) are more satisfactory than occasional, longer breaks

- informal breaks (e.g. on other tasks) are more effective in relieving visual fatigue than formal rest breaks

- breaks should be taken away from the screen

- breaks should not lead to greater intensity of work to make up for the time taken as a break

- wherever practicable, users should have some discretion as to how they carry out their task. But this should not encourage the user to forgo breaks in favour of a shorter working day, or to earn a productivity bonus of some sort.

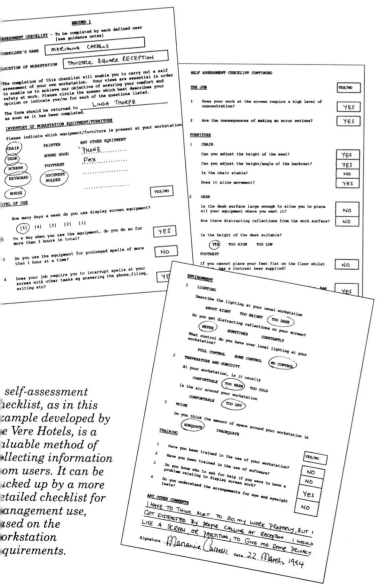

self-assessment checklist, as in this example developed by the Vere Hotels, is a valuable method of collecting information from users. It can be backed up by a more detailed checklist for management use, based on the workstation requirements.

Workstation requirements

General environment
- ☐ sufficient space for user to change position and vary movements
- ☐ adequate lighting, with appropriate contrast between the screen and background
- ☐ noise levels do not distract user's attention, nor affect speech levels
- ☐ equipment does not produce excess heat which causes discomfort to user
- ☐ adequate level of humidity

Interface between computer and user
- ☐ software suitable for the task
- ☐ software appropriate to the level of knowledge or experience of the user
- ☐ systems display information in a format and at a pace suited to the user, and give feedback on their performance

Display screen
- ☐ characters well defined, clearly formed and of adequate size, with adequate spacing between characters and lines
- ☐ image stable with no flickering
- ☐ brightness and contrast easy to adjust by user
- ☐ easily swivelled and tilted by user
- ☐ on separate base or adjustable table
- ☐ no glare or reflections liable to cause discomfort to the user (lighting levels are an important factor here, as is the position of the screen in relation to windows and doors, etc.)

Keyboard
- ☐ tiltable and separate from the screen to allow the user to find a comfortable working position avoiding fatigue in the arms or hands
- ☐ sufficient space in front of the keyboard to provide support for the hands and arms of the user during pauses in keying
- ☐ matt surface to avoid reflective glare
- ☐ user-friendly arrangement of keys
- ☐ symbols on keys adequately contrasted and legible from the user's working position

Work desk or work surface
- ☐ sufficiently large for flexible arrangement of screen, keyboard, documents, etc.
- ☐ low-reflective surface
- ☐ document holder stable and adjustable to avoid uncomfortable head and eye movements
- ☐ adequate space for user to work comfortably

Work chair
- ☐ stable, allowing the user easy freedom of movement and a comfortable position
- ☐ adjustable in height
- ☐ seat-back adjustable in height and tilt
- ☐ foot rest available to any user who wants one

 For more details refer to *Display Screen Equipment Work*, ISBN 011 886331 2, available from the Health and Safety Executive (see page 12).

Precautions against Aids

A basic understanding of what Aids is, and how the disease can spread may encourage your staff to take the fairly simple precautions required to avoid risk. Consider providing guidance to anyone who has – even on an occasional basis – to clean bedrooms, toilets and bathrooms, or handle waste materials left by customers or guests.

More about Aids

Aids stands for Acquired Immune Deficiency Syndrome. Most experts think (but not all) that it is caused by HIV, a virus which can break down the body's resistance to infections, with the result that the sufferer will eventually die.

In the majority of known cases, Aids has been passed from one person to another through sexual intercourse, or by taking infected blood into the bloodstream, for instance when drug addicts inject with shared needles. This is because the virus is carried in the body fluids, particularly semen and blood. Aids cannot be transmitted by food or drink.

Anyone can contract Aids. It is not an illness confined to drug addicts, prostitutes or gays. It is often impossible to tell if a person has Aids or is HIV positive, and so they can pass on the Aids virus. The symptoms can take years to appear.

Reducing the risk

Do not provide guests with electric shavers unless they are of the type which has a disposable head.

Use a safe disposal system for sanitary towels, nappies (diapers), etc. These should be incinerated on the premises, or stored in a sanitised container which is emptied and replaced by the supplier/contractor.

Hand-drying towels should not be used by more than one person. In public and staff toilets this will normally require disposable towels (with lidded waste receptacles), warm-air dryers or automatic roller towel dispensers.

Points to consider for work procedures

Special care is required when handling or cleaning anything that might have had contact with another person's blood or semen, e.g. used razor blades, hypodermic needles, used condoms, sanitary towels, soiled sheets, vomit or excreta.

Beware of sharp objects when emptying waste bins from bathrooms and toilets.

Dispose of used razors, razor blades, etc. in metal or hard plastic containers.

 An information sheet on Aids (on which this information has been based) is available from the Hotel Catering & Institutional Management Association, 191 Trinity Road, London SW17 7HN.

Disinfection procedure

For wiping up spills of blood, semen, mucus, vomit, and other body fluids

1 Ensure that cuts and grazes are covered with waterproof dressings.
2 Prepare disinfectant (see below), diluted in accordance with manufacturer's instructions.
3 Put on rubber gloves. If necessary wear a plastic apron.
4 Disinfect the contaminated area. Use a cloth or mop, but not a scrubbing brush as this can cause splashing. For soft furnishings, thoroughly soak the contaminated area with 'Tegodor' solution then allow to air dry.
5 Leave the disinfectant to work. How long is needed will be specified on the instructions.
6 Without removing them, rinse gloves in the disinfectant. Rinse and wipe apron.
7 Discard the disinfectant down sluice or toilet. Place the cloth in a plastic bag and put with normal rubbish, or incinerate. Wash out the mop head in disinfectant.
8 Leave gloves, apron and mop, if used, to dry before putting away.
9 Wash hands thoroughly.

Removing needles and syringes

1 Put on rubber gloves and plastic apron.
2 Pour disinfectant over the syringe and needle. Leave for 20 minutes. This applies to needles on floors or in toilets.
3 Ensure no one tampers with them.
4 Pick up the syringe carefully with tweezers or pliers. Place in the sharpsafe container.
5 Mop up the disinfectant/flush the toilet. Wash surrounding area with disinfectant.

Follow steps 6 to 9 above.

Contaminated bedlinen

1 Wear rubber gloves and apron.
2 Put bedlinen in its own plastic bag. Label as contaminated. If you have in-house laundry facilities, wash separately from other linen, on the hot cycle, using normal detergents.

What disinfectants to use

Chlorine-based disinfectants can be used for impermeable surfaces – tiles, floors, work surfaces. The chlorine is very effective and fast, but penetrates poorly. It can harm certain metals, e.g. aluminium, mild steel.

'Tegodor' is very effective in penetrating blood spills and can be used on most soft furnishings. It takes 20 minutes to work.

When using disinfectants, always:

• follow instructions carefully when making up solutions, and measure quantities accurately
• make up fresh on each occasion.

With thanks to Scottish & Newcastle plc

Precautions against legionnaires' disease

he bacteria which cause legionnaires' disease live in damp, arm conditions. They have been found in large numbers in ater systems, particularly when the temperature of the ater is between 20°C and 45°C, and in stagnant or slow oving water. When the water has been contaminated by gae, rust from metal piping and tanks, or scaling has curred, the bacteria will grow even more rapidly.

hese conditions are likely to occur in:

hot water systems in which the water temperature drops during long pipe runs, or through infrequent use – lag pipes, and if parts of the system have been unused for a period, thoroughly flush with hot water before the supply is used

cold water tanks which are badly sited so that the water gets quite warm on hot days – insulate tanks and have them cleaned regularly by contractors

air-conditioning systems which use water to collect the excess heat. The water is then cooled in special towers – employ specialist contractors to clean and disinfect.

he bacteria cause illness when they are inhaled in gnificant numbers. This might happen by breathing in the ne spray of a contaminated water supply from a shower (see x), fast running tap, whirlpool or spa. The bacteria attach emselves to the inside of the lungs, and after several days e victim is likely to suffer from headaches, muscle pain, verishness and confusion. Legionnaires' disease can be tal. It seems that middle-aged men are particularly lnerable.

Building services

eople have lost their lives, others have suffered serious juries as a result of accidents during maintenance work, or rough lack of attention to essential services such as the ater supply. The mini-case studies in the action overleaf (all sed on accidents reported to local authorities) illustrate me of the dangers.

edecorating or minor alterations: fire safety

efore making changes, check carefully that they will not fect fire safety. If doors are repainted, replace the fire tices. Some points to watch out for:

urface finishes

hese should be of the standard specified when Building egulation approval was obtained. In all other circum- ances, materials *not* acceptable on escape routes

---

Building services and cleaning

☐ all shower heads cleaned and disinfected on a quarterly basis, with additional cleaning where usage is low

☐ water storage tanks in good clean condition and provided with lids

☐ water storage tanks emptied annually, left for a period of not less than 25 hours, disinfected and rinsed

☐ air-handling plant serviced on a regular basis by a specialist company

☐ boilers, pumps and switches routinely serviced by a specialist company

☐ qualified staff regularly check these for normal working order

☐ kitchen grease filters deep-cleaned regularly by a specialist company

Extract from the audit form used by general managers in Jarvis Hotels as part of the company's system of checking.

Air-conditioned premises

All premises containing cooling towers and evaporative condensers (components of many air-conditioning systems found in larger buildings) must be notified to your local authority under the Notification of Cooling Towers and Evaporative Condensers Regulations 1992.

The form for doing this is available from the environmental health department.

Lifts and hoists

☐ Have all lifts and hoists been fully inspected and serviced within the past 6 months? Is the inspection certificate held on file and have all requirements been actioned?

☐ Are daily inspections made of lifts, emergency telephones and hoists?

☐ Are all lift and hoist shaft wells inspected at least once every 3 months for unsafe accumulation of refuse and debris?

☐ Are all lifts and hoists used solely for their respective designated uses and are all staff trained to comply with this rule?

☐ Confirm it is hotel policy that motor rooms are out of bounds for all but authorised persons and access is only possible with the use of a key

☐ Are sufficient staff trained in the manual operation of lifts and hoists to provide for a competent person to operate systems manually in the case of an emergency?

A further example from the Jarvis Hotels' audit system.

(i.e. stairways, corridors, entrance halls) include: timber, hardboard, blockboard, particleboard (chipboard), heavy flock wallpapers, and some thermosetting plastics (e.g. expanded polystyrene wall and ceiling linings).

Preventing the spread of fire or smoke

Fire or smoke should not be able to spread through ventilation trunking, holes in the walls for pipes, etc. These may need to be blocked with intumescent putty.

Fire doors to cupboards, service ducts and any vertical shafts linking floors should be kept locked shut when not in use. Other fire doors (e.g. to rooms, dividing corridors) should be fitted with self-closing devices to ensure they close fully. Cupboard doors should have a FIRE DOOR KEEP LOCKED notice fixed on the outside. Other doors should have a FIRE DOOR KEEP SHUT notice on both faces, fixed at about eye level.

Automatic door releases must be closed at a pre-determined time each night and remain closed during sleeping hours. If this is impracticable, test the release mechanism at least once a week, and check that the door closes fully. For automatic fire doors the notice must state AUTOMATIC FIRE DOOR KEEP CLEAR and, if appropriate, CLOSE AT NIGHT.

Lighting

Escape routes should have both normal and emergency lighting. If lights are not left on permanently, it should be easy for people to be able to switch them on.

British Standards relating to fire resistance of furniture and fittings

Furniture should conform to British Standard 5852: ignition source 0 (cigarette test) and ignition source 5 (timber crib test). In certain areas (e.g. a basement room used for discos), an increased performance criterion such as ignition source 7 could be justified.

Floor coverings should be tested to BS 4790 and classified as low radius of fire spread in accordance with BS 5287.

Beds and bedding should be tested to BS 6807, to resist ignition sources 0, 1 and 5.

Curtains and drapes should conform to BS 5867, both surface and edge ignition, and classified as fabric type B. In practical terms, this means choosing fabrics made from fibres which have in-built flame-retardant properties (e.g. Trevira or Temir), or those which have already been finished with a flame retardant. Alternatively, you can have the fabric of your choice treated, but this is quite expensive and can take several weeks.

 For more details, consult: Home Office/The Scottish Office, *Guide to Fire Precautions in Premises used as Hotels and Boarding Houses which Require a Fire Certificate*, available from HMSO or through bookshops ISBN 0 11 341005 0.

CASE STUDY

Building services accidents

Two ladder accidents

The assistant was standing on the ladder watering plants. The foot of the ladder was being supported by his co-worker – that until he stepped aside to give help someone else. The assistant fell, breaking his elbow.

The deputy manager was standing on mobile ladder on the dance floor. As colleague pushed the ladder, it collapse The manager suffered multiple fractures his pelvis and dislocated and fractured shoulder. One of the locking pins for th ladder was found to be defective, and th other one sheared when the ladder w pushed.

Guest found dead outside window

The guest, a 20-year-old student, had go to bed at 3 a.m., having consumed seve pints of beer. At 7.30 a.m. he was found the ground 30 feet below the open window his room. The window was the type th pivoted at its mid-point. The sill was abo 3 ft above floor level, and the mid-point of t window about 5 ft. The brackets, whi should have prevented the window openi more than about 7 inches, were found to distorted. Examination of other windows the hotel revealed a similar situation – make window cleaning easier.

Resident dies after fall down stairs

The resident, who was elderly and par disabled, was making his way from his 1 floor bedroom to the toilet on the half landi by the main stairs. He tripped on the tw steps that formed the half landing, and f down the stairway to the ground floo Artificial lighting was required throughout th day at the landing, but at the time (8 a.m both bulbs were not working.

ANALYSIS

For each of the incidents, discuss with yo colleagues:

1 Could a similar problem occur in yo workplace? If the situation described the case study could not happe because your building is single storey, example, think what other comparab problems might occur, such inadequate lighting in a corridor.

2 If so, how can it be prevented?

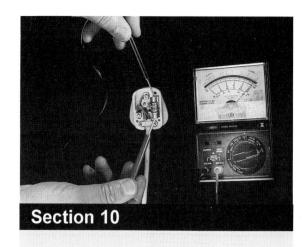

As the title suggests, this section invites you to look back at what you have covered in the book. The cycle of planning, of implementing and reviewing, is one that should underlie your whole approach to health and safety:

- *planning for change* – the world of work is in a continual state of flux, laws and regulations are changing, new equipment becomes available, and new threats emerge, particularly in the area of security

- *implementing* – safety procedures do not have many advantages in terms of arousing interest, as a new piece of equipment might, or a new recipe for a favourite food. That means you have to work hard at finding imaginative, different ways of putting across the message

- *reviewing* – how effective are safety procedures in preventing accidents? Are they understood by all those they affect? Do they meet current legal requirements? Are they relevant in the workplace of today?

Reviewing your safety performance

Contents guide.

Re-looking at safety and
security procedures 102

Monitoring and maintaining
standards 111

Towards a healthier and safer
environment 114

NVQ/SVQ level 3 checklist 115

Comments on case
studies/activities 116

How this section works

The text in this section is directly related to the core unit which covers health, safety and security for level 3 NVQs/SVQs in Catering and Hospitality Supervisory Management. Three elements make up this unit (see panel on the right), and for each element there are between five and seven performance criteria.

The number – **2e**, for example – which accompanies each of the headings in the text is a cross-reference to the performance criteria – performance criterion **e** of element **2**, in this example. The performance criteria are reproduced in the final checklist on page 115.

The text headings pick up key words from the performance criteria, for example: **How are you at anticipating problems? 1d** deals with performance criterion **d** of element **1**: *potential problems are identified and recommendations for the improvement of security / safety procedures are passed on to the appropriate people*.

Where similar performance criteria occur in two or more elements, these are dealt with once under an appropriate topic heading – e.g. relevant legislation in **1a**, **2a** and **3c** is discussed under the heading *Are you meeting legal requirements?*

  LEVEL 3

Catering and Hospitality Supervisory Management

3D1 *Monitor and maintain the health, safety and security of workers, customers and other members of the public*

which has three elements:

1 Maintain security/safety procedures in own area of responsibility

2 Monitor and maintain the health and safety of workers, customers and other members of the public

3 Maintain a healthy and safe working environment

Re-looking at safety and security procedures

Under this title the focus is the first NVQ/SVQ element, *Maintain security/safety procedures in own area of responsibility*, and four performance criteria from the third element *Maintain a healthy and safe working environment*. These relate to legal requirements, checking/investigating, taking action, and record-keeping.

Are you meeting legal requirements?   1a 2a 3c

With a vast range of Acts of Parliament, regulations, codes of practice, etc., no one can expect you to know all of them in detail. But there are some overriding principles which you should keep in mind, and specific issues to address:

- everyone at work has a legal responsibility towards the health and safety of themselves, others at work, and others who might be present in the workplace

- you (your colleagues and your senior managers) have a duty to establish what hazards exist in your workplace – that is, to make a risk assessment. This should not be a paper-exercise destined for the filing system, but a meaningful activity, leading to fewer hazards, and better safety procedures. Both assessment and procedures need to be kept up-to-date, to deal with the equipment, work processes, etc. that you and your staff are using now

- the risk assessment will need to take account of legal requirements, of course. But carried out well, it avoids the piecemeal approach, whereby certain things are done just because that is what the law requires. You should not have to rush around in panic putting fire notices on doors before the visit of the fire officer. The officer will insist that they are there, but a notice is not going to stop the spread of fire and smoke: only a strict rule, which all staff follow, that doors are kept shut

- if enforcement officers (e.g. EHOs or trading standards officers) feel you have good procedures and safeguards in place, and are willing to listen to advice, they are not likely to quote detailed legal requirements to you. But if there is a serious risk to people, or you have ignored previous advice, then the details do count (as the case study shows).

- there are certain specific legal requirements which it is essential you meet: reporting accidents, for example, or providing first-aid equipment – the legal summaries and text in earlier sections give clear guidance on these

- the law is an evolving process, so you do need to keep in touch through the trade and the national press with what is happening and changing. Obviously your employer has a responsibility to provide you with information. If you belong to a trade or professional association, you will get help through this. And your local Health and Safety Executive office, and environmental health department, are there to advise on the law, not just to enforce it.

Pub tots up 25 contraventions

In February 1991, a public house Aldershot was fined £750 (£30 eac offence) and £250 costs for 2 contraventions under the Food Hygien Regulations 1970.

The evidence presented by Rushmo Borough Council included the following:

- a greasy, dusty, chip scoop was foun lying on the floor behind a worktop in th kitchen

- cooking pots of various sizes wer stored beneath the kitchen sink in an o greasy cardboard box along with a tra containing a slimy deposit

- the internal surfaces and shelving of th refrigerator were not clean. There wa an accumulation of dried, foul smellin liquid on the floor of the refrigerator

- trays of decorating materials and boxe of new clothing surrounded the was hand basin in the kitchen

- no soap, towel or nailbrush provided the wash hand basin in the rear foo store and used by food handlers workin in the kitchen

- cleaning materials, polish and varnis stored in the wash hand basin in the rea food store.

Food Forum, IEHO Food Safety Bulletin, Issue 1, Vol. 1, September 1992

ANALYSIS

This case study suggests that little attentio was paid to their legal responsibilities b the management and staff of this pub.

1 In very general terms, and using you imagination to fill in some of the detail omitted from the case study, what do yo think went wrong with the managemer of the pub, and of the kitchens?

2 Put yourself in the shoes of the EHC who conducted the inspection. Wha action might you have taken? Why d you think the decision was made t prosecute on 25 separate offences

⚖️ LEGAL REQUIREMENTS CHECKLIST

Subject/topic	Legislation	For more details
Communicating safety	Health and Safety Information for Employees Regulations 1989	*page 12*
Contractors	Management of Health and Safety at Work Regulations 1992	*page 8*
Dangerous equipment	Offices, Shops and Railway Premises Act 1963	*page 36*
	Prescribed Dangerous Machines Order 1964, *see also Equipment*	*page 36*
	Provision and Use of Work Equipment Regulations 1992	*page 35*
Diseases, control of	Public Health (Control of Disease) Act 1984	*page 17*
	Public Health (Infectious Diseases) Regulations 1988	*page 17*
Display screen equipment	Health and Safety (Display Screen Equipment) Regulations 1992	*pages 96–7*
Equipment	Electricity at Work Regulations 1989	*pages 37–8*
	Offices, Shops and Railway Premises Act 1963	*pages 19, 36*
	Prescribed Dangerous Machines Order 1964	*page 36*
	Provision and Use of Work Equipment Regulations 1992	*page 35*
Fire	Fire Precautions Act 1971	*page 42*
	Fire Precautions (Hotels and Boarding Houses) Order 1972	*page 42*
	Fire Precautions (Places of Work) Regulations *(postponed)*	*page 42*
First-aid provision	Health and Safety (First-Aid) Regulations 1986	*pages 24–5*
Food	Dairy Products (Hygiene) Regulations *(proposed)*	*page 64*
	Food Hygiene (Amendment) Regulations 1990 and 1991	*pages 58, 59, 61*
	Food Hygiene (General) Regulations 1970	*page 58*
	Food Labelling (Amendment) (Irradiated Food) Regulations 1990	*page 62*
	Food Labelling Regulations 1984	*page 62*
	Food Safety Act 1990	*pages 57, 58, 63*
	Food Safety (General Food Hygiene) Regulations 1994	*pages 17, 58, 59, 61, 64*
	Ice-Cream (Heat Treatment, etc.) Regulations 1959	*page 64*
	Materials and Articles in Contact with Food Regulations 1987	*page 60*
Gas equipment	Gas Appliances (Safety) Regulations 1992	*page 39*
	Gas Safety (Installation and Use) (Amendment) Regulations 1990	*page 39*
Hazardous substances	Control of Substances Hazardous to Health Regulations 1988 (COSHH)	*page 29*
Health and safety at work	Health and Safety at Work etc. Act 1974	*pages 5, 6, 42*
	Management of Health and Safety at Work Regulations 1992	*pages 7–12*
Liability for guest property	Hotel Proprietors Act 1956	*page 52*
Managing health and safety	Management of Health and Safety at Work Regulations 1992	*pages 7–12*
Manual handling	Manual Handling Operations Regulations 1992	*page 26*
Noise	Environmental Protection Act 1990	*pages 23, 33*
	Noise at Work Regulations 1989	*page 23*
Notifiable diseases	Public Health (Control of Disease) Act 1984	*page 17*
	Public Health (Infectious Diseases) Regulations 1988	*page 17*
	Reporting of Injuries, Diseases and Dangerous Occurrences Regulations 1985 (RIDDOR)	*page 15*
Policy on health and safety	Health and Safety at Work etc. Act 1974	*page 6*
	Management of Health and Safety at Work Regulations 1992	*page 7*
Protective equipment	Personal Protective Equipment at Work Regulations 1992	*page 32*
Registering food premises	Food Premises (Registration) Regulations 1991	*page 60*
Registering guests	Immigration (Hotel Records) Order 1972	*page 52*
Reporting injuries, diseases, etc.	Reporting of Injuries, Diseases and Dangerous Occurrences Regulations 1985 (RIDDOR)	*page 15*
Risk assessment	Control of Substances Hazardous to Health Regulations 1988	*page 29*
	Management of Health and Safety at Work Regulations 1992	*page 10*
	Manual Handling Operations Regulations 1992	*page 26*
Safety representatives etc.	Management of Health and Safety at Work Regulations 1992	*page 12*
	Safety Representatives and Safety Committee Regulations 1977	*page 12*
Safety signs	Safety Signs at Work Regulations 1994	*page 13*
Training	*see Equipment, Fire, Food, Hazardous substances, Managing health and safety, Manual handling, Protective equipment*	*Index, page 124*
Waste disposal	Environmental Protection Act 1990	*page 33*
Workplace	Workplace (Health, Safety and Welfare) Regulations 1992	*page 19*

Are you *really* checking?

Work procedures and legislative guidance can be turned into checklists quite quickly (this is how most of those in this book have been done). The challenge is to develop an approach to checking which helps you and your staff in a meaningful way. Here are some guidelines to consider. Checklists should:

Be comprehensive but not over-detailed – contrast the Jarvis Hotels examples (page 99), with the workstation requirements for display screen equipment (page 97). The Jarvis checklist is part of a document that the general manager completes, providing the company's directors with an overview. For most items there are supporting, more detailed checklists for supervisors and staff (like the workstation one).

Cover suitable activities and work areas – by all means focus attention on well-known hazards, or areas where many people are present. But a hazard in a less-frequented area could go unnoticed until it is too late (cockroaches which make their home in under-the-counter pipework).

Meet legal requirements but do not be over-complex – take the example of fire precautions. Your fire certificate will specify the various intervals at which fire equipment must be tested and/or inspected. In a small business a simple log book will be sufficient, requiring the date and initials of the proprietor and manager.

Be backed by guidance where this helps – the Rank fire manual (extracts shown on right) includes this. The fire at Summerland (case study, page 41) is a reminder of what can go wrong if people don't understand their duties.

Be carried out at appropriate intervals – too much checking and the exercise tends to lose value. Proper checking takes time and resources. You've got to balance priorities but the danger is that safety drops to the bottom of the list – until there is an accident. The frequency and timing of checks should leave no one in any doubt that there will be checks. For some activities it is useful not to give away the exact time. If people know that at 10 a.m. on Mondays you check the fire escape routes, it's likely they will make sure they work particularly tidily on Monday mornings. For the other days of the week, confident that you won't check, soiled linen might be left in piles on the corridor, fire doors wedged open, and so forth.

Clarify responsibility – everyone needs to know what their role is. Don't give them the opportunity to say: 'I thought so-and-so did that'. Clarity about responsibilities is vital if you are using contractors or consultants, e.g to check certain equipment, for pest control, or to monitor safety standards. You need to know what it is the responsibility of the contractor/consultant to check, and who is responsible for safety precautions while the work is in progress.

Means of escape   *Fire hazards*   *Fire alarms*   *Staff training*

Checks made/activities carried out.

Frequency of checks/activity.

Rank Leisure

Each check is supported by a detailed procedure.

FIRE ALARM SYSTEM

Alarm systems will be tested weekly: on the same day and at the same time. All persons on the premises whose alarm is interlinked must be advised that a test is about to take place. Furthermore, if the system is linked to a central control or the local fire authority, they **must** be notified prior to the test, and a check made at the finish to ensure they received the alarm signal and are aware the test has been completed.

A different break glass call point will be used each week for test purposes. When the alarm system incorporates zoning, a different point in each zone will be tested each week.

All break call points will be numbered and record kept of which one(s) has/ve been tested.

During the alarm test, all audible and/or visual indicators will be checked. Any faults or failures are to be recorded on the events section form and immediately reported to the servicing contractors.

Alarm systems will be serviced by an approved contractor at least twice per year and details of the service, extent and any faults recorded.

Spare replacement glass for call points must be kept.

Any activation of the alarm system outside the specified test period is be treated as serious. The fire and evacuation procedures must be put into immediate operation.

For each check there are supporting forms to record details.

FIRE ALARM SYSTEM WEEKLY TESTS

An event includes any damaged or call point not working properly, any failure of the sounder(s) or visual indicators, any false or actual fire alarms.

Date	Call point no.	Zone no.	Tested by	Audible/visual indicators working	Faults to be entered in events sect.

In larger establishments a more elaborate system will usually be necessary to ensure everyone knows what to do, and actually carries out the tasks.

ead to action – when problems are identified, it's likely that number of people (senior management, maintenance, safety fficers, etc.) will be involved in putting the matter right. If ae same problem keeps appearing on checklist after aecklist, find out where and why the communication is iling. Audit systems which lead to a pass or fail mark (with uality grades of good and excellent to provide motivation) re a way of focusing attention on problems – see the IcDonald's Restaurant example on pages 86 and 87.

rovide evidence of what has been done – if a problem does ccur, one of the first matters to be investigated will be the aecking procedures.

s the action you take when   1c 3e
roblems occur effective?

' problems keep reoccurring, the answer is a definite no. Iopefully that extreme is unlikely, but there is certain to be range of in-between states, where you could be more ffective. Questions to think about (1, 2, 3 and 6 relate pecifically to the NVQ/SVQ performance criteria) include:

Are you and your staff familiar with your organisation's procedures (or, in the absence of these, your employer's instructions) for breaches of security and faults with safety equipment? Written procedures or your manager (or a combination of the two) have to be your first reference point for dealing with problems. Are written procedures kept in a place where people have access to them? Do your staff understand them? Do they form part of your training programmes and less formal, on-the-job instructions?

Do you and your staff know what to do for the types of security problem which might occur in your workplace? Situations might include a briefcase left on the premises (could there be an explosive device inside?), a customer who presents a stolen credit card (on the blacklist, or because you have been told by other businesses in a Hotel Secure/Pub Watch scheme), or a member of staff under suspicion for short-changing customers.

And what happens if safety equipment develops a fault? The NVQ/SVQ range list includes specialist security equipment (e.g. CCTV, identity badges, computerised key cards), fire fighting equipment (see Section 5) and first-aid equipment (see page 24). Think back to the last time you had to deal with a fault. Consider what other faults could occur and ask yourself if you know what to do.

When things go wrong, is action taken speedily? In the case study where a pub customer fell to his death down the stairs to the toilet (page 16), no action had been taken to repair the stair covers (presumably over a long period), nor was the accident reported. But what of the first few minutes after the accident occurred? If the man was lying at the bottom of the stairs unconscious, or bleeding badly, you do not have the luxury of time to find out what to do, or look for the first-aid box.

ACTION

Events like the bombing of The Carlton Club (photograph on page 107) have highlighted the need for emergency planning. (Knowledge of emergency procedures relating to fire, accident, flood and bomb alert is required for this NVQ/SVQ unit.)

There are many things that might need to be thought about in an emergency:

Security – are you evacuating the building to put everyone in worse danger (see box below), and how do you prevent other people gaining access to the building once emptied?

Is a *full* or a *partial evacuation* necessary, and in the event of an evacuation which might last for many hours or days, *where does everyone go, how do they get there, who will check that people don't get lost on the way*, and how can information be gathered to *inform the next of kin* once the news breaks that there has been a major emergency?

Read the extracts from the emergency procedures followed at Metropole Hotels (in the boxes on pages 9, 107 and 108) with regard to some of these topics, then have a go at developing suitable guidelines for a subject of your choice in your workplace.

Evacuation: making the right decision

The decision on whether to start searching, or evacuating the building or both is not an easy one. 'But with hoaxes a pattern does emerge, such as the time and the nature of the call. Once you stop evacuating, the hoaxer stops,' says Denis Hancock, head of security for Ladbroke. 'But if your are in doubt you should treat it as a genuine threat,' he stresses.

Even when the call is genuine, the decision to evacuate guests can be a difficult one. Evacuation may be exactly what terrorists want because they have planted the bomb outside, rather than inside the building as claimed. Many more lives would have been lost in the 1983 Harrods' bombing if the shop had been cleared. A phone caller claimed the bomb had been placed inside the store; in fact, it had been planted in a car outside.

Not all bomb calls are necessarily made direct to the hotel. In one incident, the police were warned that a bomb had been planted in a Park Lane hotel. No clue was given as to which, leaving the police with a major logistical headache. If every hotel had been evacuated, thousands of guests would have been spilled on to the busy streets. In the event, all the hotels sent guests to their bedrooms after deciding this would be safer. Each public room was searched by staff and police. The bomb was eventually found behind some panelling in the gents' toilets in the Hilton International.

Bally Sall, *Voice*, March 1993

5 If staff ignore safety instructions, what action can you take? Some of the accidents described in the ACTION on page 84 occurred because staff were not wearing gloves or eye protection when using hazardous cleaning materials. The suggestion was that they had ignored instructions. The problem is that it is quite easy to tell someone to do or not to do something. It is less easy to get them to take notice of what you are saying, particularly when you or other workplace pressures create conflicting priorities. There is no single answer, but a combination of good example, training and instruction, close supervision and improved motivation can usually persuade most people.

6 If all else fails, can you dismiss? The answer is yes, provided you go through the proper disciplinary procedure. For grave misconduct, summary dismissal might be appropriate. The procedures will be in your company's staff handbook, or in individual contracts of employment, or check with your manager.

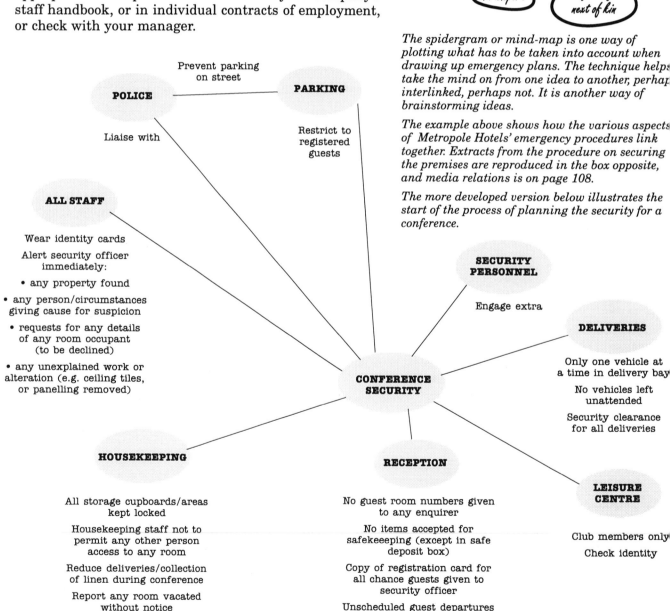

The spidergram or mind-map is one way of plotting what has to be taken into account when drawing up emergency plans. The technique helps take the mind on from one idea to another, perhaps interlinked, perhaps not. It is another way of brainstorming ideas.

The example above shows how the various aspects of Metropole Hotels' emergency procedures link together. Extracts from the procedure on securing the premises are reproduced in the box opposite, and media relations is on page 108.

The more developed version below illustrates the start of the process of planning the security for a conference.

How are you at anticipating problems? 1d

Many of the practices often tolerated in the workplace, like rubbish left in a corridor during the cleaning of bedrooms, might not have led to an accident – fortunately. Nevertheless they are *potential* problems, and in the interests of safety you need to be very honest in your assessment of how you are at anticipating problems. Your own powers of observation are an essential element:

- recognising hazardous situations throughout your workplace, not just in your own department

- recognising hazardous practices, whether they involve your staff, staff in other departments, customers or contractors working on the premises.

Of course, you need to know what to look for. Your own experience will help, as will the effort you put into risk assessments and preparing checklists. Don't make assumptions that your staff will know that a particular practice is hazardous, just because you do. Some people, for example, have no idea of the force behind the cork in a bottle of Champagne (people have lost the sight of an eye after being hit by a flying cork).

Your staff are another essential element. This means giving them the knowledge and skills to recognise problems, and building up a relationship which encourages them to bring problems to your attention – a combination of training, appreciation and being seen to take effective action. If their efforts seem to be wasted (and staff will make up their own minds on that score), this support will be lost.

Some of your customers might tell you of problems. Even if they seem to be busybodies, it's a point of view you should take seriously. The sort of customer you don't want is the one who tells you of a problem via the court.

The Carlton Club, London, after the bomb blast, June 1990.

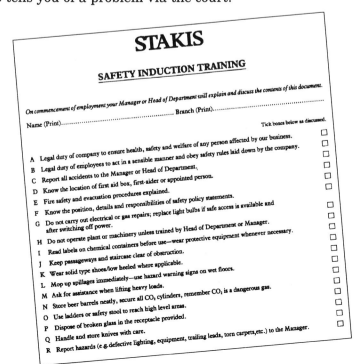

STAKIS

SAFETY INDUCTION TRAINING

On commencement of employment your Manager or Head of Department will explain and discuss the contents of this document.

Name (Print)... Branch (Print)..........................

Tick boxes below as discussed.

A Legal duty of company to ensure health, safety and welfare of any person affected by our business.

B Legal duty of employees to act in a sensible manner and obey safety rules laid down by the company.

C Report all accidents to the Manager or Head of Department.

D Know the location of first aid box, first-aider or appointed person.

E Fire safety and evacuation procedures explained.

F Know the position, details and responsibilities of safety policy statements.

G Do not carry out electrical or gas repairs; replace light bulbs if safe access is available and after switching off power.

H Do not operate plant or machinery unless trained by Head of Department or Manager.

I Read labels on chemical containers before use—wear protective equipment whenever necessary.

J Keep passageways and staircase clear of obstruction.

K Wear solid type shoes/low heeled where applicable.

L Mop up spillages immediately—use hazard warning signs on wet floors.

M Ask for assistance when lifting heavy loads.

N Store beer barrels neatly, secure all CO_2 cylinders, remember CO_2 is a dangerous gas.

O Use ladders or safety stool to reach high level areas.

P Dispose of broken glass in the receptacle provided.

Q Handle and store knives with care.

R Report hazards (e.g. defective lighting, equipment, trailing leads, torn carpets, etc.) to the Manager.

Emergency procedure

Securing the premises after evacuation

Areas of the hotel not affected by the fire will be secured against possible intrusion and theft.

As soon as evacuation is complete floor housekeepers, accompanied by a senior manager, will check all bedrooms in each wing of the hotel not affected by the fire.

Commencing with the top floor, they will check and secure each room. No personal belongings will be removed. A note of each room containing property will be recorded on a room checklist and handed to the chief security officer on completion.

As soon as a floor has been checked all stairways leading to that floor will be secured by the presence of a security officer or house porter, preventing unauthorised access to that floor.

This process will be repeated at all floor levels until the ground floor is reached. Each stairway will then be secured from the ground floor to prevent unauthorised access to that floor.

Stairways will be continually manned throughout the emergency.

Restaurants will be secured by restaurant staff under the direction of the senior food and beverage manager on duty.

Prior to evacuation all cashiers will secure all cash: by placing in secure storage within the department, or by taking it to reception and depositing it in the hotel safe.

With thanks to Metropole Hotels

Are you communicating with colleagues and bosses?

1d

Identifying a potential problem in a colleague's department may not go down well, unless you handle the situation with tact. The checklist on increasing safety awareness (page 12) included the suggestion of hazard spotting in other departments – the idea being that a fresh pair of eyes can often identify more.

Teamwork can pay great dividends, especially in security matters. One of the easiest ways for thieves to get access to guest bedrooms is by persuading housekeeping or room service staff that they are *bona fide* guests, who have accidentally got locked out of their rooms. A phone call to reception would soon establish that the claim was not legitimate, but if reception and housekeeping staff are in a state of feud (and such feelings often work their way down from managers and supervisors), information is unlikely to be shared.

Good communication to your managers, to head office health and safety managers, and to maintenance and security managers, is critical if changes are to be made successfully. These people rely on you for information. You (together with all other employees) have a legal responsibility to bring your employer's attention to shortcomings in health and safety arrangements (see page 8). Depending on your workplace, there will be three main channels for communicating concerns and recommendations:

- checklist action points, accident investigations, audit reports, etc.

- attendance at health and safety meetings and/or department meetings where health and safety is a regular topic for discussion (see box and page 12)

- memos, reports, formal and informal meetings with colleagues and superiors.

About your record-keeping?

1e 3a

The room attendant's claim for damages after a fall (case study on page 18) was finalised nearly 2½ years after the accident. Over this time there were requests for more and more detailed information. The analysis asked you to consider your ability to provide the responses sought. Would you (and would your managers) be as confident as Michael Gottleib (see box) that the reporting and record-keeping system was sufficiently watertight to defend a hoax claim for damages?

If you have a role in designing forms and records, consider:

- what is the purpose of the record, why is the information required, what conclusions will be drawn from it?

Emergency procedure

Contacts with the press/media

From the outset enquiries can be anticipated from international, national or local agencies, depending on the nature of the crisis.

The media must not be ignored. Indeed, it is extremely important to plan press and media liaison in advance. Carefully undertaken, such planning will lead to the success of the recovery operation.

Statements on behalf of the company may only be made by the spokesperson nominated by the managing director, or company secretary. All statements must be carefully prepared. It is essential to avoid contradictory, conflicting, incorrect or premature statements.

Requests for interviews with key personnel involved must be referred to the managing director for approval.

In major incident cases where interest is likely to be intense and the recovery operation protracted, press conferences may be held in conjunction with the police and fire brigade.

With thanks to Metropole Hotels

Dealing effectively with the media in a crisis situation relies on good internal communication lines to the top of the company, and everyone knowing the limits of their responsibility.

Defending a hoax claim for damages

A customer at one of Smollensky's Restaurants in London demanded £5000 damages for loss of earnings, distress, and so forth. She claimed to have broken her wrist when she slipped on some food left on the floor of the restaurant. In court she produced doctor's, employer's and psychologist's reports. She had noted the name of the manager, waiter and receptionist on duty at the time (who remembers all that without ulterior motives?), and had as a witness the person she had dined with.

Because the event had not happened, Smollensky's had no witnesses. The first lawyer advised the restaurant to cut its losses and settle. A second lawyer agreed to take on the case, but warned it might cost up to £10,000 and the chances of winning were no better than 75–25 against, in spite of the restaurant's practice of scrupulously recording every customer complaint and incident. Even if the restaurant successfully fought off the claim, the lawyer added, it would not get costs, since the claimant would not have the means to pay them.

Faced with this, Smollensky's agreed to settle out of court, paying £3000 to the alleged victim, £2000 for her legal costs and £2500 for its own legal costs.

Michael Gottleib, proprietor of Smollensky's Restaurants, writing in *Caterer & Hotelkeeper*, 17 March 1994

- who will see it – others within your organisation, or external people (e.g. the environmental health department), or a combination?

- who will have to fill it in? – for some of your staff the format may have to be very straightforward (the display screen assessment form on page 97 is for staff use)

- can some of the information be given in the form of yes/no answers, or by ticking boxes (as the COSHH training form on page 31 and the medical questionnaire on page 17)?

- when space is required to give an answer, have you allowed sufficient? Risk assessment forms pose a particularly difficult design challenge. While not much space is required to describe the activity itself (e.g. moving conference furniture), and four columns seem to provide a neat way of indicating the level of risk (i.e. none, low, medium, high), rather more space is needed to describe the methods of reducing the risk. Indeed, if you follow this example through, you might question how useful this approach will be. After all, there are many other facts that have to be considered when you decide the level of risk (e.g. the strength of the person doing the handling, the distance the items have to be carried, how much time is available, what exactly has to be carried – see page 26).

When you come to fill in a form for the first time (such as the one for reporting accidents, see page 15), spend time reading the whole form before you put pen to paper. Otherwise you could find yourself giving an answer in the wrong place – to take a simple example, writing the postcode as part of your address, then finding that a separate box is provided for it.

The records which your NVQ/SVQ assessor is likely to focus on are the accident book (see page 14 or in-house equivalents as shown on the right), incident book (the security report on the next page is a version of this), wastage book and damage mark-downs book. The last two mentioned provide a way of accounting for stocks of food or drink, for example, that have had to be destroyed (e.g. because of a fridge breakdown, see the temperature recording sheet on page 71), or equipment, fixtures and fittings which have become unsafe to use.

You are quite likely to encounter other records in your career, including those for detailing customer complaints about food (see box), and faults that have occurred with equipment (example overleaf). Record-keeping is essential for showing that you have tested fire equipment and held fire drills for your staff (Section 5), and tested electrical equipment (Section 4). It is also an invaluable way of showing that your staff have had training in safe procedures for manual handling, the use of personal protective equipment and so forth, and that you have taken reasonable precautions to prevent an infestation of pests.

A further range of industry forms are reproduced overleaf.

The layout of the original form gives appropriate space for each answer.

METROPOLE HOTELS

PERSONAL INJURY REPORT NUMBER 8.94

00004

(handwritten personal injury report form — injured person: Wilson, Neil; details of accident and injury; treatment; investigation; action taken; administration)

Food Complaints Record Sheet

Name and address of complainant

....

....

....

Tel ....

Date received .... Time

....

Products/food concerned ....

....

Nature of complaint ....

....

Person receiving complaint (name, job title, department) ....

....

Information to be obtained:

If products/food involved brought in: supplier/ manufacturer ....

....

Product made on site: list of ingredients ....

....

Any details noted on delivery ....

....

Action taken ....

Complainant advised: date ....

With thanks to University of St Andrews

EQUIPMENT SERVICE HISTORY CARD

21

Model No. **213-DF**   Serial/ Code No. **218-021-25/5/91**   Equipment Type **REG TOASTER**

Date	Ref. No.	Description of Work		Engineer to initial appropriate box	
10.9.91	02	**Service Company** I.HC **Engineers Name** C L R	Electrical test (needs new flex)	Equipment left in good working order	
				Work outstanding but equipment operational	✓
				Equipment in poor condition. DO NOT USE	
7.9.92	02	**Service Company** D+C **Engineers Name** ChR	Electrical Test. Flex has come out of stuffing gland. TESTED OK.	Equipment left in good working order	
				Work outstanding but equipment operational	
				Equipment in poor condition. DO NOT USE	✓
17.9.92	02	**Service Company** JAC **Engineers Name** CXO	Repair gland above. rectified	Equipment left in good working order	✓
				Work outstanding but equipment operational	
				Equipment in poor condition. DO NOT USE	
30-12.92		**Service Company** H.C.S. **Engineers Name** JB.	Harold. New power switch fitted along with power cable & plug.	Equipment left in good working order	✓
				Work outstanding but equipment operational	
				Equipment in poor condition. DO NOT USE	
7/93	02	**Service Company** JAC **Engineers Name**	Electrical Test.	Equipment left in good working order	✓
				Work outstanding but equipment operational	

TRAINING RECORDS

The Company keeps a record of each individual's training, these records are kept by the Personnel and Training Manager of your branch. You will be asked to sign to confirm that you have received training in specific skills and tasks.

All of these records will be monitored by the Company Training Manager.

JONES A.

RoadChef

NAME:

Date of joining:

INDUCTION	Date training completed	Trainer's initials	Trainee's initials
Welcome to Roadchef			
Introduction to other staff/management			
Personal presentation and hygiene			
Health and safety responsibilities			
Accident reporting			
First-aid provision			
Manual handling			
Fire, bomb scares			

SECURITY REPORT

Alleged theft, loss or damage of property

Report No ....   OB Ref ....

Name of Loser/Complainant ....

Address .... Post code ....

Tel No .... Date of depar...

Room No. .... Date of arrival .... Date of depar...

Property lost/stolen/damaged ....

.... Previous losses

Total value ....

Classification of allegation ....

Date & time last seen correct by complainant ....

Date & time loss/theft/damage discovered ....

PARTY COVERED BY INSURANCE

Details of insurance co ....

Staff having access .... Police officer ....

Date police notified .... Reference ....

Station ....

Police classification .... Date

Report completed by ....

This report on the theft of a customer's handbag shows the value of CCTV in helping to identify suspects – in this incident, the descriptions of the witnesses and the victim were not much help.

Security report

At approximately 20.25 hours on Monday 11 October 1994, I was called to the Rivoli Bar regarding an alleged theft of a lady's handbag.

The loser is Ms Sharon Aburthnot, a non-resident. She was with a girlfriend sitting at the bar. The bar was quite busy with a mixture of guests and non-guests. Ms Aburthnot had placed her handbag behind her back on the stool and was pressing against it as the stools have back rests. Her friend Mrs Martha Williams was sitting to the left of her. They had only been in the bar a couple of minutes and received their order when two white males leaned across the bar to ask the barman what time the bar closed. This is when she felt movement behind her back and realised her bag was missing. She tried to run after the two men but they had vanished by the time she reached the main lobby. Several descriptions have been received but all differ. The doorman did not notice any young white males hurrying out of the hotel.

Bruno, senior barman, gave the following description:

- white male, approx. 20–23 yrs, tall, black hair, smart blue suit and blue tie, American accent
- white male, approx. 19 yrs, glasses, scruffy dress with barbour jacket.

Ms Aburthnot gave this description:

- two males, one white and one coloured, not sure as only had a glimpse as they went to the lobby and only saw them from behind.

Details of the alleged losses

Black leather shoulder back, maker HENREY, zip up, value approx. £175, house keys and address, black leather wallet value £75, Halifax card, Lloyds cash card, approx. £200 mixed cash.

Action taken to help loser

Ms Aburthnot was escorted to Redley Police Station. The police contacted the credit card companies and a locksmith was also called to replace her house locks. A local police constable would be in attendance until she arrived home.

The loser is not insured. I have explained the hotel has no liability as the loss occurred in a public area. Ms Aburthnot understood and thanked the hotel for its help.

From the video playback

Tape no. 21, time 20.21.34, camera main lobby entrance:

- male early 30s, 5' 10", medium-heavy build, short dark hair
- male early 20s, 5' 5", slim build, curly dark hair, metal rim glasses.

David Whatmore
Security Officer

With thanks to Le Meridien London. Names and details have been changed or omitted for confidentiality.

Monitoring and maintaining standards

Under this title the focus is on the second NVQ/SVQ element: *Monitor and maintain the health and safety of workers, customers and other members of the public.*

Good housekeeping standards applied to everyone?   2a

Professional housekeepers achieve high standards by:

- communicating to their staff what these standards are

- establishing cleaning routines that enable the job to be done well, within the time and resources available

- combining these routines with a schedule that ensures items are cleaned as often as necessary, whether this be repeatedly during use (e.g. a wiping cloth), daily (guest bedrooms), weekly (high surfaces) or periodically (carpets shampooed twice-yearly)

- monitoring and checking that standards are met consistently.

Why should you apply similar principles to your area of the workplace if you are not a housekeeper? Quite simply, because clean workplaces are much more likely to be safe. The process of cleaning:

- removes waste materials that are a tripping and fire hazard

- prevents build-ups of grease and other soiling – also a tripping and fire hazard

- keeps under control the growth of harmful bacteria – a health and hygiene risk

- discourages pests – which carry disease and bacteria

- provides a more pleasant environment – for customers, guests and staff

- prevents damage and improves the performance of equipment

- reduces maintenance costs

- promotes a more favourable image to customers, so the business performs better and there are more resources available to improve safety performance.

Some cleaning agents are hazardous – because of their toxic nature. Some cleaning activities are hazardous – because they involve taking apart equipment with sharp blades, for example. Your cleaning routines will need to reflect these safety concerns (see Sections 3 and 4).

Alarm bells rang

The environmental health officer stopped at a popular quick-service restaurant around mid-day for his coffee break. The restaurant was very busy, so he took his coffee to the upstairs seating area. There he noticed that a member of staff was standing outside the entrance to the customers' toilets, preventing people from using them. 'Alarm bells rang'.

On his way downstairs, he noticed that large areas of the floor in the main preparation area behind the service counter were covered with cardboard packaging material, some of which was saturated. (Customers standing at the service counter were not able to see the floor area, which is why the EHO hadn't noticed anything unusual when he was served with his coffee.)

After making himself known to the duty manager, the EHO made a closer inspection. Sewage effluent from the customers' toilets had seeped through the inspection chamber in the centre of the kitchen floor. It had blocked immediately after the inspection chamber. The wash hand basin connected above the blockage, so was out of commission (this meant that there were no facilities for food handlers to wash their hands). The sinks were connected below the blockage and were still in use.

Satisfied that there was an imminent risk, the EHO served an emergency prohibition notice closing the restaurant immediately.

Richard Evans, assistant chief environmental health officer

ANALYSIS

1 Sewage effluent swirling over the kitchen floor obviously does not suggest good housekeeping standards, but in every other aspect this restaurant met extremely high standards of cleanliness and hygiene. Assuming the problem occurred on a bank holiday, how would you deal with the situation? List all the factors you would take into account.

2 Do you think this was the first time the problem had occurred? What clues have you based your conclusion on? If you think the answer is no, what does this suggest had gone wrong?

No hazards to spot? 2b

Frankly it's most unlikely your working area will be free from hazards. Many are unavoidable – electrical equipment has the potential to cause harm, the accepted definition of a hazard. A number of common items of kitchen equipment fall into the category of 'prescribed dangerous machines'. But there is much you can do to:

- keep the hazards as few as possible
- establish safe methods of working so that there is the minimum risk of accident or injury from those hazards you cannot remove.

From the first page, this book has set out ideas and approaches for tackling both areas.

No problems left to get worse? 2c

This returns to the themes discussed earlier in relation to security and faults with safety equipment:

- identifying problems
- rectifying them where possible
- and for those you cannot sort out, reporting them to the person who will.

The general manager who failed to report a series of thefts (see box) may have had good reasons – guests sometimes do not want to press charges – but by leaving the problem he didn't help the guests who were subsequently robbed.

Maintenance on time? 2d

Health, safety and maintenance checks will be a waste of time if they are not done with some regularity. If you have the sort of cascade system described on page 104, where general managers do an overall check, you check the activities that are involved in your work area, and your staff check those that relate to their job, then the frequency will vary from level to level. This is right, because there has to be a balance between the time involved and the degree of risk.

The risk assessment should help identify how often checks need to be done (page 10). In some cases the law is quite clear (e.g. on lifts, see page 99). In other cases, the law puts the onus on the employer to decide the frequency of checks (as with portable electrical equipment, see page 37, and eye tests for those who do a lot of computer work, page 96).

Whatever system you follow, do make a reminder in your work diary or on computer or some sort of planner of when checks should be made. It will be too late, if on the eve of the fire officer's visit, you discover it is several weeks since the alarm call points were tested, or that the fire extinguishers have not had their annual maintenance check.

Valuing your staff

Alert staff are worth more than the most sophisticated crime prevention equipment.

'Crime prevention is about staff awareness,' said David Williams at the Metropolitan Police's Hotel Intelligence Unit. In his experience staff often saw something suspicious when a crime was being committed – but they weren't trained how to react. And if they did raise a query with the duty manager, they were ignored.

Managers often didn't take enough interest in crime prevention, and even if staff acted quickly, and criminals were arrested, the staff sometimes weren't even thanked.

But others made much more effort. 'They have things like employee of the month schemes. If a member of staff helps catch a criminal they may well get some premium bonds.'

Kate Trollope, *Hotel & Restaurant Magazine*, March 1992

Footnote

The hotel's new general manager found he had one or two thefts taking place. He went back over his predecessor's records to find 27 allegations of which only seven were reported to the police. When we helped him put it all together, we found that one member of staff was on duty every day. Had the previous manager not tried to hide it, he would have eliminated that problem.

Interview with David Williams, *Inside Hotels*, September 1993

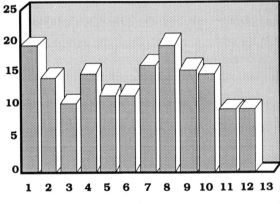

REPORTED ACCIDENTS

Month

Accident statistics have been used at several points in earlier sections to put the particular messages across, and fire statistics formed the basis for the training session suggested on page 45. They also have value as a motivational tool, and in larger organisations where trends can be clearly established, they help identify priorities for action at all levels of management. An example of this is shown here.

earning from accidents? **2e**

he need to report and record accidents accurately, and notify
iem to the appropriate authority has been discussed. There are
ear legal requirements (see pages 14–18), and should you need
irther convincing, return to the Smollensky story (page 108).

ccident records have another value – when carefully
impleted they provide the means for examining what went
rong and putting better safeguards in place to prevent a
ipetition. This is why many employers prefer their own
:cident recording forms to the standard book available
irough HMSO (see page 14).

quipment and fixtures used as **2f**
itended by their manufacturers?

ection 7 made the point that general safety procedures had to
ike second place to instructions from the manufacturer. This
intrast is apparent by comparing the information on
iicrowave ovens (identifying various wrong uses to be avoided),
impiled from one manufacturer's manual (page 85), with the
Ivice on testing swimming pool water (step 3, page 92).

more comprehensive explanation of how to test pool and spa
ater for chlorine, bromine, pH, alkalinity, calcium hardness,
angelier balance and cyanuric acid would run to many pages.
it if you heard the news that a famous actress had fallen ill
fter swimming in a health club pool which was found to have
00 times the approved level of bacteria (and this did happen),
ould you not review your procedures to check that staff were
irrying them out fully, and check with your supplier that you
ere indeed using the most effective tests?

he work equipment and personal protective equipment
gulations (summarised on pages 35 and 32 respectively)
iake clear everyone's responsibilities to use equipment as it
: intended to be used by the manufacturer.

afety signs doing their job? **2g**

afety signs perform a valuable communication role,
iforming people in a clear, readily understandable way about
safe route, alerting them to the need to take caution,
rohibiting or requiring a certain action or activity. You have
legal duty to use the signs properly (see page 13). There is
Iso a strong common-sense argument for doing so: people
ind to ignore signs when the hazard doesn't seem to exist.

or example, a CAUTION WET FLOOR sign should be removed
hen the floor is dry. If it is consistently left in place for hours
fter the floor has dried, people may stop taking care. Then
ie day comes when they find, too late, that the floor really is
et. Do you always slow down on a motorway when speed
estrictions are flashing, but there is no sign of any problem
head?

Equipment engineers offer some advice

Certain boilers, expresso coffee machines, steam-jacketed boiling pans, tilting kettles, combination ovens, etc. have internal pressure vessels. They should be maintained, inspected and certificated on an annual basis, by a competent engineer. (The Employers Association of Catering Equipment Engineers points out that some caterers may not be aware that such equipment has an internal pressure vessel, and therefore of the need for checks.)

Earth bonding (often found on the pipework to sinks, wash hand basins, etc.) might be treated as a nuisance especially when it comes to cleaning. Remind staff that it is there to protect their safety and should never be removed or tampered with.

Aluminium equipment (e.g. parts from food mixing machines) reacts with certain chemicals used in dishwashers, leading to serious corrosion. Check with your supplier first.

Beware of unscrupulous dealers of second-hand, refurbished equipment, bankrupt stock, etc. If incorrect chemicals have been used to clean the equipment, damage may be caused to internal working parts and surfaces. This is not obvious at the time of purchase, but could be the reason for subsequent deterioration.

Pre-rinse spray arms on dishwashers, like shower heads, can become a breeding ground for legionella bacteria. Dismantle regularly, thoroughly clean and disinfect.

and give some cautionary tales

After repairing the gas range, the engineer is asked by the catering manager to look at a mixing machine which is not working. Thinking he is helping his firm by obliging the customer, he attempts the repair – but unsuccessfully. The manufacturer of the mixer is called in and the first thing their engineer says is 'Which cowboy has been at this?' Not a cowboy, but someone who should have been able to say 'no'.

An engineer used '3-in-1' oil to ease the door of a steamer. He had considerable experience, but in an engineering environment, and didn't realise that oil and greases for catering equipment had to be food compatible. The product he used sets up a reaction in the presence of heat and moisture, creating a hazard to any food which was steamed.

On a recent visit to a new kitchen, it was noted that the extractor system was off and the chef was reluctant to use it. When he did turn it on, we could understand why: all the swing doors suddenly swung into the kitchen. The small fan under the dishwasher ran against its windings in a reverse position, and some of the gas burner flames were seen to be 'lifting', creating unspent gas release. When the extraction system was commissioned, no allowance was made for relief air or combustion air.

Towards a healthier and safer environment

Four of the performance criteria for the third element, *Maintain a healthy and safe working environment*, have been covered on earlier pages (3a on page 108–110, 3b on page 104–5, and 3c on page 102).

Training and retraining   3d

There is a lot of information to absorb on health and safety for those in a management or supervisory position, or training and working towards that responsibility. If you have found this, then you will sympathise with the point of view of your staff that they want it broken down into manageable chunks and confined to what they need to do their job.

Note how the training plan on page 36 and the instructions for the basic lift (opposite page) are broken down into steps. Consider the recap questions (reproduced below) which are used to complete the session on using a mixing machine, and the points to remember for the basic lift. The cartoon example opposite shows another way of assessing levels of knowledge, which might be adapted for your younger staff and trainees.

The training checklist on this page follows the process through from selection of trainees to signing off the training record. Steps which relate specifically to equipment could be readily adapted to more general training.

The management of health and safety regulations requires you to consider the capabilities of your staff when you give them tasks to do, and to provide health and safety training (see page 11). To be effective, this process has to be on-going, starting from the time the employee joins you, added to, refreshed and updated as responsibilities, activities or equipment change. It seems inconceivable that the awful conditions described in the case studies on hygiene in Section 7 could be tolerated, but did the people involved see them in a different light because they didn't know better?

Keeping safety uppermost is not easy in the pressures of business. But with effective training, what should be done for safety reasons will be one and the same with what is actually done.

Verbal recap
1 Why must the machine be switched off at source prior to connecting any attachments?
2 Why do we use bowl clamps?
3 How do we fit the attachment to the spindle?
4 Why do we always start the machine in a low gear?
5 What could happen if you had loose items of clothing?
6 Why do we never leave the machine unsupervised?
7 How do you dismantle the machine?
8 How do you lift a heavy bowl?

With thanks to The University of Sheffield (see page 36)

 CHECKLIST

Training in safe use of equipment

- how is the trainee to be selected?
- who is to supervise the training?
- who is to do the training?
- what training and guidance can equipment suppliers provide?
- what records of training will be kept?

Assessing the trainee

- what is the trainee's existing knowledge?
- has the trainee worked similar equipment elsewhere?
- if trained elsewhere, has the trainee an adequate knowledge of safe working practices?
- has the trainee special needs, for example language difficulties?

Basic instruction

- prepare checklist of all the points that the trainee must remember – there may be need for multi-lingual notices or easily understood graphics
- explain how the equipment works
- explain the dangers that can arise from the use and misuse of the equipment
- explain the safety features of the equipment and how they protect the operator
- explain how to operate the equipment and how to follow any emergency procedures, including isolation from electrical, gas or steam supplies
- explain how to clean the equipment safely. No one under 18 years of age should be allowed to clean machinery if there is a risk of injury from a moving part or that of any adjacent machinery
- explain what to do if the equipment is or seems to be faulty

Supervised working

- ensure that the supervisor has sufficient knowledge of all the equipment, processes, hazards and precautions, and fully understands the responsibilities involved in training staff
- set the trainee to work under close supervision ideally following a prepared training programme
- make sure the supervisor has sufficient time and knowledge to supervise effectively
- make sure the supervisor watches for bad habits or dangerous practices that may develop, and stops them

Finally assessing the trainee

- check that the trainee knows how to use and clean the equipment properly and safely
- make sure that the trainee can be left to work safely without close supervision
- complete and sign the training record

With thanks to the Health and Safety Executive (for details of source see top of page 83)

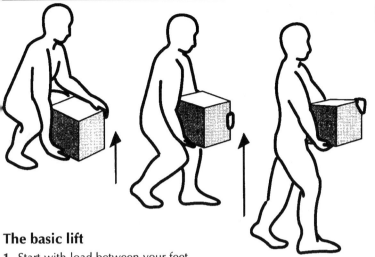

The basic lift

1 Start with load between your feet.

2 Get down to the level of the load – bend your knees and hips, keep your back straight from head to tail.

3 Get a firm grip on the load.

4 Stand up in one smooth movement, looking ahead to help keep your back straight. Keep the load close to your body – don't jerk.

5 Reverse the above procedure to lower the load. Keep your back straight and bend your knees and hips.

Reproduced from the poster in *Backbreakers*, a video-based training package on manual handling, available from HCTC. With thanks to Whitbread Inns.

POINTS TO REMEMBER

1 Do not carry too much.

2 Keep passages clear.

3 Keep heavy loads at body level.

4 Do not twist while lifting or carrying.

5 Wear sturdy shoes and gloves where appropriate.

6 Do not stack heavy loads too high.

What are the main rules you should follow to avoid each of these accidents?

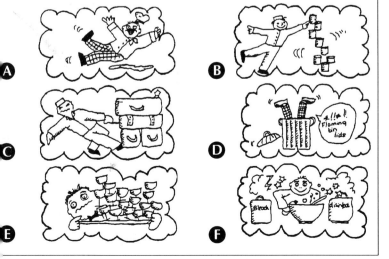

ne of the ways you might test individual staff awareness.

andouts used on some of HCTC's youth and adult training programmes, with anks to Jane Howard

CHECKLIST

3D1.1   *Maintain security/safety procedures in own area of responsibility*

☐ **1a** procedures for maintaining operations in accordance with relevant legislation are fully maintained

☐ **1b** premises and equipment are regularly checked

☐ **1c** breaches of security and faults with safety equipment are promptly dealt with according to organisational policy

☐ **1d** potential problems are identified and recommendations for the improvement of security/safety procedures are passed on to the appropriate people

☐ **1e** all relevant information is accurately recorded in a suitable format and made available to the appropriate people

3D1.2   *Monitor and maintain the health and safety of workers, customers and other members of the public*

☐ **2a** cleaning standards/routines are carried out in line with relevant legislation and company procedures

☐ **2b** the working area is free from hazards

☐ **2c** problems are identified, rectified if possible or promptly and accurately reported to an appropriate authority

☐ **2d** health, safety and maintenance checks are carried out regularly

☐ **2e** all accidents are dealt with, reported and recorded accurately, completely and legibly in the accident book and notified to the appropriate authority if necessary

☐ **2f** manufacturers' instructions and legislative requirements relating to the safe use of all equipment and fixtures are fully complied with

☐ **2g** all necessary health and safety signs are displayed effectively

3D1.3   *Maintain a healthy and safe working environment*

☐ **3a** relevant records are complete and accurate

☐ **3b** damage, infestation, contamination and potentially unsafe features in the working environment are investigated and immediate action is taken

☐ **3c** health and safety standards are implemented in line with current legislation

☐ **3d** on-going training and instruction are made available to enable staff to perform their work safely and efficiently

☐ **3e** problems with staff not complying with the health and safety standards are identified and dealt with according to organisational policy and relevant employment legislation

Comments on case studies/activities

 Ladder safety   *Section 1, page 3*

1 Precautions which should have been taken

The ladder should not have been used. It is not clear why the handyman ignored its dangerous state, or whether he had secured the ladder properly – tied at the top to prevent it slipping along the wall, staked or 'footed' at the base (i.e. with someone holding it in place); at the right angle and on a firm base (see box).

The hotel owner should have recognised that wooden ladders are prone to damage and must be regularly examined. He should have provided the handyman with guidance on the safe use of ladders.

2 Human failings

The hotel owner seemed to give little importance to safety. This attitude is bound to have spread through the organisation.

The handyman seems to have given higher priority to carrying out the owner's instruction, than to his safety. Why didn't he hire a better ladder, or, if this required approval, wait until the owner was back?

The handyman underestimated the risk of using a ladder which was in poor condition and not secured properly. The case study does not reveal what other risks he underestimated. Could he manage the sign on his own (considering its weight and shape)? What were the weather conditions like? A strong gust of wind might have blown the handyman off the ladder, especially if it caught the sign.

It is a reasonable assumption that there was no notice on the ladder to say it was unsafe. It might have been used by someone else who would not have recognised it as unsafe, say an assistant manager who had to replace a light bulb when the handyman was off duty.

In the owner's absence, there must have been someone in charge of the hotel. Apparently the handyman did not see any need to involve that person in his work. Perhaps he believed that in the owner's absence he was responsible for his own activities. This role-playing may have been encouraged by the owner.

Further discussion points

What aspects of the management of health and safety regulations and the work equipment regulations would help prevent this sort of accident? (Refer to page 8: *employees' duties*, pages 10 and 35.)

What observations would you make if the handyman was not an employee of the hotel, but a local person whom the owner had contracted to do the work? (Refer to page 8 if you need help.)

 *Human factors*   *Section 1, page 4*

The bomb scare, which made such an unfortunate start to the American couple's visit to the UK, might have arisen from inadequate information: the person who took the telephone call not asking the questions which would help the police and management distinguish between a genuine threat and a hoax call (see page 56). Perhaps someone failed to report suspicious behaviour. Perhaps a briefcase or package was left unattended.

The second and third photographs show the dangers which arise from misuse of cleaning materials (pages 29–31): because the risks are underestimated, or priorities are mistaken (not making the effort to wear goggles or gloves).

Safety hazards from ladders

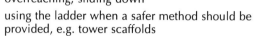

- not securing the ladder properly
- unsafe use of the ladder, e.g. overreaching, sliding down
- using the ladder when a safer method should be provided, e.g. tower scaffolds
- using a ladder with a defect
- unsuitable base for a ladder
- insufficient handhold at top of ladder or at stepping-off position
- insufficient foothold at each rung
- using a ladder near overhead electricity cables, cranes
- ladders at an unsafe angle, swaying, springing, etc. – the recommended angle for a ladder is 70 to 75 degrees
- insufficient overlap of extension ladders

 Safety awareness   *Section 2, page 11*

These are some of the activities your review might have covered:

- copy of HSE poster displayed, or employees given leaflet HSC5 plus the relevant addresses (page 11)
- information (and training) on safety provided to new employees and when there is a change of responsibilities etc.
- refresher training and workplace reminders provided
- work procedures emphasise safety aspects
- safety signs used as necessary (page 13).

In looking at other methods for reinforcing safety messages, did you consider the points on page 12 (*Consulting on safety* and *Some ways to increase safety awareness*)?

To what extent do your staff understand the health and safety information they are provided with? What provision do you make for individuals with language or reading difficulties? Did you check your accident book, to see what problems have arisen because of inadequate training or lack of awareness of safety procedures?

 Bandsaw accident   *Section 2, page 14*

1 Not reporting the accident

It is possible that the accident was described in such a way to the council that it did not appear to be serious. The claim that an attempt was made to report the accident would be more believable if the name of the council employee who took the call had been noted.

2 What led the accident to be reported

It is possible that the company only realised the seriousness of the injury when the wound had to be operated on. The company might also have become worried that the chef would submit a claim for damages (as in the *Fall in corridor* case study on page 18).

3 Removing the guard

Guards sometimes seem to make the job more difficult. Many bandsaws have an adjustable blade guard which fits over the blade and which should be set as low as possible. If the bones were of different sizes this might have meant constantly turning off the machine to readjust the blade guard, or setting the guard high enough to accommodate all bones, or removing it altogether.

Responsibility for checking that there was a guard

The restaurateur had a responsibility to provide safe equipment, even if it was borrowed.

Why borrow the bandsaw?

You probably had a lot of difficulty in thinking of a reason. It might be that the restaurant's usual supplier had been unable to get veal bones, and alternative suppliers were unwilling to supply them cut.

Weakness in management

Getting the job done seems to have been considered more important than how safely it was done. Management should have been more familiar with the regulations on reporting accidents.

High fine

The fine was high to make an example of the restaurant and because of the seriousness of not providing a guard.

The Environmental Health Department at Reading, responsible for the prosecution, added further details not clear from press reports:

as a result of the accident, the chef was unfit for work for three days – in these circumstances, there could be no confusion about the obligation to report the accident

the bandsaw was not borrowed, and the pre-cut bones story they regarded as 'far fetched'. The bandsaw had been bought off bankrupt stock, with the guard missing

it was a tabletop model, and there was no suitable work area in the kitchen to locate it (bandsaws should be sited where the operator cannot be pushed, bumped or distracted). After the case, the bandsaw 'disappeared'.

Fatal fall down pub steps   Section 2, page 16

What went wrong and why

The staircase was dangerous and should have been replaced (as it subsequently was). But whether it was or not, the metal covers should have been fixed so they could not slide when someone walked on them, and these and the rubber strips in them regularly checked. A second handrail, better lighting and signs warning of the steepness and uneven heights of the steps would all have helped.

The company should have had a policy statement and given it to the manageress with health and safety arrangements for the pub and her health and safety information and guidance.

The death should have been reported immediately to the environmental health department. While the regulations (RIDDOR, page 15) do not specifically mention the need to report accidents involving customers, they could be interpreted as applying, because notifiable accidents are those 'arising out of or in connection with work'. In any case, common-sense would lead to the conclusion that a serious incident of this sort would be investigated by the enforcement authorities. Taking the initiative to inform them would indicate a willingness to cooperate and put matters right.

Charges brought against company

Two charges were brought under the Health and Safety at Work Act:

all three defendants (the company, the company secretary and a senior officer) for failure to discharge the duty of an employer to conduct his/her business so as not to expose persons not in his/her employment to unreasonable health and safety risks

all three defendants for failure to prepare and as necessary revise a written policy statement about health and safety matters, and the arrangements for carrying out that policy, and to bring these to the notice of all staff.

And two charges under the reporting of injuries, etc. regulations, against the company and the company secretary for:

- failure to give immediate notification of a fatal accident
- failure to report the incident in writing within seven days.

After extensive legal arguments on whether a business had to notify serious accidents to customers as opposed to accidents to staff, the magistrate dismissed the reporting charges. Camden are appealing against this to clarify the law.

3 The main costs of the accident

In addition to the fines and lawyers' bills (over £20,000), you probably mentioned: bad publicity, loss of goodwill and loss of customers. There were also damages for the man's widow. The cost of replacing the staircase would have been the only expense if this had been done six months earlier.

Non-financial costs included the loss of the man to his widow and children, trauma for the manageress and her staff.

Further discussion points

If you took charge of this pub before the accident, what would you do to improve safety standards, bearing in mind that the British operation was apparently in financial difficulties?

(The Trade Union Reform and Employment Rights Act 1993 gives employees who are dismissed, or otherwise put at a disadvantage because they have expressed reasonable health and safety concerns, the rights to compensation.)

Follow-on activity

The contraventions cited in the improvement notice on page 6 related to the Health and Safety at Work etc. Act 1974. In a similar situation today (re-read the schedule on page 6), the EHO might have made references to three 1992 regulations (see pages 10, 19, 26). Describe, in general terms, what further actions the employer might have been asked to take to comply with these regulations.

Fall in corridor   Section 2, page 18

1 Records to provide information

Remind yourself of the questions which you would be asked on the Department of Social Security's form BI 76 (summarised in the bullet points on page 18). Clearly a well-designed *accident reporting form* would supply much of the information. You might also need to look at the *job description* for a room attendant to establish whether the claimant was authorised to collect clean linen.

The *duty rota* and *time sheet* would indicate what hours the claimant was expected to work, and what time she came on duty. The accident form would give the time of the accident.

Payment records would be required to establish how much Miss Moxon earned in the period up to the accident, and the details for Mrs Wayne for a 2½ year period.

2 How easy to provide this information

Clearly this is a question only you can answer. Try putting a financial cost to the time it would take you and your colleagues to collect the information, deal with the visits of insurance inspectors, reply to various letters, etc. – even if you only make a rough estimate of 3 or 4 person-days, the cost would be substantial.

Further discussion points

Identify the occasions when floors, passageways and gangways in your workplace might become obstructed, the reason(s) and what should be done to avoid a tripping accident.

Manual handling Section 3, page 28

The main purpose of this activity was to introduce some of the factors that you need to consider when assessing the risks involved in manual handling. As you will realise, any one operation may involve risk because of the task, the load, the working environment and individual capabilities.

To turn the activity into a risk assessment, you could therefore start by listing all the manual handling operations (see Boddingtons checklist below). It is likely that you would be able to classify some as low risk without further analysis (e.g. collecting glasses), while for others you will have to work through the four stages.

Follow-on activity

Draw up some questions and answers for a recap at the end of a training session on manual handling (see the text and industry examples on pages 26 and 27).

Another suggestion is for a 'pick and match' session: on a flip chart or OHP slide, draw a series of illustrations (these can be quite simple to do, yet very effective, as those reproduced here), then ask the trainees to come up with a matching safety message.

With thanks to Formecon Services Limited, Gateway, Crewe CW1 1YN from a placard on manual handling, in a comprehensive health and safety series

The themes illustrated here are:
1 check the load first, 2 divide heavy loads or use a trolley, 3 don't obstruct your vision, 4 know the route (floor surfaces, steps, etc.) before setting off. Can you match them up?

Some manual handling tasks that might be overlooked — The BODDINGTON Group plc

- ☐ Lifting of cellar flaps
- ☐ Moving/lifting/use of fire extinguishers
- ☐ Moving of one-arm bandits and similar amusement machines
- ☐ Moving of garden furniture
- ☐ Opening/closing garage doors/roller shutters
- ☐ Emptying/filling bottle shelves
- ☐ Replacing bottles on optic stands
- ☐ Collecting glasses
- ☐ Cleaning inside and outside areas
- ☐ Handling cash register drawers (including cash)
- ☐ Carrying cash to/from bank
- ☐ Moving catering equipment to clean
- ☐ Carrying or moving step ladders (bulb changing etc.)
- ☐ Disposal of refuse

 Dough machine Section 4, page 36

What led to the accident

This accident is typical of many, when a combination of factors com together with disastrous consequences – on their own, they a tolerated because they do not cause an obvious problem.

1 The employee behaved recklessly – rigging the machine so th it kept running while the guard was removed.

2 The company's policy of permitting staff to finish early if they ha completed an agreed quota encouraged undue haste.

3 There was a lack of supervision – no one stopped the employe tampering with the machine's safety mechanism.

4 The employee had not been given training in the use of th dough machine, or it was inadequate.

5 The company and its management failed to realise the potenti dangers of the machine. They also failed to replace the seals o the machine sufficiently often to prevent the dough seeping in the drive area.

6 The poor design of the interlock switch which allowed it to b rigged comparatively easily was a manufacturing fault, but th employer has a duty to provide suitable equipment. Under th Provision and Use of Work Equipment Regulations 1992 (se page 35), work equipment must be suitable for the purpose fo which it is used or provided. In this case suitable means 'suitab in any respect that is reasonably foreseeable'. In other words, the misuse of a machine is reasonably foreseeable then the ris assessment exercise must investigate and pre-empt such use

In this example, the misuse of the dough divider was entire foreseeable. The machine should have been designed original or subsequently modified to reduce the need to access th dangerous area of the machine, and to improve the safet protective devices when access was necessary.

 Leisure centre fire Section 5, page 41

1 Why things went wrong

By his own admission, the general manager underestimated the ris of fire, and overestimated the ability of his staff to get people o safely, having had no special training in what to do. In other word the real problem was people, not other factors such as failure of th fire detection equipment or the alarm system.

As a consequence, the staff:

- wasted 20 minutes trying to fight the fire, and were so pre occupied that no one remembered to call the fire brigade

- overlooked the automatic alarm system, using a publi telephone to call the fire brigade

- switched off the electricity putting an emergency exit in darknes

- did not notice that the emergency lighting had not come on. I the week before the fire, there had been some trouble with th electrical system. It is possible that in the course of repairs, a isolating switch to the standby generator that provided power t the emergency lights had been left in the 'off' position.

Fire training for staff would have left them better prepared on th emergency procedure, and regular checking of the emergenc lighting would have identified the problem of the generator. Th combination of abnormal circumstances (a fire, lack of fire drill, an the failure of the emergency lights) threw the staff into unde standable confusion.

Would all your staff know what to do

[ob]viously this is a question only you can answer. This is one of the [re]asons why it was recommended in the text (page 48) that [ob]servers should note the behaviour of people during a fire drill.

[Fu]rther discussion points

[At] the Stardust disco in Dublin, 48 people lost their lives on St [Va]lentine's day in 1981. The managing director said in his evidence [to] the inquiry that he did not think that there was a fire risk or hazard [in] the club. He had not given doormen any instruction on what to do [in] the event of a fire. 'There were enough doors on the premises and [on]ce they were open, the people could get out.' (The exit doors were [loc]ked from 10 p.m. until sometime around midnight, and there was [a p]ractice of wrapping chains and padlocks around the bars on the [do]ors, to keep out gate crashers.) What similarities does this [inc]ident have with the Summerland fire?

[Fol]low-on activity

[Wh]at can hotels and other residential [es]tablishments do to encourage [pe]ople with mobility or [co]mmunications difficulties to ask for [sp]ecial attention in the event of a fire? [A s]pecial room door card, as shown [he]re, is one suggestion.

[Co]ntact your tourist board or the [Ho]liday Care [Se]rvice to find out [wh]at practical steps [yo]u can take to make [yo]ur facilities as safe [an]d accessible as [po]ssible, so that [dis]abled people and [oth]ers with particular [ne]eds enjoy their visit, [as] ordinary travellers, as [ind]ependently as [po]ssible.

[Ho]liday Care Service, [O]ld Bank Chambers, [St]ation Road, Horley, [Su]rrey RH6 9HW

Your Personal Safety

If you have any difficulty in hearing or for any reason you may require assistance in the event of an hotel evacuation please display this card outside your bedroom door before retiring

Smouldering cigarette   *Section 5, page 49*

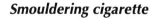

[W]hat should have been done/not done

[Th]e room attendant should have been trained by the housekeeper [to] empty all ashtrays into a metal bin, preferably with a hinged lid.

[It i]s not clear where the room attendant left the vacuum cleaner and [pil]e of soiled linen, but the spread of the fire suggests they were in [the] corridor. If so, this would have created a fire hazard (by causing [an] obstruction in the emergency escape route). This also indicates [a l]ack of training and supervision.

[Th]e manager should have agreed a safe work plan with the [en]gineers before they started work on the alarm system. Provision [wo]uld then have been made for the fire doors to be closed manually, [an]d for staff to be instructed to keep the doors shut (this would [pro]bably make their work more difficult, so the instruction would [ha]ve to be backed by supervision).

[Val]uable time was lost before calling the fire brigade. Why didn't the [rec]eptionist call 999 immediately? There is an implication that the [ma]nager did not trust his staff to recognise the seriousness of the [fire], having to go and check before he called the fire brigade.

 £45,000 fine   *Section 7, page 65*

1 The manager's reaction

There is no way of knowing whether the woman who met the EHOs understood the significance of the visit, and conveyed the information to the manager. It was certainly a poor start to arrive smoking, and then extinguish his cigarette in the sink.

The manager would have been advised to retain his right to silence when asked about the chopping board, the rice and the toilets. (The caution was 'You are not obliged to say anything, but what you do say will be written down and may be given in evidence.') His answer about the chopping board made the offence more serious. His answers to the rice and toilet questions cast doubt on his honesty. With the toilets it led the EHOs to observe a situation that was arguably worse (that food handlers had to use the family's bathroom).

2 Contraventions

The contravention against the Food Safety Act was selling food unfit for human consumption – any food on the premises is assumed to be intended for human consumption unless the opposite is proved. Contraventions against the Food Hygiene (General) Regulations – similar offences would apply under the 1994 regulations – included:

- insanitary premises, with evidence of infestation by vermin
- food exposed to risk of contamination
- premises not clean, nor in such a condition that they could be effectively cleaned.

3 Hazards in photographs

Sink and preparation area: cooked food next to uncooked food, work surfaces not clean or capable of being effectively cleaned, open waste bin, waste bin not capable of being effectively cleaned, refuse in food room (beyond what would be normal).

Close-up of floor and pot: cooked rice in saucepan on floor, cigarette butt on floor, floor very dirty.

Cooking area: badly scored chopping board in foreground, open waste bin, tiled wall not clean, nor capable of being cleaned.

Preparation room: overloaded electrical socket, food equipment not clean (potato peeling machine), wall surfaces not clean.

 Food poisoning outbreak   *Section 7, page 67*

1 Practices which led to outbreak

The chicken drumsticks were not allowed to thaw fully – it is most unlikely that an almost solid, single mass of drumsticks (310 drumsticks would weigh about 60 lbs) would defrost in a refrigerator over a period of just 21 hours.

This meant they were inadequately cooked the following morning. Subsequent handling, storage and heating procedures gave ample opportunity for the surviving bacteria to multiply to dangerous levels.

Chicken is known to be a high risk food in respect of salmonella. Analysis of stool samples provided by guests who had been ill isolated *Salmonella enteritidis*. One of the catering staff involved in the buffet preparation was also positive for this organism, but there were no grounds for suspecting that he was the source of the outbreak.

The chicken drumsticks taken home by two of the guests were found to contain high levels of the same organism. The salmonella were present inside the meat.

2 Preparing food in advance

The chicken drumsticks should have been cooked, breadcrumbed and deep fried on the day of the function. Before the initial cooking, they should have been checked to establish that they had completely defrosted. After this 'roasting' in the fan-assisted oven, a temperature probe should have been used to check that the temperature at the centre of each drumstick (i.e. a representative sample) had reached at least 75°C (some experts recommend 82°C for food which might be contaminated at the centre).

Cooling before breadcrumbing should have been as quick as possible. Ideally, cooling should have been done in a blast chiller.

After breadcrumbing, the drumsticks should have been stored at below 5°C, until a short time before service when they would be deep fried in batches (the food was served over 3 hours) and, if necessary, held above 63°C. Before service the core temperature of the drumsticks should again have been checked (above 70°C).

 **Scenario Two**   *Section 7, page 69*

The hazards you identified at each stage would probably be similar to those on page 73. Fewer safeguards in Scenario Two mean more critical control points (compared with Scenario One).

Receipt

As the burgers are purchased from a local supplier, the restaurant would have to check from time to time that the burgers are conforming to the purchase specification – perhaps by sending samples away for analysis. Temperature on delivery is a very important protection against harmful bacteria.

Storage

The traying-up introduces a risk of contamination – from poor personal hygiene, lack of cleanliness of equipment, and cross-contamination from other products during storage. There is a risk that the temperature of the cold room and refrigerators rises above 5°C, when bacteria are able to multiply. Poor stock rotation could mean some burgers are several days old before they are cooked.

Preparation and cooking

By contrast to Scenario One, there seems to be an abundance of hazards during this stage.

Critical control points

Delivery
- temperature of burgers checked.

Storage
- unpacking process (including staff personal hygiene, cleanliness of trays, stock rotation)
- temperature of refrigerators and cold room
- cleanliness of refrigerators and cold room, and separation of stock to avoid cross-contamination.

Preparation and cooking
- food handling practices of staff, including personal hygiene
- core temperature of burgers after cooking
- core temperature of burgers during hot display
- stock rotation of cooked burgers.

Further discussion points

Inadequate supervision at the take-away restaurant in Scenario Two might quite easily lead to the sort of letter reproduced on page 76. Read it again, identifying the control measures recommended.

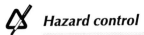 *Hazard control*   *Section 7, page 73*

From this activity you may also have got an idea of the sort of control and monitoring procedures that would be helpful for the take-away in Scenario Two, e.g. check suppliers on site, check temperatures of refrigerators, supervise and check working procedures, etc.

Look back at the industry examples on pages 70 to 72. The McDonald's audit sheet shows great attention to detail. CCG use more general headings. The Ind Coope procedure for checking food deliveries is comprehensive. The J D Wetherspoon temperature log book is designed to be readily accessible and easy to complete. The Stakis policy on frozen foods rules out certain thawing practices, as well as the freezing of food on the premises. Why?

You might get further ideas from the industry procedures on page 83 (washing-up) and page 85 (using a microwave, pest control).

Remember that controls are only effective when the people carrying them out understand what has to be done. For example, there is no point in recording the temperature of food if the probe has not reached the centre of the item, or tested the temperature at various places in a large dish. And if the probe is not sanitised between each use, it may spread bacteria from one dish to another.

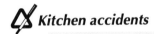 *Kitchen accidents*   *Section 8, page 84*

Accidents 1, 2 and 3 suggest a need for more effective training in the safe use of hazardous substances, and better storage practices. You might have suggested reviewing/updating the company's COSHH assessment, investigating whether any of the substances could be replaced by safer alternatives, or less concentrated solutions, and contacting suppliers for communication aids. You probably also suggested a check on what protective clothing was provided, and better supervision to ensure it was always worn. And what about first-aid provision? It's important that the right action is taken after an accident.

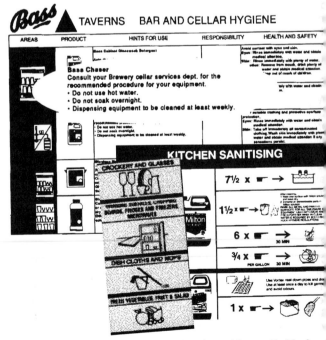

Two further examples of communication aids available from suppliers (top Lever Industrial, below Procter & Gamble).

Accidents 4 and 9 are well-recognised dangers in a kitchen. A moment's lack of thought, over-hastiness, less-than-ideal design of the kitchen, or not entirely suitable floor surfaces are some of the factors that can contribute to the hazards. It would be unwise to comment on what might have caused these problems without knowing more of the circumstances. Nevertheless, you might start to tackle the problem by:

- updating the risk assessment which is required under the management of health and safety regulations (see page 10)

- refresher training and improved supervision to raise safety awareness levels of staff

- fully investigating any incident, and seeking to eliminate contributory factors. The employer in *accident 9* erected a partition to stop similar incidents occurring in the future.

Accident 5 is particularly difficult to comment on without knowing the circumstances. Could the operation have been made safer by moving out the fryer and other units first? If not, could the assistant have waited until the oil in the fryer was cool? Is this sort of task not better done by a specialist kitchen cleaning contractor?

Accident 6 – it's with this sort of problem in mind that the precautions relating to fryers on page 82 were written. Of course, these need the support of training and supervision to be really effective. Remember, because you know something is dangerous, do not assume that other people recognise the danger. It probably never occurred to the young chef that the hot oil would melt the plastic container.

Accidents 7 and 8 might be turned into valuable training points, for many people underestimate the risks of using knives. There is no shortage of good advice on using knives (the eight points on page 83 could be expanded to double that number without difficulty), but these remain ineffective when the matter is treated light-heartedly. Safe knife use should be part of a professional chef's skills.

 ### Building services   Section 9, page 100

Two ladder accidents

The problems associated with the use of ladders have already been discussed (page 116). People performing a safety role or engaged in a dangerous task should not be distracted – whether this takes the form of a poorly-timed request to do something else, as happened here, or a conversation on a social or work-related matter, as happened in the second knife accident on page 84 (No. 8).

Guest found dead

Why the student went to the window or why he fell out will never be known. Whoever was responsible for distorting the restraining brackets obviously hadn't considered the possibility that someone might fall out of the window. The hotel owners should have spotted the problem during safety audits or the risk assessment. It is too easy to think that no one would lean so far out of the window as to fall out, but if you are running an establishment open to the public, you cannot make assumptions about people's behaviour. The workplace regulations require windows to be of a design or so constructed that they can be cleaned safely.

Resident falls down stairs

Check against the requirements of the workplace regulations for traffic routes and safe lighting (see boxes on page 20) that the risks of a similar sort of accident happening in your workplace are low. It seems unlikely that both bulbs could have gone at the same time. Given the time of the accident (8 a.m.), why didn't any of the staff who came on duty that morning get the bulbs replaced?

 ### Pub's contraventions   Section 10, page 102

1 Comments on the management

Standards had obviously been allowed to slip. The problems described are not likely to be one-off matters, following an exceptionally busy period, or staff shortages. It is interesting that all the problems relate to the kitchen, which presumably could not be seen by customers. Perhaps the food side of the business was not considered very important by the publican.

2 The EHO's response

The decision to prosecute confirms poor management standards. Asked to comment on this case study, Rushmoor Borough Council gave the author three reasons for deciding to prosecute:

- the occupier had ignored previous advice over a period of time

- the number of offences indicated a serious risk to health

- they had no confidence that further advice or informal action would lead to the required work being done.

 ### Emergency planning   Section 10, page 106

Many of the hotels in the Metropole group sleep several hundred guests or more, posing a major logistical problem in an emergency. Added to this, their location in city centres, at major conference centres like Blackpool and Brighton, and major exhibition centres like the NEC Birmingham, make them attractive targets for terrorism. A well-developed emergency procedure is essential.

However, if you work for a small establishment, you may have asked what relevance an emergency plan has to your situation? You might find it useful to scan back through the book and prepare your own checklist of possible emergencies, e.g. serious accident, gas leak (mains or CO_2), bomb threat, death, fire/flood requiring evacuation of the premises for a prolonged period, food poisoning complaint, breakdown of refrigerator, theft involving customer's property, violent attack on staff. Would you know what to do?

 ### Alarm bells   Section 10, page 111

1 Dealing with the situation

You would no doubt have made an attempt to contact your manager or head office to get instructions and authority to close the restaurant immediately, call an emergency plumber to unblock the drains and then get the whole kitchen thoroughly cleaned.

If it was your own restaurant, the decision to close would be more difficult. All that bank holiday trade would be lost, and customers would be left wondering what had happened. You might be tempted to persuade yourself that the risk was not all that great, since the cardboard was doing a good job in soaking up the effluent. But what if a splash from the floor landed on a food preparation surface, or on someone's hands or uniform and then came in contact with food?

2 Had the problem occurred before

The evidence suggests it had. It would take some working out to know that effluent from the customers' toilets, and drainage from the kitchen wash hand basin connected above the blockage. Why not simply hang an OUT-OF-USE notice on the doors to the toilets? But what if a customer ignores the notice and uses the toilets? Why was the floor not mopped? Was there an awareness of the risks of splashing effluent everywhere, hence the use of cardboard?

Restaurants robbed   *Follow-on case study*

London, March

It was about 1 a.m. when Jenny and Sue, young but experienced managers, carefully locked the night's takings in a safe in their basement office. Satisfied that the premises were secured, they prepared to leave the restaurant through a side door.

As they pushed the door open they encountered their worst nightmare: three men wearing balaclavas. One brandishing a handgun, forced them back inside. They wanted money, and made it clear they would shoot if they didn't get it.

Realising that the men were agitated enough to pull the trigger if they failed to comply, the two terrified women led their assailants into the basement where they handed over £10,000. They were left handcuffed to a pipe.

Glasgow, April

A man posing as an environmental health officer walked into a popular mid-spend restaurant in broad daylight and politely asked to be taken into a back office for a chat with the manager.

No one checked his identity. Once inside the office he produced a handgun and demanded the contents of the safe. He made a clean getaway with 'thousands of pounds'.

Dublin, May

A gunman strolled through the restaurant's front door at the start of the day, while staff were laying up the tables. Securicor had just removed the previous night's takings, so the gunman escaped with only the float of a few hundred pounds.

Several days later, an armed gang burst into the restaurant a few moments after Securicor's arrival. The guards, staff and customers were forced at gunpoint to lie on the floor. The gang got away with £10,000.

DISCUSSION POINTS

The *Caterer & Hotelkeeper* article, on which the case studies were based, ended by quoting one of the victims: 'We're living in an aggressive society, with crime and violence all around us. We never thought we'd end up as victims, and we did. Investment in security and staff awareness should be a matter of course.'

It would be wrong to say that restaurants are now a major target for gun-wielding criminals, *Caterer's* reporter Penny Wilson admits. But four factors are making them more vulnerable:

* the traditional targets – banks, building societies, betting shops, security vans, etc. – get increasingly sophisticated crime prevention equipment, which means the criminals are being forced further afield

* restaurants are portrayed and perceived as offering rich rewards because people spend a lot of money in them – the downside of the higher public profile the sector has established, with many chefs and proprietors appearing regularly in the media

* there are regular points in the restaurant day when staff are on their own and when sizeable sums of money may be on the premises

* it is fairly easy to 'case out the joint' by posing as a customer – 'Let's face it', a crime prevention officer told Penny Wilson, 'you can't hang around in a bank or building society like you can in a restaurant.'

 Ploys to extract money   *Follow-on activity*

Discuss with a group of colleagues and/or staff how you would deal with each of the following scenarios. Once you have had some initial ideas, broaden the discussion by revealing the real experience.

Dry cleaning claim

Scenario: You receive a letter from someone demanding that you pay for the dry cleaning of a jacket which a member of your staff spilt wine over.

A real experience: In January 1992 police arrested a man in Camberley. He admitted obtaining property by deception after a roll of 60 laundry bill stubs, several cheques from hotels and a copy of the *Good Food Guide* had been found at his home. The man admitted to sending requests for money (£5.75 in each instance) to the first 60 hoteliers listed in the England section of the guide.

Two blackmail threats

Scenario: You receive a letter demanding a large sum of money, otherwise you will be hurt or killed. A few days later a man phones with instructions on where the money should be left.

A real experience: Terry Holmes, managing director of The Ritz Hotel, received a letter demanding £140,000 otherwise the hotel's guests and staff would be attacked and even killed. The blackmail failed when a man telephoned to arrange a rendezvous. A detective posing as a Ritz executive met the blackmailer. An arrest was made, and subsequently the man, a radiographer, was jailed for 10 years. (Reports in *Caterer & Hotelkeeper*, 29 April and 29 July 1993.)

Scenario: A man phones to say that he has photographs showing cockroaches on tables and walls, taken at a wedding reception at your establishment the previous week. He wants compensation for his distress at seeing the creatures. You tell him it's nonsense, but the man phones on three more occasions, finally demanding £3000 or he will show the photographs to the press.

A real experience: After receiving a series of blackmail demands from a man who claimed to have taken photographs of cockroaches crawling around the furniture during a wedding reception he had attended at a hotel in West Yorkshire, the managing director and co-owner called in Rentokil and her EHO. After receiving the all-clear, she contacted the police.

Then she agreed to meet the blackmailer to see the photographs. She secretly tape-recorded the conversation in which he demanded £3000. Explaining it would take a few days to raise this money, the blackmailer agreed a subsequent meeting. When he returned, the police moved in to arrest him.

Man poses as an EHO

Scenario: A man arrives, says he's an environmental health officer and has come to make an inspection. He says that you do not appear to have been registered and there will be a heavy fine to pay. When you protest, he suggests you accompany him to his offices where the matter can be checked. As they are not far, you agree. You are taken into a meeting room in the town hall. After a while the man reappears and says that there is definitely no record, a registration is not valid until it has been received, and you must pay an on-the-spot fine of £250 or risk prosecution.

A real experience: Sheffield police issued a warning to look out for a thief posing as an EHO, after a restaurateur had been taken to Sheffield City Hall, shown into an empty room and asked to pay £270 to be registered. The man said he would return with the paperwork, but disappeared. The restaurateur said that going to the City Hall had convinced him the man was genuine. (Report in *Caterer & Hotelkeeper*, 2 April 1992.)

Index

Accident records 14–15, 109
Accident statistics 19, 35, 112
Aids, precautions against 98
Air-conditioning, health and safety 99
Assessing risks 10, 26, 29, 96–7, 109
Assured Safe Catering (ASC) 66–73
Attitude to safety 1–4

Bar, closing time management 78
Bar safety 77–9
Beer pipe cleaner, safe usage 29
Blackmail 122
Bomb threats 55–6
Building services, safety and security 99–100, 121

Car park security 52
Carbon dioxide as hazardous substance 11, 29, 80–1
Cash security 53
CE mark on appliances/equipment/clothing 31–2, 35, 37, 39
Cellar flaps 2
Cellar safety 2, 80–1
Children's facilities 40
Closed circuit television system (CCTV) 94
Closing time control 78
Computers see Display screen
Confidence tricks 122
Consulting on safety 12
Contractors and suppliers
  cooperating: food safety 69–73, 113
  cooperating: safety 8, 113
Cooling towers/evaporative condensers 99
Counterfeit money 53
Crime watch 54
Critical control points for food see Hazard analysis (HACCP)

Dangerous machinery 36, 82, 116–18
Death on the premises 95
Deliveries
  arrangements with suppliers 2, 8
  cellar 80
  food deliveries 66–9, 71–3
Disabled people, care of 94, 119
Disaster plans 9, 105, 106, 107, 108
Discotheques (in relation to noise) 23
Diseases which have to be reported 16
Display screen, safety using 96–7
Door safety 20
Drinking glasses, safe handling 2
Drugs use, dealing with and prevention 79
Due diligence 57, 63

Elderly customers/guest security 94
Electrical equipment 37–8
Emergency procedures 9, 46, 48, 54–6, 105–8, 121
Employees' duties, for health and safety at work 6, 8
Employers' duties for health and safety at work 6, 8
Enforcing officers 5, 6, 20, 57, 58, 63, 64, 74–6
Entertainment licences 42, 43
Environmental health officers see Enforcing officers
Equipment safety 20, 35–9, 59, 82–5, 110, 113
Evacuation see Emergency procedures
Extinguishers (fire) 50

Falls see Slips, trips and falls
Fire certificates 43
Fire prevention 41–50, 82, 100, 104, 107, 118–19
First-aid arrangements 24–5, 84
Fitness suites/gymnasium 91
Flambé lamps 87
Floor and personal traffic route safety 20
Food
  allergies 62
  Assured Safe Catering 66–73
  bacteria (food poisoning) 67, 119
  best-before labelling 62
  complaints records 109
  deliveries (hygiene) 66–9, 71–3
  display cabinets, correct use 87
  freezing 62
  frozen foods handling 72
  handlers, personal hygiene 58, 61, 64
  hazard analysis and critical control points (HACCP) 66–73, 120
  hygiene prosecutions 65, 67, 102, 119, 121
  inspections (by EHO) 74–6
  irradiation 62
  labelling/menu descriptions 62
  microwave cooking/defrosting 85
  premises 58, 59, 61
  safety of food 57–76
  shellfish 64
  storage safety 72–3, 84
  temperature controls 58, 60, 70–3
  training of food handlers 58, 64
  transportation 61
  use-by labelling 62
  washing facilities 59
  waste disposal 33, 59
  wrapping materials 60
Fraud 93–4, 122

Gas equipment 39
Glass safety 2
Guest security 52, 94

Hazard analysis and critical control points (HACCP) 66–73, 120
Hazardous substances 29–31, 84, 111, 120
Health & Safety Executive information and advice 12
Holiday Care Service 119
Hotel Secure Scheme 54, 105
Housekeeping safety 88, 111

Ice-cream, hygiene laws 64
Improvement notice 5–6, 63, 75–6
Information security 94
Information to employees on health and safety 11–12
Inspections (food hygiene) 74–6

Keg moving safety 26
Key security 53
Kitchen safety 82–4
Knife, safe handling 83

Ladders, safe use 3, 116, 121
Legionnaires' disease 99
Leisure centre safety 87, 90–2
Lifts and hoists, safety 99
Lighting safety 20–1
Liquefied petroleum gas (LPG) cylinder 87
Local Authorities Coordinating Body on Food and Trading Standards (LACOTS) 61, 76
Lost property 53

Managing health and safety 7–12
Manual handling 26–8, 115, 118
Microwave ovens 85

Noise as a nuisance/health hazard 23
Notifiable diseases 17

Office safety/security 89

Penalties for offences 5, 57
Personal protective equipment 31–2
Pest control 85, 88
Play areas and equipment safety 40
Police, cooperating with 54, 112
Policy statement on health and safety 7, 117
Portable electrical equipment 37
Portering safety 89
Pots and pans, care of 82
Press/media contact 108
Prohibition orders/notices 5, 63

Index *continued*

Prostitutes 95
Protective clothing equipment 32
Pub Watch 54, 105

Reception safety 89
Recording accidents *see* Accident records
Registering food premises 60
Registering guests 52
Reportable diseases 16
Reportable injuries and illnesses 15, 109, 112
Restaurant safety 86–7
Right to search employee's person or property 53
Risk assessment *see* Assessing risks
Room service safety 87

Safety representatives/committees 12
Safety signs 13, 113
Saunas 90
Searching the premises 56
Security 51–6, 89, 93–4, 102–10, 112, 122
Shared workplace safety 9
Shower heads, cleaning 93

Slips, trips and falls 18, 21, 117
Smoking in the workplace 21, 64
Social Security accident claims 18, 117
Storage (in the kitchen) 84
Sunbeds 90
Swimming pools 91–2

Telephone bomb threats 55–6
Temperature in the workplace 21
Temporary workers and non-employees' safety 8
Terrorism 55–6
Theft 110, 122
Toilet and washing facilities 22, 58
Training
  dangerous machines 36
  fire 48
  food handlers 64
  hazardous substances 31
  health and safety 11–12, 107, 110, 114–15
  induction training 107, 110
  manual handling 26–7, 115, 118
  young people 36, 115

Violence in the workplace 34, 77–8

Washing-up 83
Waste disposal 33, 59, 84
Water supply 59
Welfare facilities for employees at work 22
Women customers/guest security 94
Work equipment safety 20, 35–9, 82–5, 113

Other help in finding your way around this book

Checklist of legislation (in topic order) 103
Checklists in this book iv

Index to legislation

Control of Substances Hazardous to Health Regulations (COSHH) 29
Dairy Products (Hygiene) Regulations (proposed) 64
Diplomatic Privileges Act 52
Electricity at Work Regulations 37–8
Environmental Protection Act 23, 33
Fire Precautions Act 42
Fire Precautions (Hotels and Boarding Houses) Order 42
Fire Precautions (Places of Work) Regulations (postponed) 42
Food Hygiene (Amendment) Regulations 58, 59, 61
Food Hygiene (General) Regulations 58
Food Labelling (Amendment) (Irradiated Food) Regulations 62
Food Labelling Regulations 62
Food Premises (Registration) Regulations 60
Food Safety Act 57, 58, 63
Food Safety (General Food Hygiene) Regulations 17, 58, 59, 61, 64
Food Safety (Live Bivalve Molluscs and Other Shellfish) Regulations 64
Ice-Cream (Heat Treatment, etc.) Regulations 64
Immigration (Hotel Records) Order 52
Gas Appliances (Safety) Regulations 39
Gas Safety (Installation and Use) (Amendment) Regulations 39
Health and Safety at Work etc. Act 5–6, 42, 117

Health and Safety (Display Screen Equipment) Regulations ... 96–7
Health and Safety (First-Aid) Regulations 24–5
Health and Safety Information for Employees Regulations 12
Hotel Proprietors Act 52
Immigration (Hotel Records) Order 52
Management of Health and Safety at Work Regulations 7–12
Manual Handling Operations Regulations 26
Materials and Articles in Contact with Food Regulations 60
Noise at Work Regulations 23
Notification of Cooling Towers and Evaporative Condensers Regulations 99
Offices, Shops and Railway Premises Act 19, 36
Personal Protective Equipment at Work Regulations 31–2
Prescribed Dangerous Machines Order 36
Provision and Use of Work Equipment Regulations 35
Public Health (Control of Disease) Act 17
Public Health (Infectious Diseases) Regulations 17
Reporting of Injuries, Diseases and Dangerous Occurrences Regulations (RIDDOR) 15, 117
Safety Representatives and Safety Committee Regulations 12
Safety Signs at Work Regulations 13
Trade Union Reform and Employment Rights Act 117
Workplace (Health, Safety and Welfare) Regulations 19